IMAGES
of America

AFRICAN AMERICAN TOPEKA

Page No. 34

SCHEDULE 1.—Free Inhabitants in Topeka Township in the County of Shawnee State of Kansas enumerated by me, on the 25th day of June 1860. J. Flemming Ass't Marshal.

Post Office Topeka.

	Dwelling-houses—numbered in the order of visitation.	Families numbered in the order of visitation.	The name of every person whose usual place of abode on the first day of June, 1860, was in this family.	Description: Age.	Description: Sex.	Description: Color, White, black, or mulatto.	Profession, Occupation, or Trade of each person, male and female, over 15 years of age.	Value of Estate Owned: Value of Real Estate.	Value of Estate Owned: Value of Personal Estate.	Place of Birth, Naming the State, Territory, or Country.	Married within the year.	Attended School within the year.	Persons over 20 y'rs of age who cannot read & write.	Whether deaf and dumb, blind, insane, idiotic, pauper, or convict.
	1	2	3	4	5	6	7	8	9	10	11	12	13	14
1			Martha Cook	15	f					Penn				
2			William	2	m					Ohio				
3	301	286	Samuel Brown	33	m		Farmer	1500	1000	do				
4			Catharine	30	f					do				
5			Mary	6	f					do				
6			Eliza	4	f					do				
7			Minerva	2	f					do				
8	302	287	Gabriel Wright	35	m		Laborer		500	Penn				
9			Rebecca	33	f					do				
10			Edward	9	m					do				
11			Ellen	7	f					do				
12	303	288	Andrew Miller	44	m		Farmer	800	250	Ohio				
13			Rachael N	30	f					N Carolina				
14			Rebecca J	2	f					Indiana				
15			Lucy A	1	f					do				
16			Jemima	15	f					do				
17			Jacob	6	m					do				
18			Joseph Proctor	21	m		Farm Laborer			Ohio				
19	304	289	Wm H Kilpatrick	[illegible]8	m		Farmer	3000	300	Kentucky				
20			Nancy A	34	f					Penn				
21			Thomas D	8	m					Indiana				
22			Margaret J	6	f					do				
23			R Ford	3	m					do				
24			Wm J	3	m					Kansas				
25	305	290	[illegible] H Slayton	32	m		Farmer	2800	300	N York				
26			Lavina F	30	f					Penn				
27			Clara F	6	f					do				
28	306	291	Joseph Cox	28	m		Farm Laborer			Indiana				
29			John Ellis	27	m		do			Germany				
30			Elisa Ellis	21	f					Ohio				
31			Elijah	1	m					do				
32	307	292	Clements Chatteau	38	m		Farmer	1500		Mo				
33			Ann	40	f	B				do				
34			Elisabeth	14	f	M				Kansas				
35			William	12	m	M				do				
36			Francis	9	m	M				do				
37			Margaret	8	f	M				do				
38			Laura	6	f	M				do				
39			Adele	4	m	M				do				
40			Henry	1/12	m	M				do				

No. white males, ___ No. colored males, 4 No. foreign born, ___ No. blind, ___ No. idiotic, ___

No. white females, 6 No. colored females, 4 No. deaf and dumb, ___ No. insane, ___ 9600 2050 No. paupers, ___ No. convicts, ___

Ann Davis Shatteo (Chattilon). This 1860 US census for Topeka shows Ann Davis Shatteo (with the arrow pointing to her name) and her family. She was born free in Illinois around 1817. At a young age, she was stolen and taken as a slave to Missouri. Because she was an undocumented slave, Ann was allowed to hire herself out to buy back her freedom. In 1847, she moved with Samuel Lewis, her employer at that time, from Fort Scott, Kansas, to Shawnee County. After purchasing her freedom, she and her husband, Claymore Chattilon, bought land in Topeka on the Shunganunga Creek, where they raised their family. (Courtesy of Heritage Quest.)

On the Cover: Father and Son Banquet. This 1935 Father and Son Banquet, sponsored by St. John African Methodist Episcopal Church, was a gathering of many of the men of Topeka and their sons. It took place in the Monroe School building, where many social gatherings in the black community occurred. Prominent men in this photograph include Elisha and Charles Scott, Dr. G. Robert Cotton, and Joe Douglas and his father. (Courtesy of the Kansas Historical Society.)

IMAGES
of America

AFRICAN AMERICAN TOPEKA

Sherrita Camp

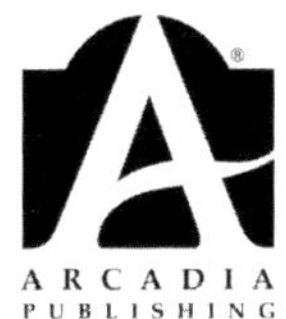

ISBN 978-1-4671-1068-6

Published by Arcadia Publishing
Charleston, South Carolina

Printed in the United States of America

Library of Congress Control Number: 2013934879

For all general information, please contact Arcadia Publishing:
Telephone 843-853-2070
Fax 843-853-0044
E-mail sales@arcadiapublishing.com
For customer service and orders:
Toll-Free 1-888-313-2665

Visit us on the Internet at www.arcadiapublishing.com

I dedicate this book to my husband, Dwayne, for his patience, and to our children and grandchildren, who are the descendants of great Topekans.

Contents

Acknowledgments

I am grateful to the many strong and talented African American Topekans who paved the way for all the generations to come. Those who laid the groundwork in education, entrepreneurship, and ingenuity have made me proud to be a Topekan. I am also thankful for the spirit of my ancestors, who were an integral part of Topeka history.

Sincere and heartfelt thanks go to the wonderful research librarians in the Topeka Room at the Topeka and Shawnee County Public Library. Charity Rouse and Jeanne Mithen provided a mountain of help in uncovering files on African Americans in Topeka. Likewise, Debra Dandridge, curator at the Spencer Research Library at the University of Kansas, was immensely helpful in locating historical documents and photographs within the Kansas Collection. I would also like to thank the *Topeka Capital-Journal* for giving me access to its many photographs.

Many thanks also to Nancy Sherbert and her team at the Kansas Historical Society for granting me access to black newspapers and helping me locate photographs and critical stories about African Americans in Topeka. Thanks to Martha Imparato from Washburn University Archives for her help with information about the Washburn alumni. This work would not have been complete had it not been for two special people: Donna Rae Pearson, who contributed her expertise in black history, and Carol Christensen, whose editing is beyond reproach. Most precious of all were my sister LaDawndra Robbs and my daughter Rah Gist, who were a great inspiration and support to me throughout the entire writing process. Last, but not least, I express gratitude to the many Topekans who contributed their photographs and stories to this project. Please inquire for a list of sources used for the captions.

The images in this volume appear courtesy of the Kansas Historical Society (KHS), the Topeka & Shawnee County Public Library (TSCPL), the Spencer Research Library Kansas Collection at the University of Kansas (KSCOLL), or as otherwise noted.

Introduction

The history of African Americans in Topeka is unique in US history—not just because slaves escaped through the Underground Railroad to Topeka or because, prior to and during the Civil War, Kansas was a free state that bordered the slave state of Missouri. Other cities can claim the same. The history of African Americans in Topeka is unique for four distinct reasons. First, the final battle over slavery started in Topeka with the Free State Constitutional Convention of 1856, two years after Kansas became a territory. Here began the process of creating a territorial government that outlawed slavery in its new constitution, a development helped lead to the Civil War. Second, shortly after the Civil War, a mass exodus of former slaves came from the South to make Topeka their home. Third, the US Supreme Court's 1954 ruling in *Brown v. Board of Education of Topeka* changed education and civil rights in the nation forever. Finally, many famous blacks had their starts in Topeka. Through photographs, this work showcases this rich history, telling the story of these distinctive people and the events that involved and impacted them.

The conflict over slavery began when part of the vast region that had been Indian Territory became Kansas Territory in 1854. The Kansas-Nebraska Act of 1854 opened up this land, which was inhabited by many Native American tribes, for westward expansion of the United States. It also effectively repealed the Missouri Compromise of 1820 by allowing the new settlers to decide if they wanted to allow slavery in their territory. At this same time, the history of African Americans in Topeka also began.

In the early years of the Kansas Territory, Topeka became a haven for runaway slaves, as well as conductors who aided them on the Underground Railroad. Those who escaped slavery and traveled the Underground Railroad to Topeka found safe passage north because of the assistance of abolitionist friends such as James Lane, John Ritchie, John Brown, Jacob Willites, Daniel Sheridan, and Rev. Lewis Bodwell, who helped them at the peril of their own lives. Some of the African American Topekans documented in this book could trace their family history back to those years before Kansas became a state.

The expansion of settlements into the new Kansas Territory also meant the opportunity for the extension of slavery into the area. This possibility caused both the pro-slavery forces and the abolitionists to flood Kansas with supporters who sought to influence the vote in their favor. The clash of these two groups resulted in bloodshed, with each side determined to have its own way. The troubles in Kansas between these two forces eventually played out on the national stage and, in 1861, erupted into the Civil War.

In January 1862, Gen. James Lane, an abolitionist, declared that it was the duty of Kansas to make Missouri a free state. After January 1863, African Americans were officially allowed to fight for the cause in the US Army. The 1st and 2nd Kansas Colored Troops were the first all-black regiments in Kansas to fight against slavery. Their valiant efforts during Civil War battles have been duly noted in history books, and a memorial now stands in Washington, DC, as a testament to their valor.

At the beginning of the Civil War, hundreds of slaves escaped into Kansas after Union troops occupied Missouri. After leaving their masters, they traveled along with the military units. Many Missouri slaves also escaped to Kansas in 1862 after the Missouri River froze. Those refugees were aided by the Underground Railroad, which traveled through Lawrence to Topeka, then north on Lane's Trail and beyond.

Some blacks came to Topeka after the Civil War. Many had fought in the conflict and settled in Topeka during the Reconstruction era to take advantage of opportunities they had never before experienced: chances for political office, education, employment, and a rich social life. For the first time, these African Americans began to enjoy some of the freedoms and rights of American citizenship.

Topeka also became a beacon to the freed slaves who wanted to escape the harsh laws in the South that followed the abolition of slavery. Looking for a better way of life, blacks began to leave the South to organize colonies in Topeka and in other towns on the eastern border of Kansas. After the end of Reconstruction, however, the migration known as the Great Exodus of 1879 found blacks fleeing the South by the thousands. During this period, the Exodusters left the South and headed for Kansas, where former slaves found freedom from the continued threat to their liberty and their lives.

The black newspapers in Kansas carried information from one black community to another throughout the state and the nation. The black community was just that: a community. It did not matter where in Kansas these African Americans lived, they all were a part of the same community, and the black newspapers were the connectors. Topeka had many black newspapers over the years. The longest-running publication was the *Plaindealer*, which carried the news to black communities all over Kansas. The chronicles in these newspapers are now important sources for the history of African Americans in Topeka.

Thomas Cox used the *Plaindealer* as a foundation for his research on the black history of Topeka. He documented his work in his book, *Blacks in Topeka, Kansas: 1865–1915, A Social History* in 1982. A longtime Topekan whose ancestry included generations of community leaders, Cox used insights and information from his family in writing his influential work. Like Cox, this author of *African American Topeka* has generations of Topeka relatives and strong ties to the spirit of the black community. This work will build on Cox's work by using images that illustrate the significance of historical events, places, and African Americans in Topeka.

The images of *African American Topeka* show the role that Topeka has played in the African American experience in Kansas and in the United States. They also illustrate many of the experiences that blacks in Topeka shared with African Americans from many other parts of the country during the last 150 years: for example, their efforts to build a strong community during the Jim Crow era, when "separate but equal" policies for schools and other segregation and discrimination existed. This book also shows that the all-black elementary schools and businesses became a viable asset in the formation of the black community in Topeka and that churches, civic organizations, and recreational activities became its strength and foundation.

As time brought changes for African Americans throughout the country, change also came to Topeka. Today, African Americans in Topeka have permeated all aspects of society. Black leaders have continued to thrive in business, education, the arts, and local, state, and national government. The presence of African Americans in public life gives a distinct leadership presence in the city and the black community. These pages are offered as a tribute to those who are or have been leaders in Topeka's black community and those who struggled to lay the foundation for future generations.

One

The Beginning

Territorial Days to the Turn of the Century

The history of African Americans in Topeka is intertwined with Kansas history like the fibers of a woven cloth. One story cannot be told without the other. Their histories are inseparable, and their stories are ones of struggle and triumph.

The first documented African American to live in the Topeka area was Ann Davis Shatteo (also known as Chattilon). She was born free but stolen as a child from her home, taken to Missouri, and enslaved. Ann was hired out at the age of 30 at Fort Scott and later at a trading post in Uniontown. She was living there among the Pottawatomie Indians when she married Claymore Chattilon (Shatteo). They purchased her freedom on March 14, 1849, and settled in Topeka on the Shunganunga Creek, where they raised their family.

During the territorial days of Kansas in the mid- to late 1850s, escaping slaves made their way on the Underground Railroad to Topeka and surrounding area. Continuing research reveals additional information on Underground Railroad activities previously unknown.

With the collapse of the post–Civil War Reconstruction, the Compromise of 1877, and the subsequent pullout of Union soldiers from the Southern states, opportunities for full citizenship for blacks in the South began to fade. These changes left the freed slaves unprotected and unable to defend themselves against the cruelties of many Southern whites. They lost their property and experienced lynchings and many other atrocities. Fear and a desire for a better life prompted thousands of blacks to leave the South and head for Kansas.

From the mid-1870s to the early 1880s, ex-slaves flooded into Kansas. Many of them made Topeka their home. Topeka became a place of refuge, a place where a large community of African Americans began to thrive in spite of continued difficulties. This chapter illustrates some of the early African Americans who came to Topeka as fleeing slaves prior to and during the Civil War and also as Exodusters during the mass exodus between 1879 and 1880.

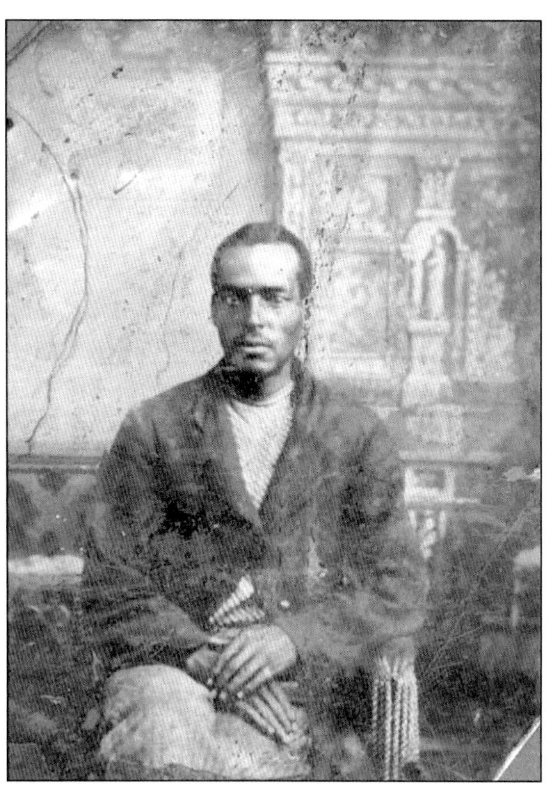

Allen Williams. Born in Tennessee in 1838, Allen Williams moved to Kansas in the early 1860s with his father, Nelson, and seven siblings. The Williams family settled south of the Topeka area in Auburn, where they farmed the land. They were among the earliest black settlers in the Topeka area prior to the Exodus. Williams married Armilda C. Benning (below) in Topeka in 1873, and together they had seven children. This tintype is dated between 1865 and 1870. (Courtesy of KHS.)

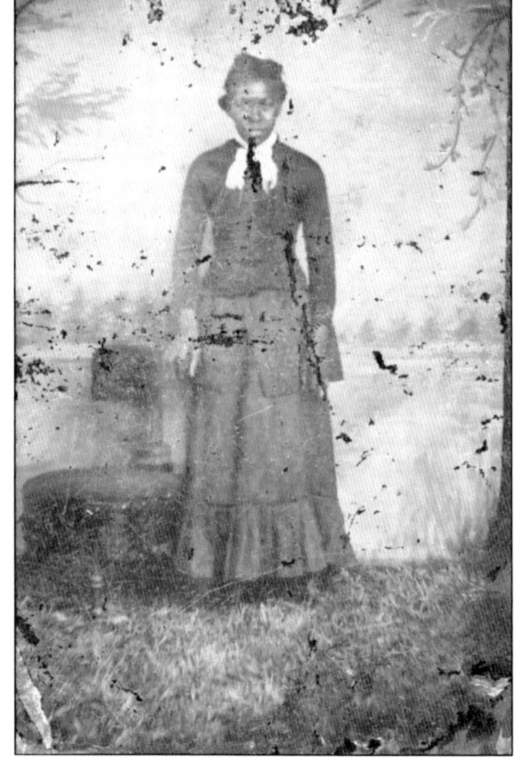

Armilda Benning Williams. Armilda was born in 1848 in Missouri and was the oldest of 14 children. She and her husband, Allen, raised their family in Waveland, an area just south of Topeka, in present-day Auburn. Her father, John Benning, was an escaped slave from Weston, Missouri. At the beginning of the Civil War, he crossed the Missouri River to Leavenworth, where he worked for two years before returning to Weston with soldiers for his family. Shortly after Quantrill's Raid in 1863, he moved his family south through Lawrence to Waveland. Armilda told her family story in 1941 in the *Topeka State Journal*. This photograph was taken in the 1860s. (Courtesy of KHS.)

SARAH P. BENNING. Like her sister Armilda, Sarah was born in Missouri and was one of 14 children of John (born in Winchester, Kentucky) and Angeline Wallace Mosby Benning (born in Missouri). Her family was enslaved by Jenny Lafferty Brassfield in Weston, Missouri. Following their emancipation, Sarah grew up in Waveland, an area located just south of Topeka. (Courtesy of KHS.)

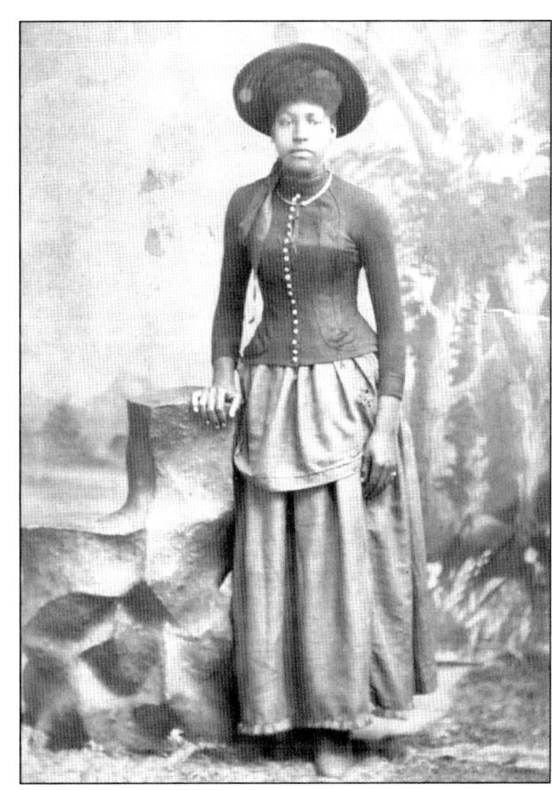

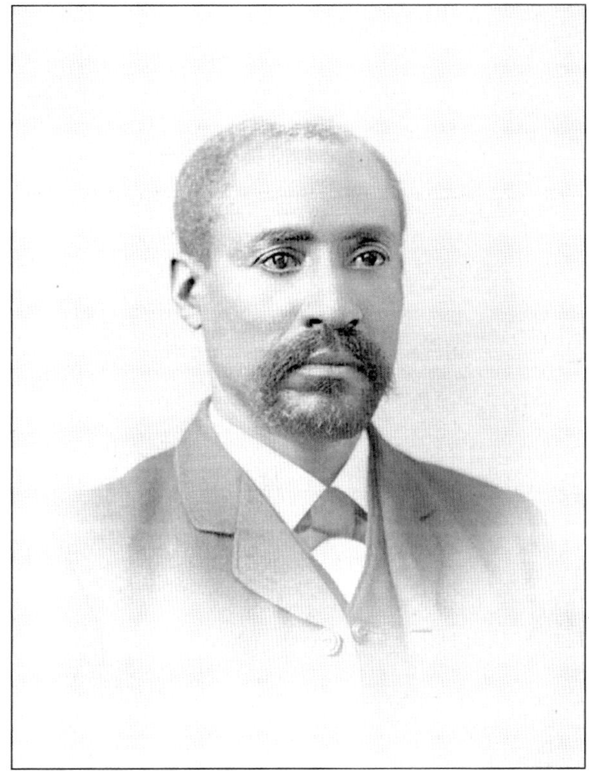

DAVID WARE. Ware was born a slave in 1839 in Missouri. He escaped to Kansas during the Civil War and served in the 1st Kansas Colored Infantry. He obtained a job at the state capitol as a janitor, a job that was well respected in the black community. When he died in 1888, the state flag was lowered in his honor, and the legislators observed a moment of silence. Many in the black community called him "Captain Ware" as a sign of respect. He was an esteemed member of the Second Baptist Church. This photograph was taken between 1865 and 1870. (Courtesy of KHS.)

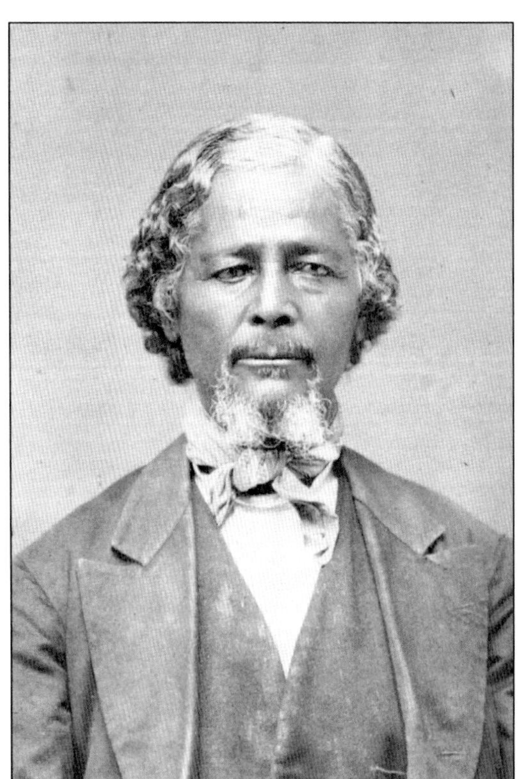

Benjamin "Pap" Singleton. Pap Singleton is considered the "Father of the Exodus." He escaped from slavery in Tennessee to freedom in Canada. After emancipation, he returned to Tennessee to encourage other African Americans to strive for a better life. He tried to persuade African Americans to buy land and own their own farms. When those efforts failed, Singleton formed the Tennessee Real Estate & Homestead Association in order to buy land in Kansas. He then recruited families to move to Kansas and established several colonies, including Tennessee Town in Topeka. (Courtesy of KHS.)

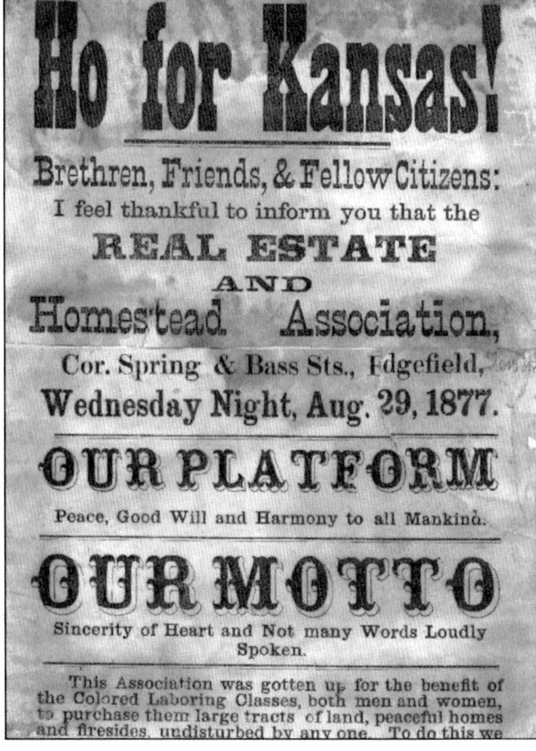

Ho for Kansas!

Brethren, Friends, & Fellow Citizens:
I feel thankful to inform you that the
REAL ESTATE
AND
Homestead Association,
Cor. Spring & Bass Sts., Edgefield,
Wednesday Night, Aug. 29, 1877.

OUR PLATFORM
Peace, Good Will and Harmony to all Mankind.

OUR MOTTO
Sincerity of Heart and Not many Words Loudly Spoken.

This Association was gotten up for the benefit of the Colored Laboring Classes, both men and women, to purchase them large tracts of land, peaceful homes and firesides, undisturbed by any one. To do this we

Ho for Kansas Flyer. Pap Singleton created this flyer for the Tennessee Real Estate & Homestead Association in order to encourage African Americans to immigrate to Kansas. It was circulated in Tennessee and across the South to promote African American land ownership in Kansas. (Courtesy of KHS.)

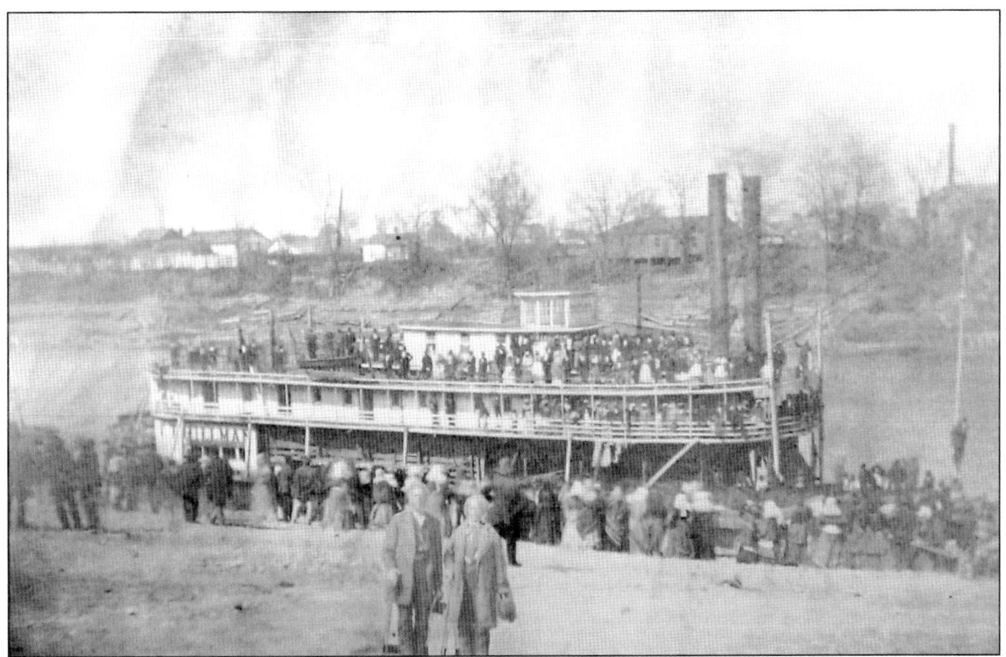

Steamboat for Kansas. An image of Pap Singleton (right) and his associate, S.A. McClure, is superimposed onto the foreground of this 1876 photograph of the steamboat *Hillman*, which was filled with Exodusters from Nashville, Tennessee. After the circulation of Tennessee Real Estate & Homestead Association advertisements, groups of African Americans gathered to form organized settlements in Kansas, including in Topeka, Nicodemus, and Dunlap (Emporia). The migration of Exodusters started after one of these initial groups of 300 immigrants headed for Kansas. (Courtesy of KHS.)

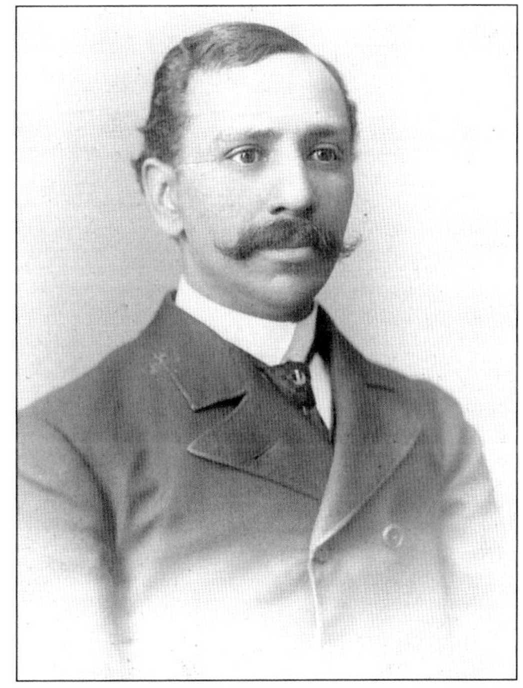

Edward P. McCabe. Edward McCabe was known for his promotion of black settlement in both Kansas and Oklahoma. He was born in 1850 in Troy, New York, and traveled the country after working as a clerk on Wall Street and for the federal treasury in Chicago. He moved to Nicodemus, Kansas, prior to the Exodus in 1878, and then to Topeka, where he worked as a lawyer and real estate agent. He then moved to Oklahoma and established African American colonies there. McCabe died in Illinois but was buried in Topeka. (Courtesy of KHS.)

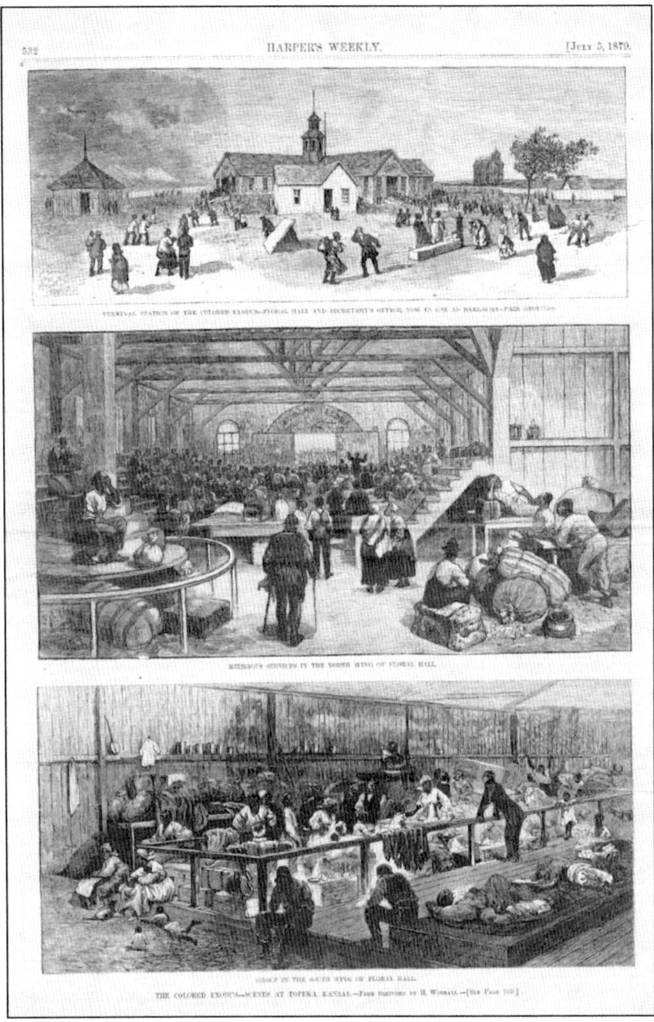

532 HARPER'S WEEKLY. [July 5, 1879.

TERMINAL STATION OF THE COLORED EXODUS—FLORAL HALL AND SECRETARY'S OFFICE, NOW IN USE AS BARRACKS—FAIR GROUNDS.

RELIGIOUS SERVICES IN THE NORTH WING OF FLORAL HALL.

GROUP IN THE SOUTH WING OF FLORAL HALL.

THE COLORED EXODUS—SCENES AT TOPEKA, KANSAS.—From Sketches by H. Worrall.—[See Page [illegible].]

Colored Exodus Scenes. This page comes from the July 3, 1879, issue of the weekly news and editorial journal *Harper's Weekly*, which ran from 1857 to 1916. It was published in New York and had subscribers from all over the country. This page illustrates the Exodusters at various points in their journey. The sketches were made by the Topeka artist Henry Worrall. His illustrations promoted life in Kansas and were considered "journalism in pictures," often capturing ideas that photographs could not. (Courtesy of KHS.)

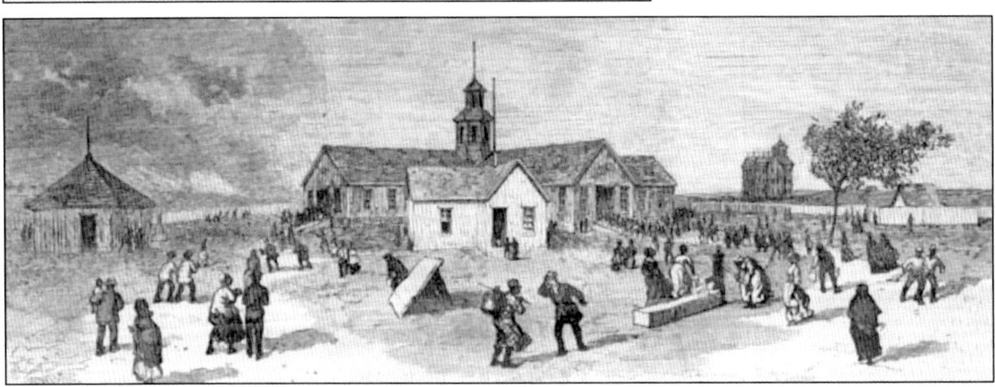

Terminal Station of Colored Exodus. This is the first drawing from the July 3, 1879, *Harper's Weekly*. The flood of African American Exodusters fleeing to Kansas caused a severe housing problem. The City of Topeka provided temporary housing at Floral Hall and the secretary's office at the fairgrounds (now the site of the Kansas Expocentre). The building in the distance on the right is Washburn College. (Courtesy of KHS.)

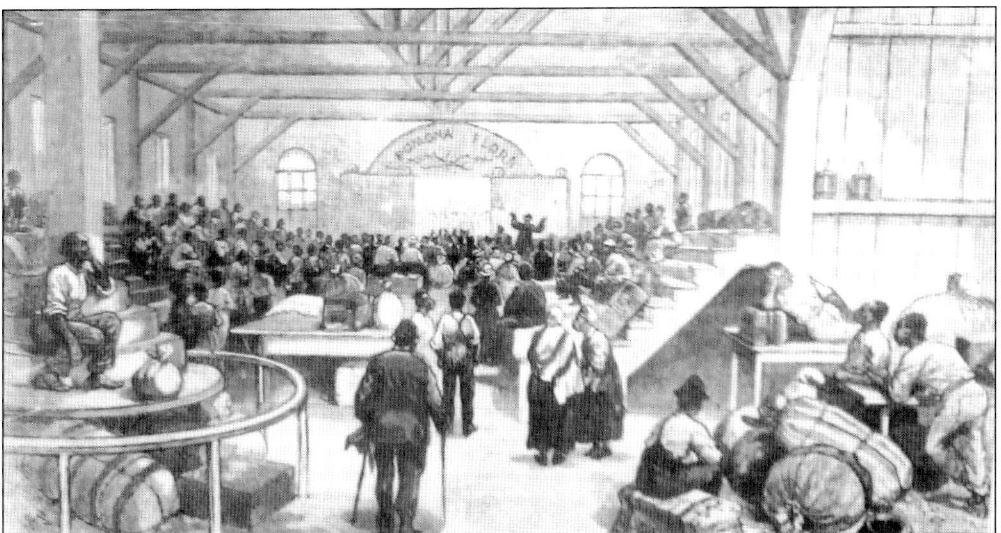

Religious Services in Floral Hall North Wing. Seen here is the second drawing from this issue of *Harper's Weekly*. Deeply rooted in religion as their foundation, the Exodusters attended church services at the north wing to keep themselves encouraged. Various churches in the community were involved in the aid of their African American brothers and sisters. They participated in the relief association by providing food, clothing, support, and, in some cases, shelter. (Courtesy of KHS.)

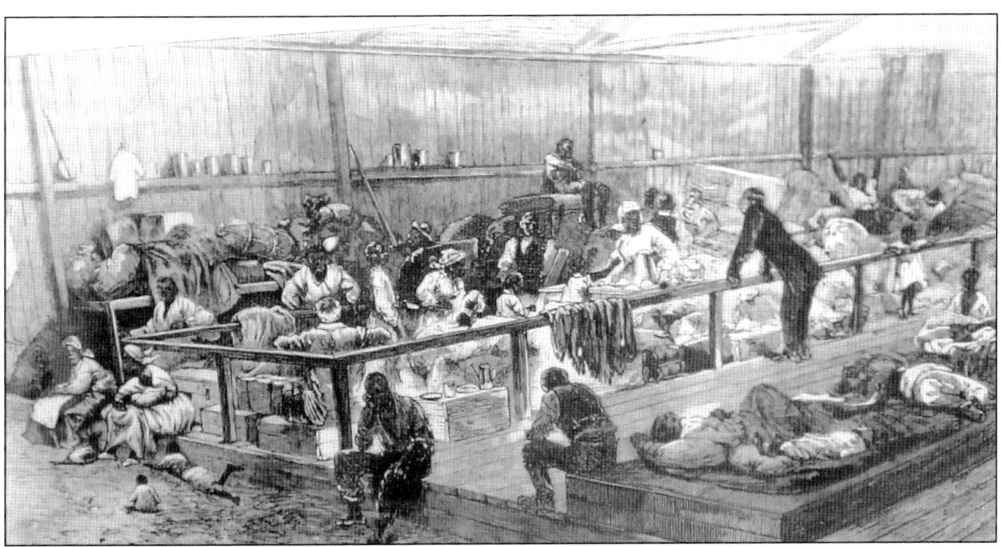

Group in Floral Hall South Wing. This is the third of the three drawings from the issue of *Harper's Weekly* dated July 3, 1879. Many of the Exodusters had no money and no means to provide their own housing. Hundreds, and then thousands, of Exodusters had only enough money to get them from their Southern homes by boat on the Mississippi River to St. Louis, Missouri. They were then taken to Wyandotte (present-day Kansas City, Kansas) and eventually arrived in Topeka by train. Destitute and homeless, the Exodusters found help from their new neighbors. (Courtesy of KHS.)

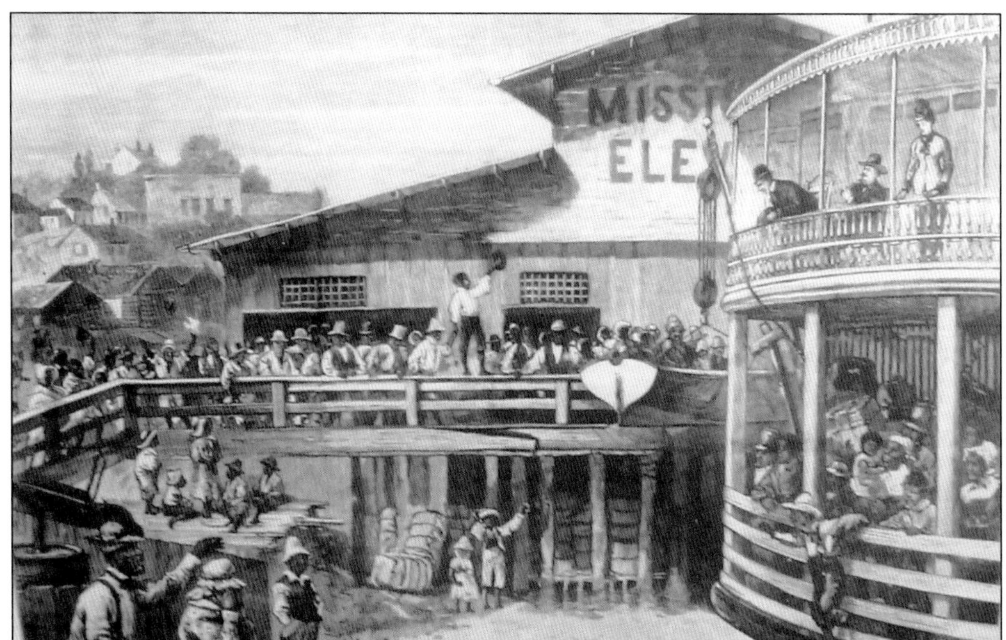

Scene on the Wharves at Vicksburg, Mississippi. A large gathering of African American Exodusters congregates at a steamboat docked in Vicksburg, Mississippi, in this drawing by James H. Moser that appeared in *Harper's Weekly* on May 17, 1879. Thousands of people waited along the Mississippi River at wharves much like this one to travel to Kansas. The boats they could obtain passage on would drop them off in St. Louis, where another boat would take them to Wyandotte. (Courtesy of KHS.)

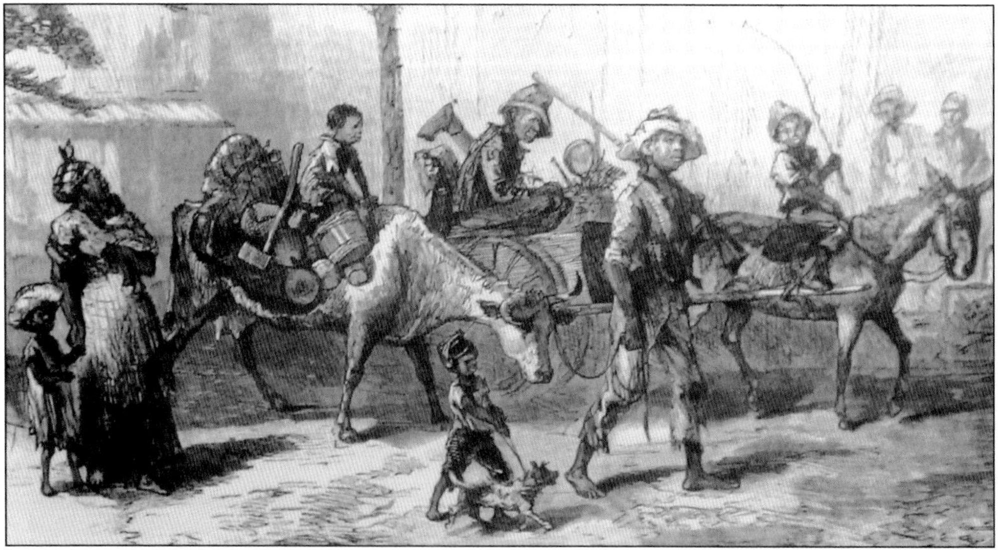

Fleeing from the Yellow Fever. Yellow fever was prevalent throughout many of the river towns, and as the Exodusters traveled through en route to Kansas, they came into contact with the disease. Sickness and death became rampant among them, and their host cities became afraid they were disease carriers. Unable to have proper hygiene, many Exodusters died. This drawing by H.J. Lewis, which was printed in *Harper's Weekly* on August 16, 1879, depicts African Americans fleeing the river towns to avoid yellow fever. (Courtesy of KHS.)

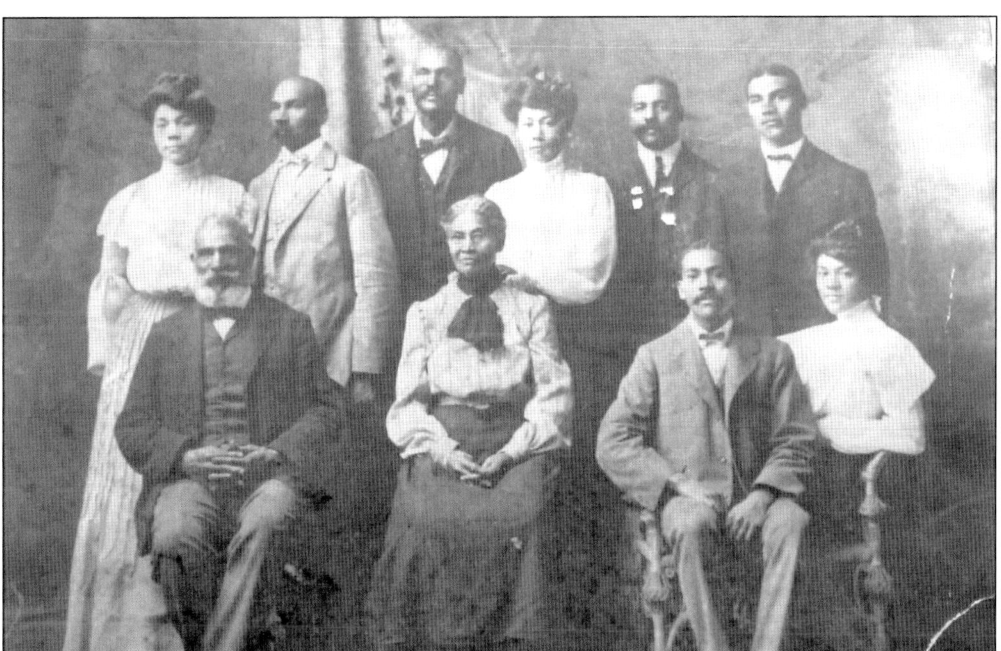

The Page Family, 1896. John Page was a freeman, and his wife, Mary Ellen (Forte) Page, was a former slave from Port Royale, Tennessee. John's father, Richard Page, settled in Wichita, while John and his wife and children came to Topeka with the Exodusters in 1879. John, who worked as a cobbler, died in Topeka. Pictured are, from left to right, (first row) John Page, Mary Ellen (Forte) Page, James Page, and Ellen Page; (second row) Minnie Page, Joseph Page, Gaitha Page, Mary Charlotte Page, Wesley Page, and John Page Jr. (Courtesy of Khadijah Matin.)

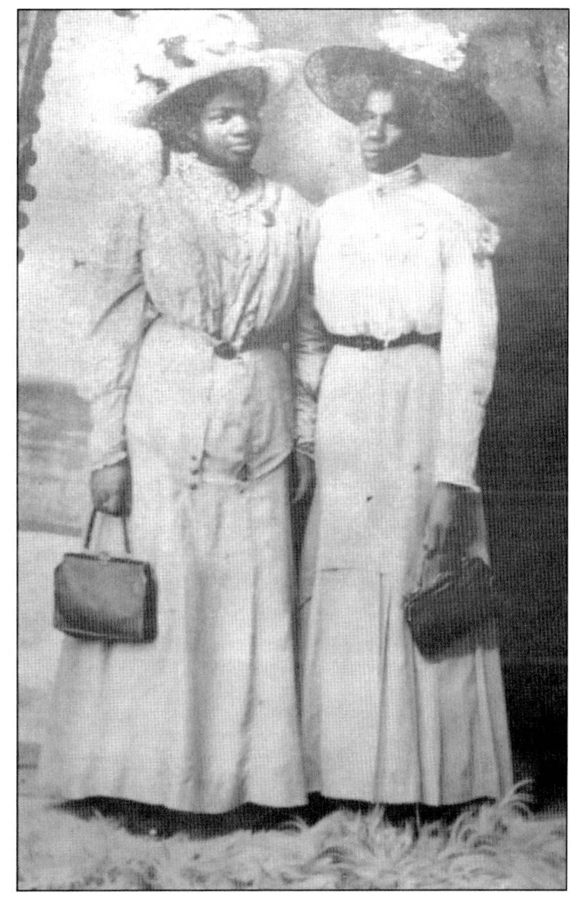

Geneva and Alberta Hall. This photograph is from Geneva Hall's photograph album, which was donated to the Kansas Collection at Spencer Library. It illustrates the style of clothes worn at the turn of the 20th century. While Geneva did not label the photograph, it likely shows her and her sister Alberta Hall, born in 1887 and 1884 respectively. (Courtesy of KSCOLL.)

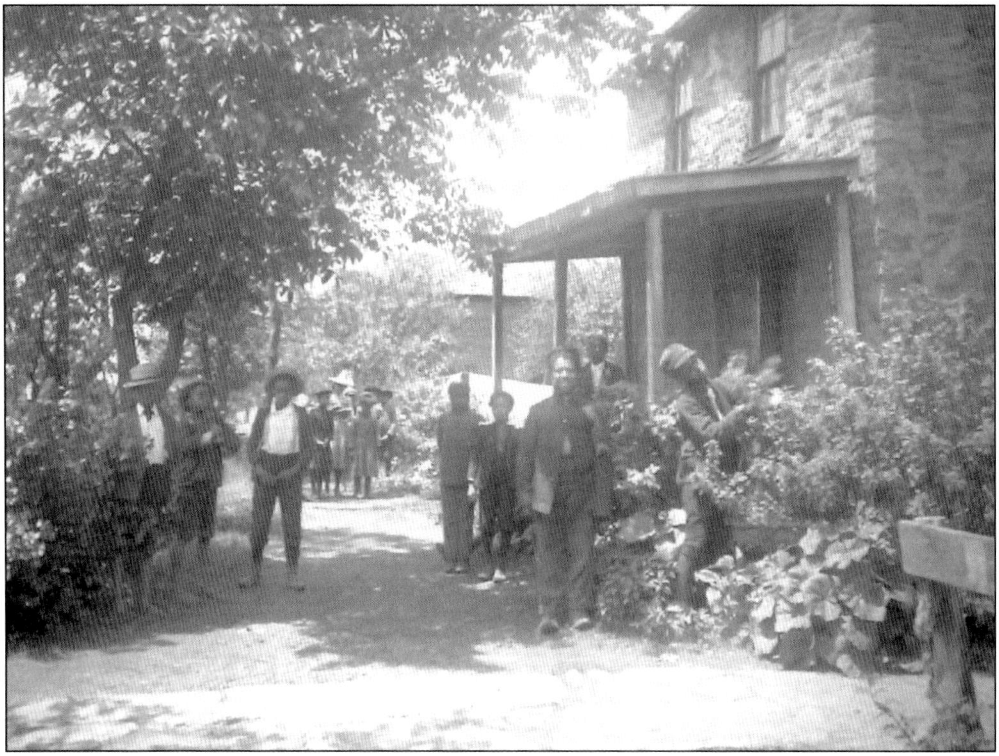

TENNESSEE TOWN CHILDREN. The Exodusters who arrived in Topeka settled in an area that came to be called Tennessee Town. The area was so named because of the many people who came from Tennessee during the migration. It was located in what was then the southwestern edge of Topeka in what is known as King's Addition. This photograph pictures the children of Tennessee Town in about 1900. (Courtesy of KHS.)

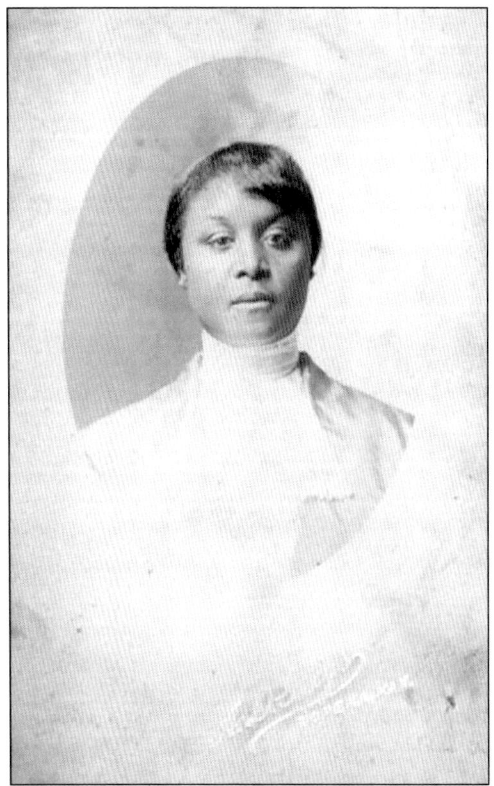

MAGGIE FITCHUE, 1910. Maggie, born in 1874 in Kansas City, Missouri, was one of 10 children of Joseph Fitchue Sr. and Sylvia Freeman Fitchue. The family moved to Lawrence in 1876 and then to Topeka. A pillar of the Topeka community, Maggie belonged to Calvary Baptist Church, the Golden Sheaf Temple No. 7, and the Sisters of the Mysterious Ten. While all of her siblings moved to other states, Maggie remained in Topeka with her father, who died in 1916. She died in 1927, one week after marrying Robert Skearce, a local barber. (Courtesy of Anita Hewitt-Williams.)

Two

FAITH THE FOUNDATION OF THE COMMUNITY

The church is and always has been the backbone of the black community. African Americans took care of one another through the church and its many branch organizations. The best example of this was shown by local congregations during the mass exodus from the South. As thousands of African Americans made their way to Topeka, they were helped by church communities in both Missouri and Kansas. The black churches raised funds to help pay for emigrants' transportation from St. Louis and Kansas City to Topeka. They provided food and clothes for the large groups of African Americans who migrated to the city without means to care for themselves. In addition, the most immediate need—shelter—was provided by local black churches for their brothers and sisters who arrived without lodging.

According to a 1939 *Topeka State Journal* article, the first congregation was established in the early 1860s by Rev. John Freeman, who came to this area as a free African American from Indiana in the 1850s. He reportedly started a missionary church at the corner of Second and Jackson Streets (where Adams Business Forms is now). The African and Colored Methodist Episcopal churches and the Baptist church were organized in Topeka not long afterwards and became the foundation of the Topeka black community.

Topeka has quite a few African American churches. Those depicted here are from the earliest years. These congregations have celebrated anniversaries in excess of 80 years, and many have spawned other organizations, including various gospel choirs and civic organizations, such as the Black Women's Clubs, the Links, Living the Dream, and countless others. This chapter makes mention of just a few of these groups to illustrate their commitment to the black community.

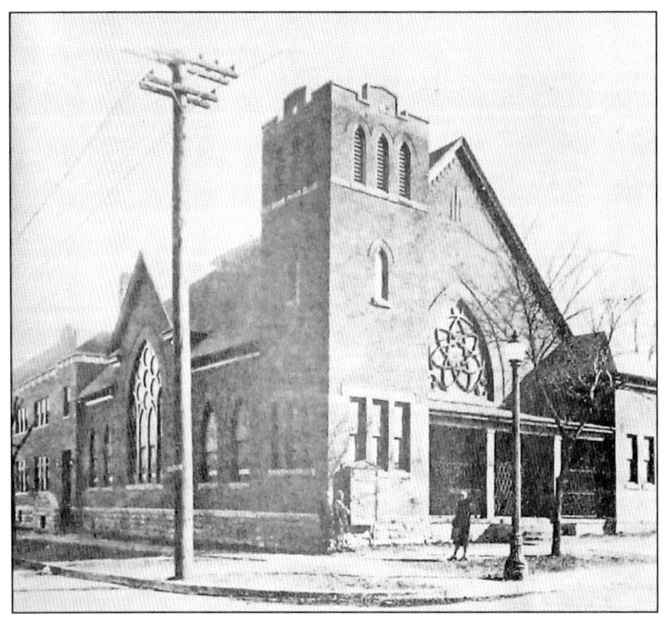

CALVARY BAPTIST CHURCH, 1895. Established in 1865, Calvary Baptist Church was the third black congregation in Topeka. It was initially called the First Colored Baptist Church of Topeka and was located on the north side of First Avenue, between Madison and Jefferson Streets. The original building, shown in this photograph, burned and was rebuilt. The church later moved to the southeast corner of Quincy and Third Streets. After several additional moves, it then relocated to its current site at 433 SW Street Harrison. (Courtesy of KHS.)

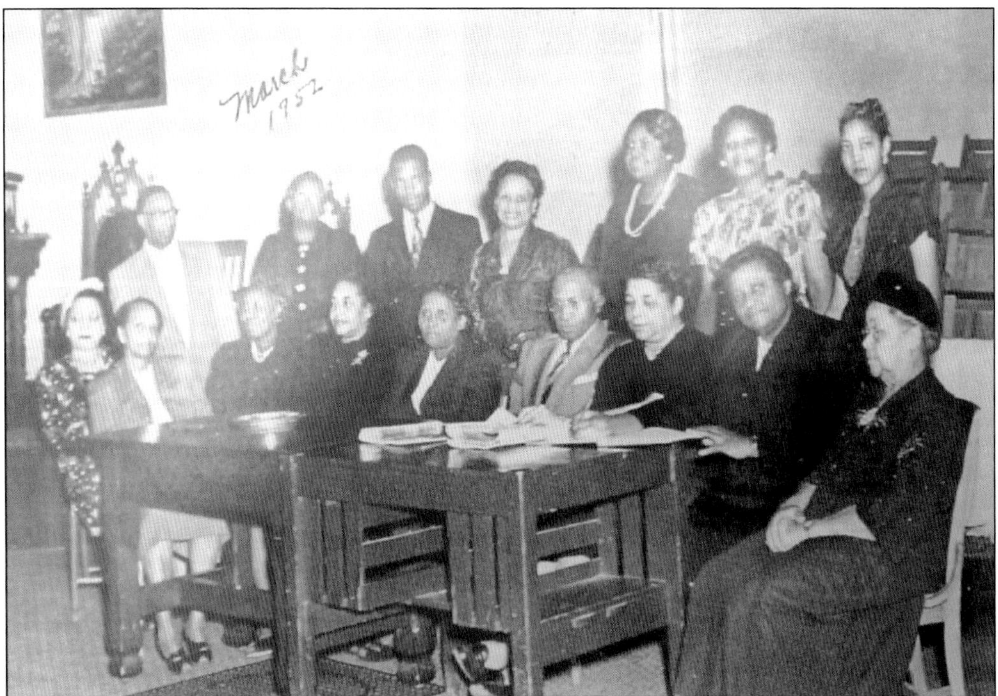

CALVARY'S *BIG BROADCAST*. In 1952, Calvary Baptist Church launched a program called the *Big Broadcast*. In this photograph, the planning committees are pictured together. The brainchild of Beatrice Gurden, the radio program continued until 1962. It featured local musical talent, fashion reviews, hairstyling tips, dramas, and a variety of other programming. In this image are, from left to right, (first row, seated) Beatrice Gurden, Mattie L. McIntosh, Leatha Bradley, Willie Pettit Wagner, Beatrice Byrd, Rev. E. Bernard Hurd, Lodie L. Hutton, Luella Reese, and Susie A. Washington; (second row, standing) F.R. Hutton, Josie Thomas, Gerald Walker, Gertrude Elzea, Beatrice Johnson, Bessie Farmer, and Octavia Anderson. (Courtesy of TSCPL.)

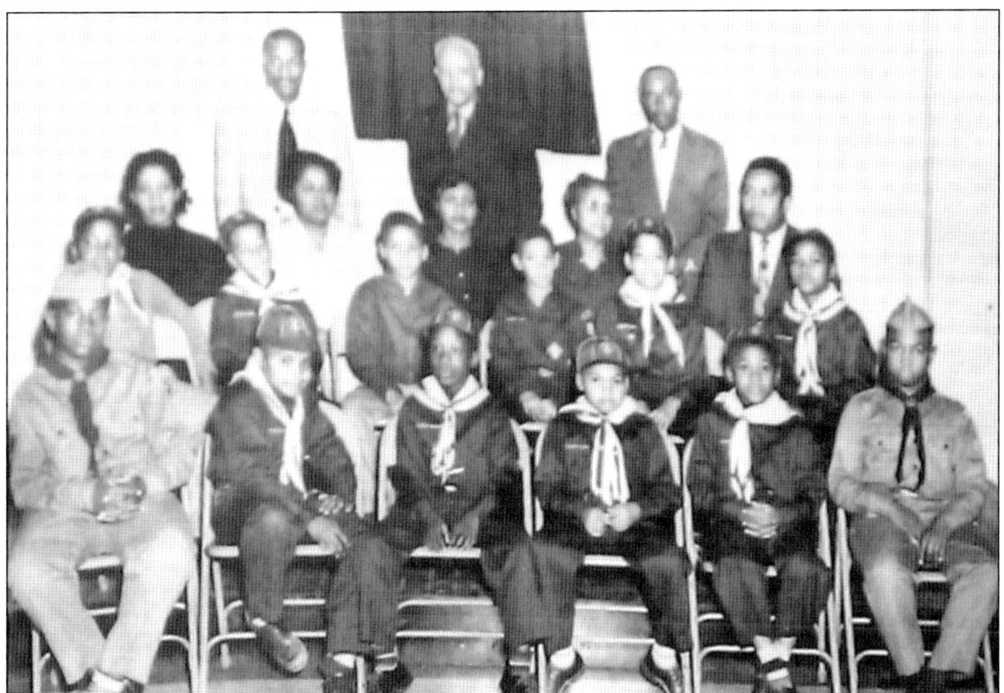

CALVARY BOY SCOUTS AND GIRL SCOUTS. Some of the youth activities at Calvary Baptist Church included Boy Scout and Girl Scout troops. The Boy Scouts met regularly for many years, participating in the church and citywide functions. The church also sponsored Girls Scout Troop No. 416, which began in 1961 with 17 girls from around the city. (Both photographs courtesy of TSCPL.)

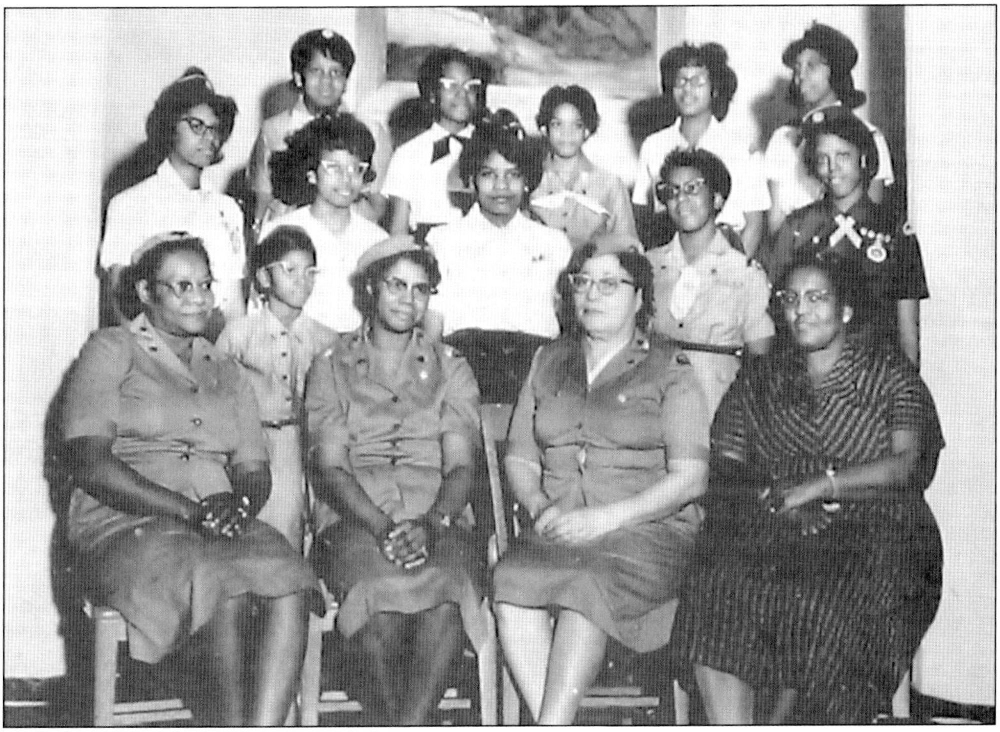

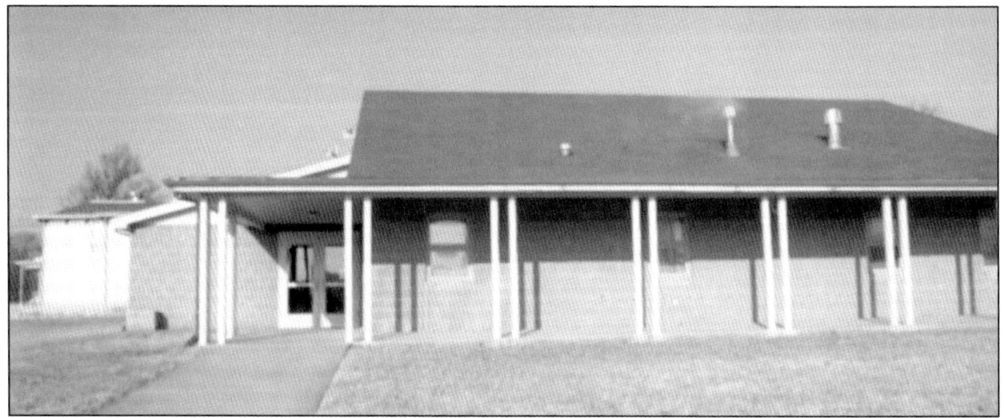

Calvary Baptist Church Today. Calvary has been through many changes over the years. It has changed its name, building, and location and has survived fires, floods, tornadoes, and urban renewal. In the 1960s, after urban renewal, it moved across the street from Fourth and Quincy Streets to its current location, 433 SW Harrison Street. Rev. Bernard Hurd currently serves as pastor. (Courtesy of Betty Young.)

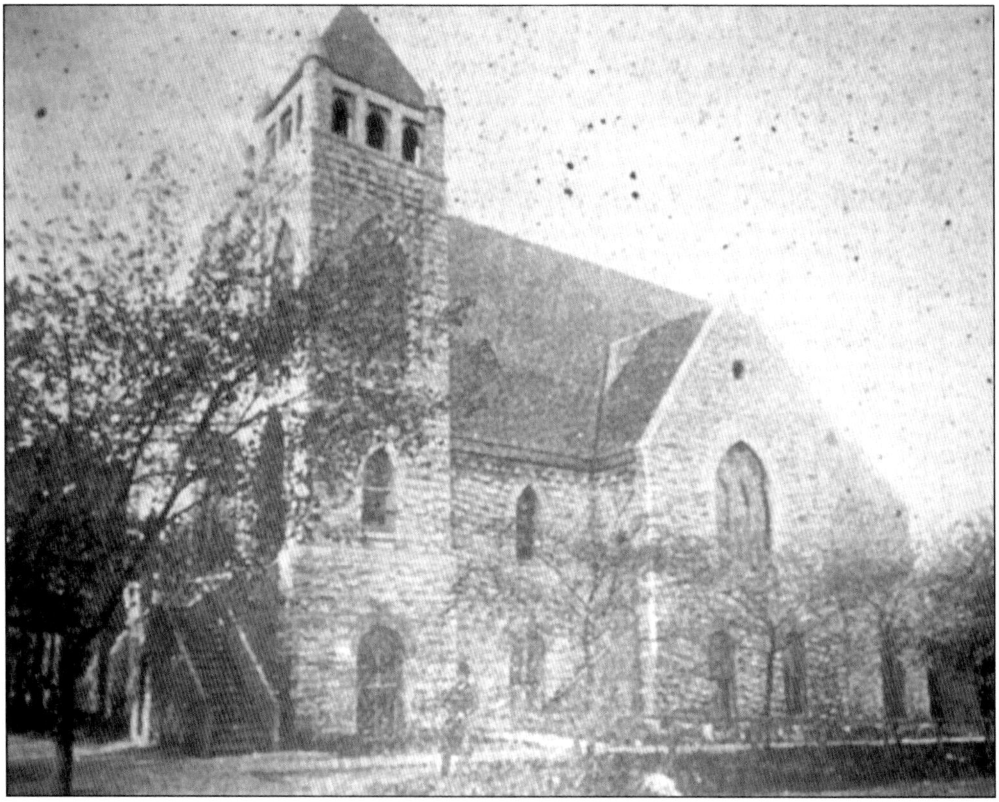

St. John African Methodist Episcopal Church Jubilee Celebration. St. John is located on the corner of Seventh Street and Topeka Boulevard. It was established in 1868 but was not located at its present site until 1886. This undated photograph comes from a leaflet advertising a jubilee celebration. Here, it is evident that the church had a different look than it does now. Apparently, this older building had a tower on the south side. The tower is not a part of the current building. (Courtesy of TSCPL.)

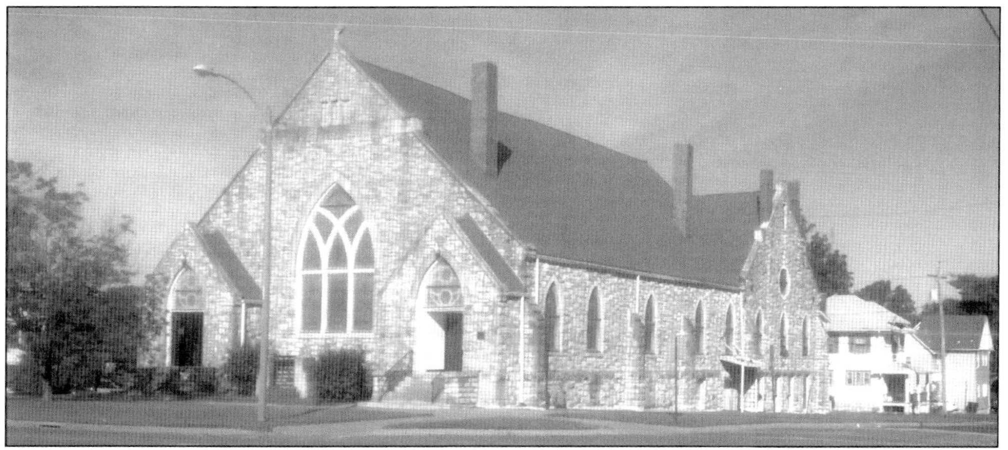

St. John African Methodist Episcopal Today. St. John has changed over the years. It went from a small prayer circle meeting at Second and Madison Streets to a large congregation that purchased land and moved to its present location at 701 SW Topeka Boulevard. It is the longest-standing African American church building in Topeka. Rev. V. Gordon Glenn III is the current pastor. (Courtesy of TSCPL.)

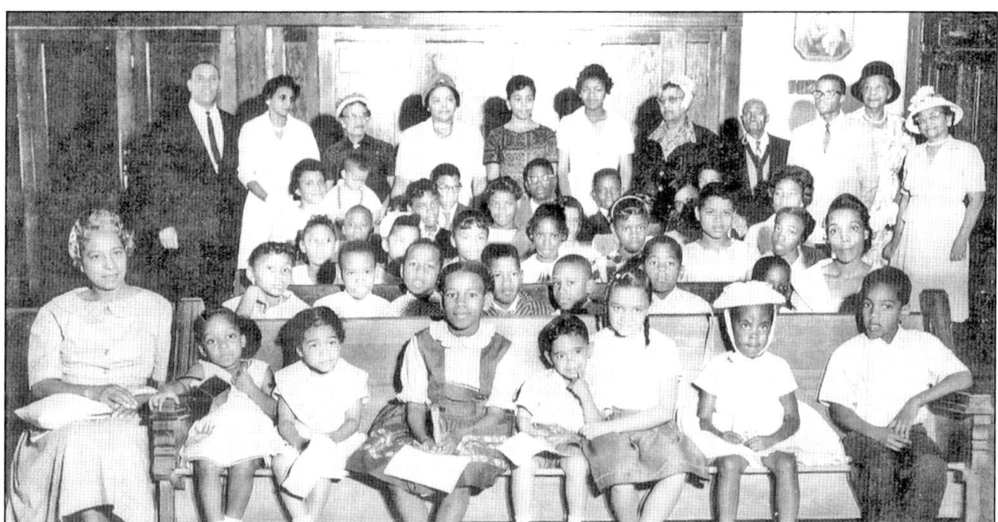

St. John AME Youth Sunday School Class, 1940s. This photograph from the 1940s shows the children and teachers of the youth Sunday school of St. John AME. The adults standing, left to right, are Rev. Grady Brown, Gertrude Logan, Esther Fisher, Ida Sheffield (Norman), Vickie Henderson, Norman Norman, Ethel Jamison, R.B. Moten, John Bryant, Daisy McDonald, and Jennie Robinson. Among the seated children and teachers are Ophelia Butcher, Tarlton ?, Yolanda Lisa ?, Joyce Blackwell, Stewart Blackwell, Emmett Bufford Jr., Cecile Butcher-Wilson, Jimmie Coleman, Jessie Cushinberry, Paula Cushinberry, Wanda Cushinberry, J.R. Edwards, Rodney Frank, James Logan, Pat Logan, Wesley Marshal, Kathryn Newman, Audrey Norton, Michael Norton, Karla Rhea, Carmen Wells, Connie Sawyer, ? Stamps, and Janice Tyler. (Courtesy of Maxine Dawson.)

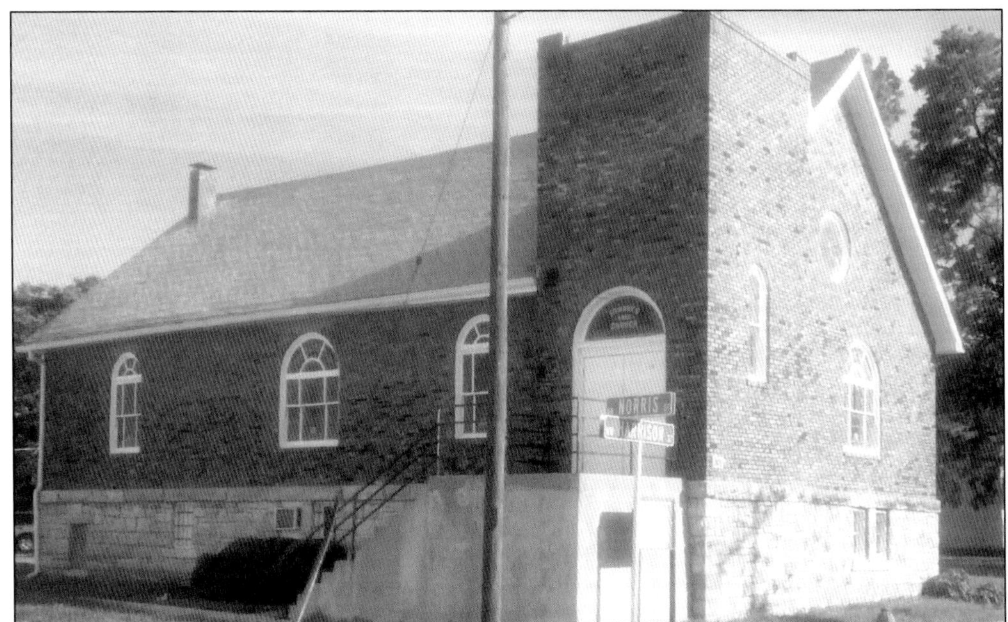

St. Mark's African Methodist Episcopal Church. St. Mark's was created by a group of Exodusters who arrived in North Topeka during the spring of 1879. In 1880, the North Topeka Mission was established as an AME church. The original members met in each other's homes until they constructed their first building on land donated in 1881 at Harrison and Railroad Streets. The church was not named St. Mark's until 1883. The land where it is currently located, 801 NW Harrison Street, was donated by Charles Curtis, a Topekan and former vice president of the United States. It came from parcels of land originally owned by his Kaw Native American ancestors. Rev. Shirley Heermance is pastor. (Courtesy of TSCPL.)

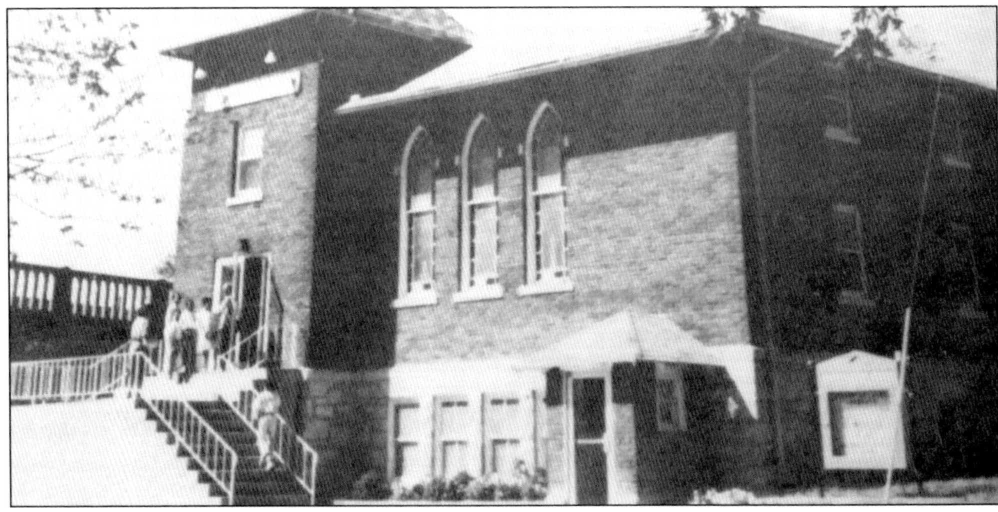

Second Baptist Church. Second Baptist Church was originally known as B Street Baptist Church and was located in North Topeka on North Tyler and Railroad Streets. It was first established in 1878, prior to the Exodus, and quickly outgrew its building. During the 1903 flood, it was the only place of refuge for hundreds of people. After it was destroyed by fire in 1907, a new stone-and-brick building was erected in 1910 at its current location on the corner of Laurent Street and Topeka Avenue. Rev. Bill Nicholson Jr. is the current pastor. (Courtesy of KHS.)

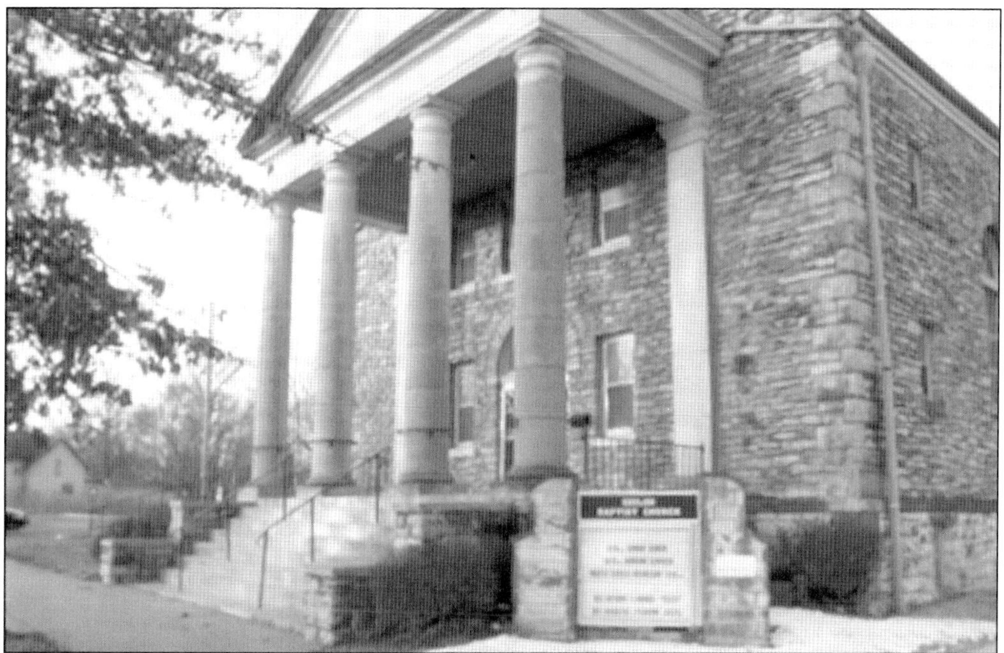

SHILOH BAPTIST CHURCH. Shiloh Baptist Church was organized in 1881 by the Tennessee Town residents who had been meeting in prayer groups since 1879. The original building was torn down in 1926, and the current structure was built on the same site at 1201 SW Buchanan Street. Shiloh was a popular meeting place, and many civic groups took photographs in front of the beautiful pillars on the front steps. Rev. B.C. Clark is pastor. (Courtesy of TSCPL.)

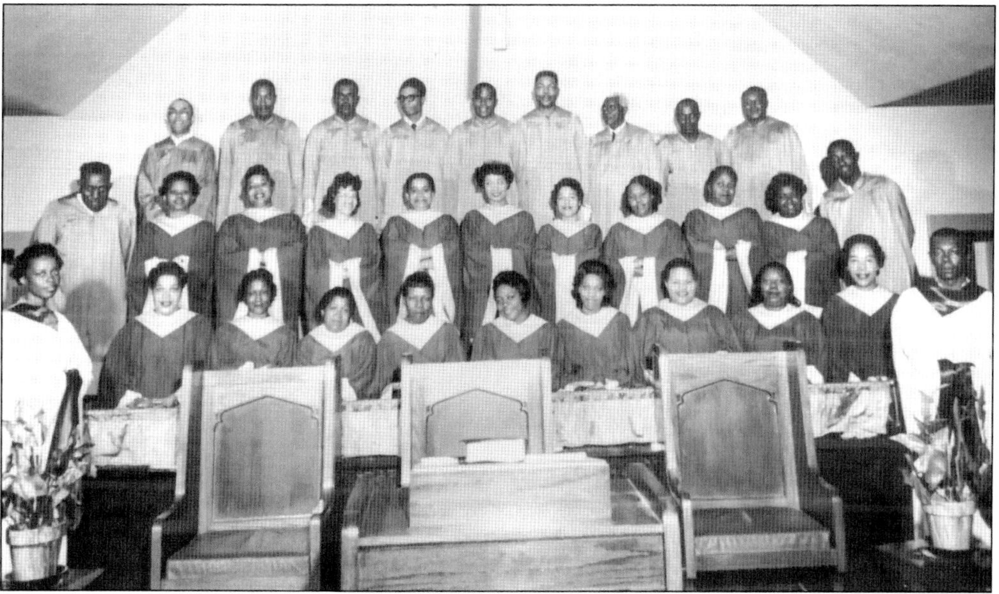

SHILOH BAPTIST CHURCH CHOIR. Shiloh was the central location for many activities that occurred in and around Tennessee Town in the black community, and other activities and civic groups evolved from it. Among its notable members were Mamie Williams and Ben and Emma Gaines, who owned Gaines & Son Mortuary. Ben and Emma Gaines also directed the popular Negro Festival Choir, which included many of their fellow church members. (Courtesy of TSCPL.)

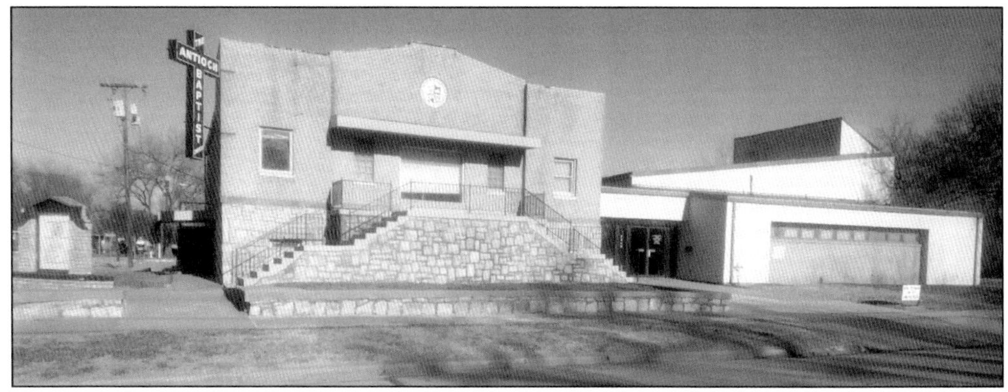

Antioch Missionary Baptist Church. Established in 1920 at 1100 SE Washington Avenue, this church has served its community well. It has sponsored the Spot, a teenage program; Harvesters, a community food bank; and, with the purchase of the former Highland Park North Elementary School, a community outreach program called the Antioch Family Life Center. The Antioch Family Life Center creates a strong sense of community for the church members and their east Topeka neighbors. T.D. Hicks is pastor. (Courtesy of the author.)

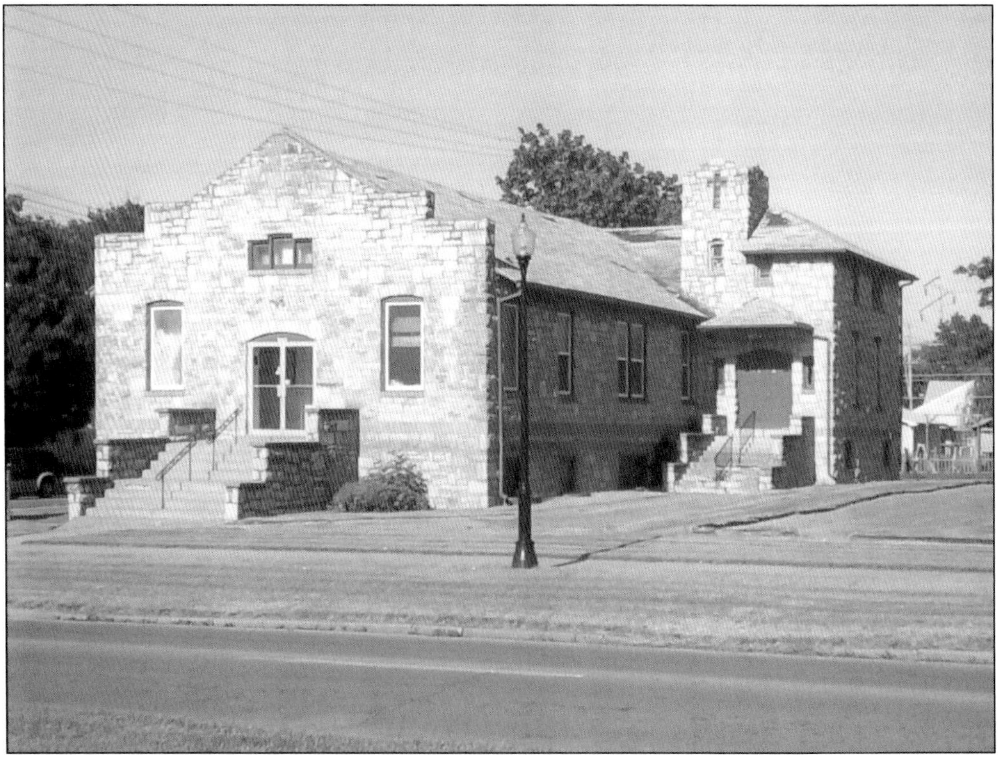

Lane Chapel Christian Methodist Episcopal Church. Organized in 1883, Lane Chapel was originally named Lane Chapel Colored Methodist Church and was located at the corner of Van Buren and Fourteenth Streets. After the 1966 tornado destroyed its building, the congregation relocated to 1600 SW Harrison Street. The current location was built after 1925 in Tennessee Town at 1200 SW Lane Street. Rev. Nicky Wickliffe is pastor. (Courtesy of KHS.)

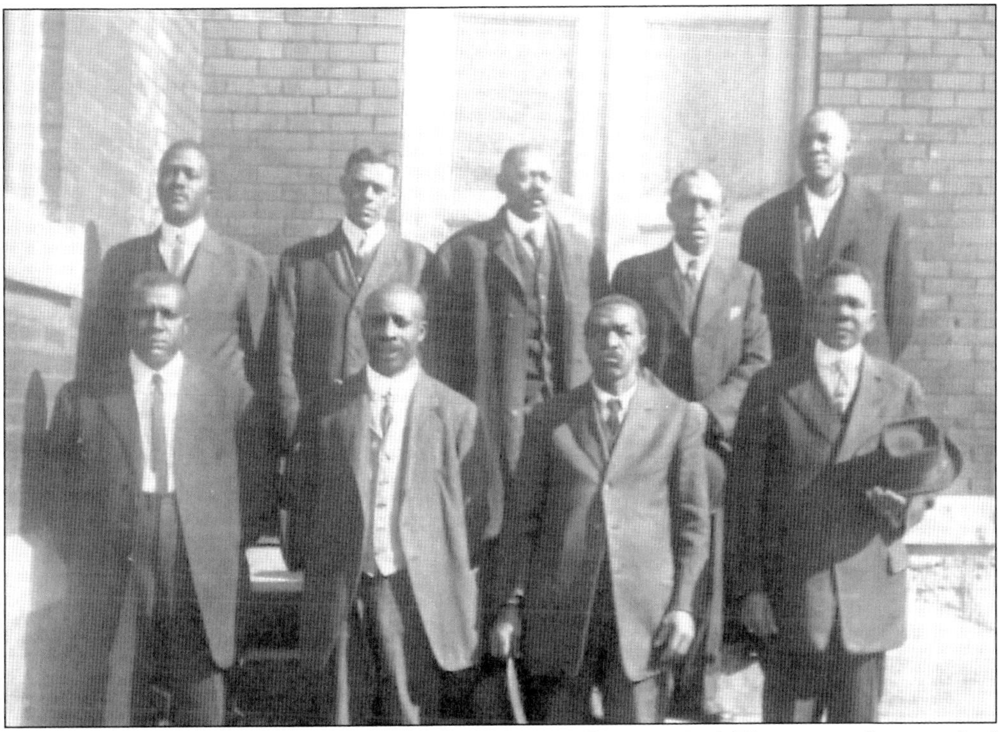

Lane Chapel Colored Methodist Episcopal Steward Board, 1916. These men, photographed outside the Harrison Street location, were responsible for assisting the pastor with many of the functions of the church, including spiritual leadership and the parish's financial affairs. (Courtesy of KHS.)

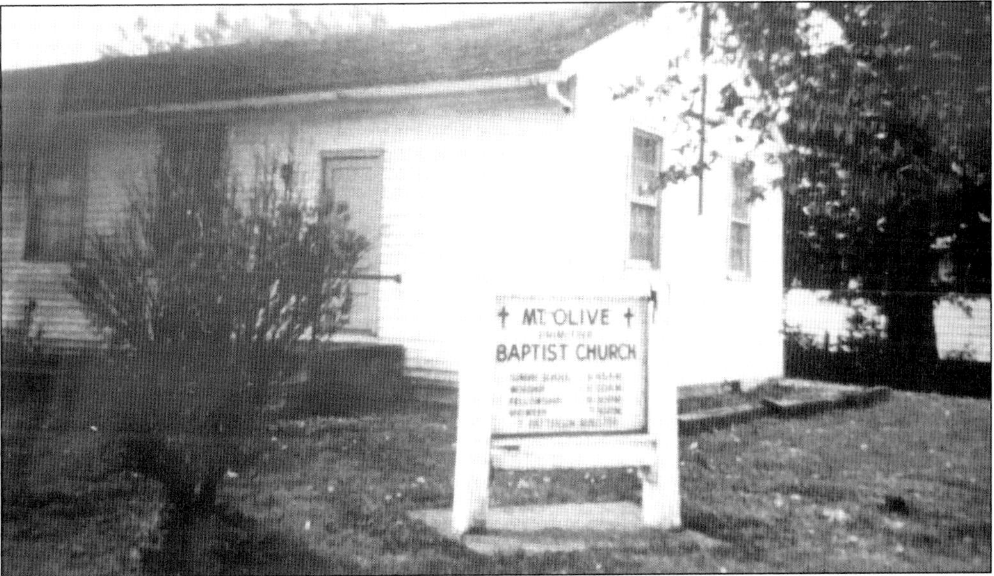

Mount Olive United Primitive Baptist Church. Originally organized in 1893, the church was destroyed by the flood of 1951 and then relocated to 701 North Gordon Street. Not much of its history survives. In 1971, the church was moved again, just across the street, to its current address at 700 Northwest Gordon Street. Rev. Jimmy Love is pastor. (Courtesy of Jimmy Love.)

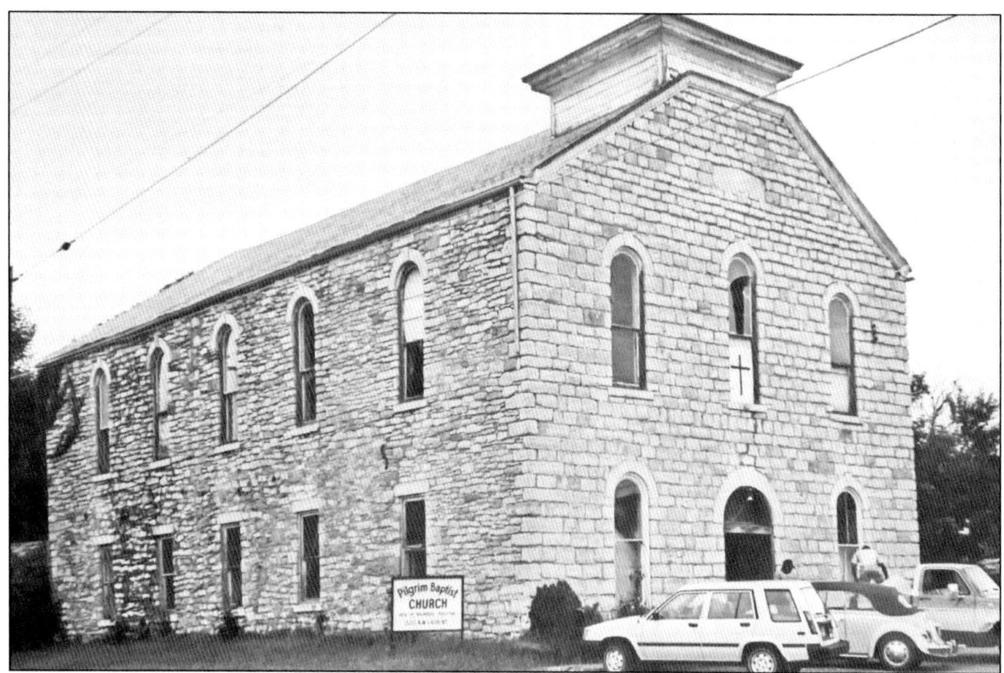

Pilgrim Missionary Baptist Church. This building, located at 316 NW Laurent Street, was erected between 1871 and 1879 by members of North Topeka Baptist Church, who hauled and placed each stone. In 1921, it was purchased and established as Pilgrim Missionary Baptist Church by Lemon and Essie Clark and their nephew and niece Clarence C. and Alberta Clark, all former members of Shiloh Baptist Church. The church is located now at 531 SE Thirty-Third Terrace. Rev. Kenneth Anderson Sr. is pastor. (Courtesy of the *Topeka Capital-Journal.*)

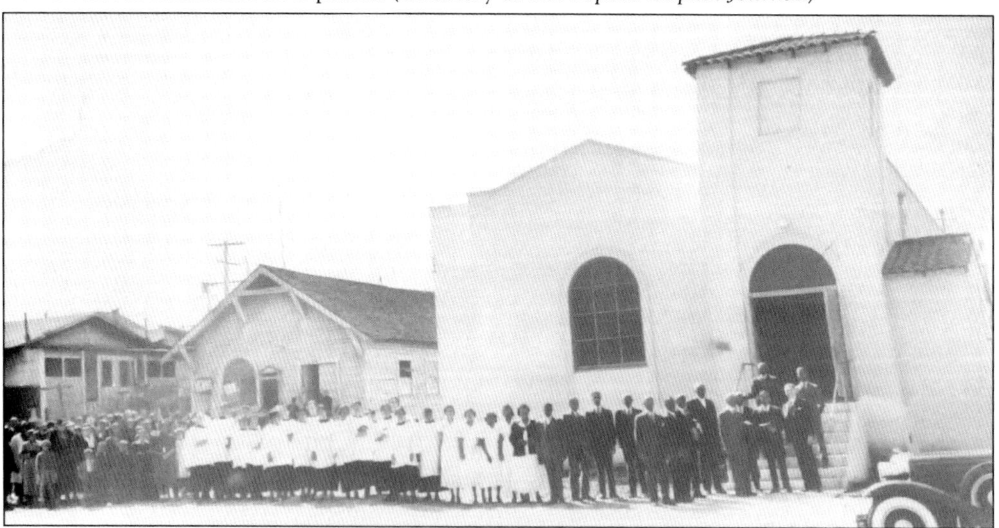

Mount Carmel Missionary Baptist Church Rededication. Mount Carmel Missionary Baptist Church was established in 1909 and is currently located at 610 SE Lime Street. After being remodeled, this building was rededicated in February 1937. Compared to the congregation's stone building today, the church in this photograph is much smaller, and the facade is made of stucco. The church has seen many changes since the members stood outside for this group photograph to celebrate the 1937 rededication. Rev. Marcus Clark is pastor. (Courtesy of KSCOLL.)

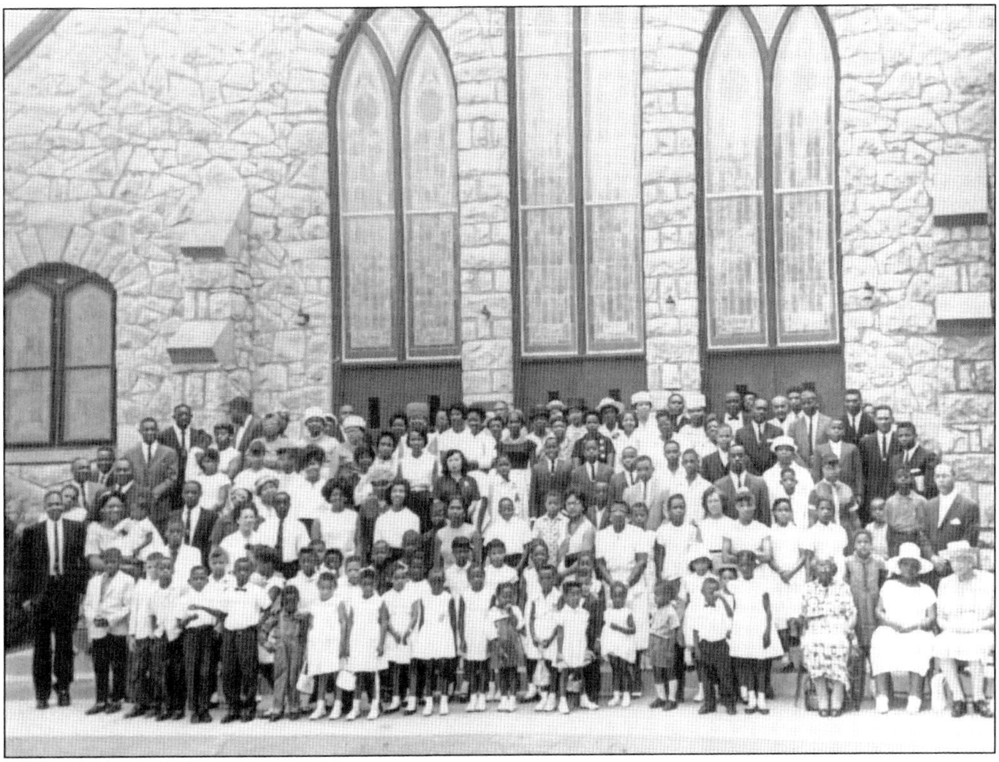

MOUNT CARMEL MISSIONARY BAPTIST CHURCH MEMBERS. This photograph, which was taken sometime in the 1930s or 1940s, depicts the church at 610 SE Lime Street as it still looks today after additional remodeling and renovation to the front of the building. The congregation had grown by this time, with the youth making up a large part. (Courtesy of KSCOLL.)

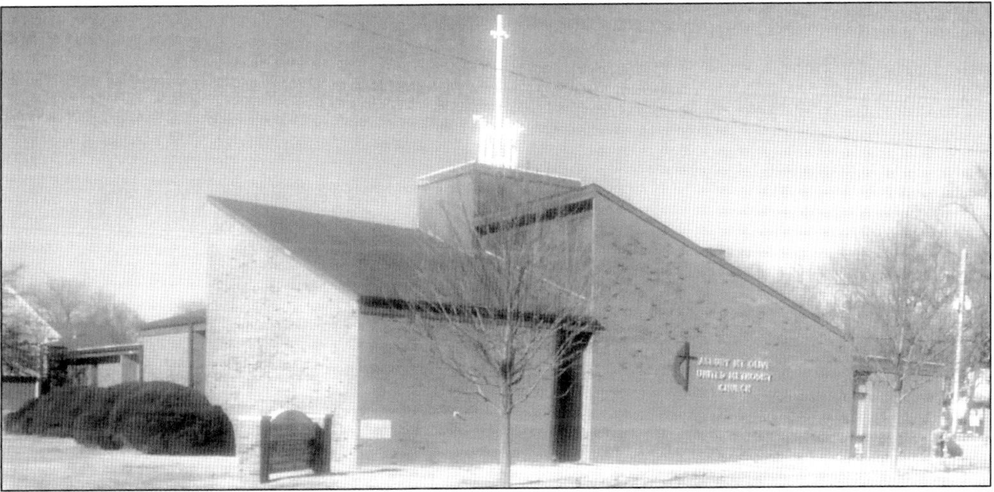

ASBURY MOUNT OLIVE UNITED METHODIST CHURCH. Asbury Mount Olive United Methodist Church was organized from two churches: Asbury Methodist and Mount Olive Methodist. Both were incorporated in the 1880s and merged in 1970. They were originally located in two separate areas of Topeka—Asbury, in the north, and Mount Olive, in central Topeka's Tennessee Town. The present building, constructed in 1974, is located in Tennessee Town at 1191 SW Buchanan Street. (Courtesy of the author.)

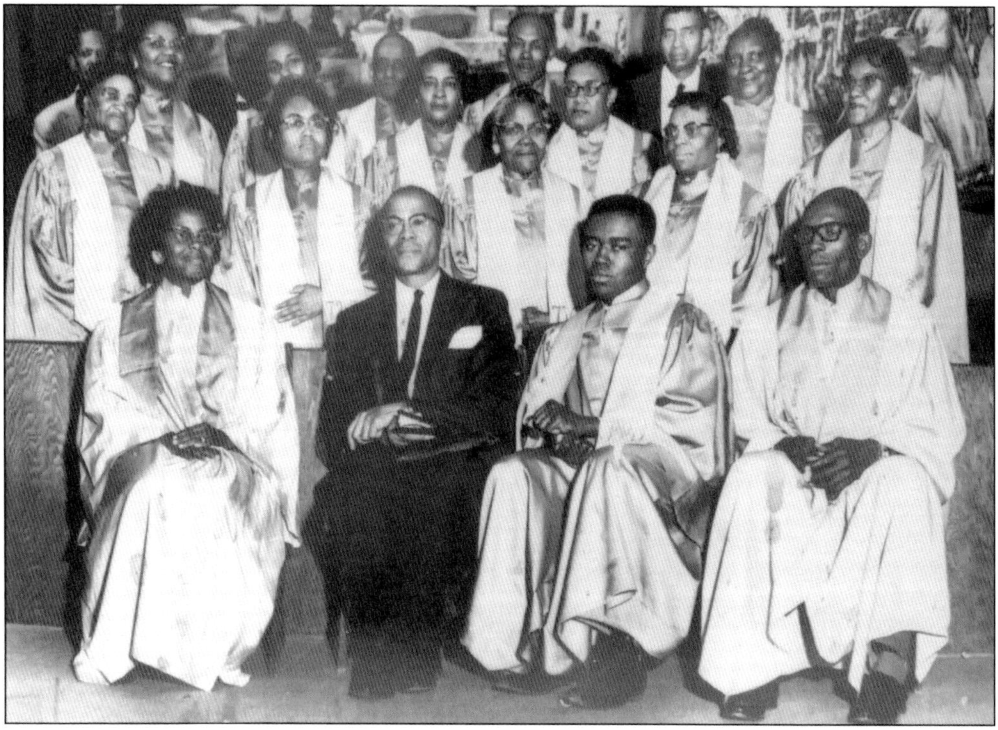

TRUE VINE MISSIONARY BAPTIST CHURCH SENIOR CHOIR. In this 1950s photograph, the choir poses with Rev. Melvin C. and First Lady Leola Wakes. (Courtesy of KHS.)

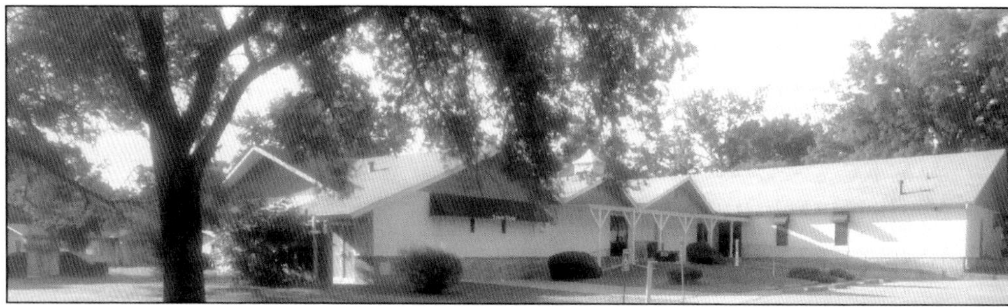

TRUE VINE MISSIONARY BAPTIST CHURCH. True Vine, originally established in 1927, is located at 307 SE Tefft Street in East Topeka. Rev. Melvin C. Wakes, who served as pastor for 22 years, passed away in 2004. His wife, the former first lady of the church, Leola Wakes, was considered the mother of the parish. The current pastor is Rev. Larry Jones. (Photograph by the author.)

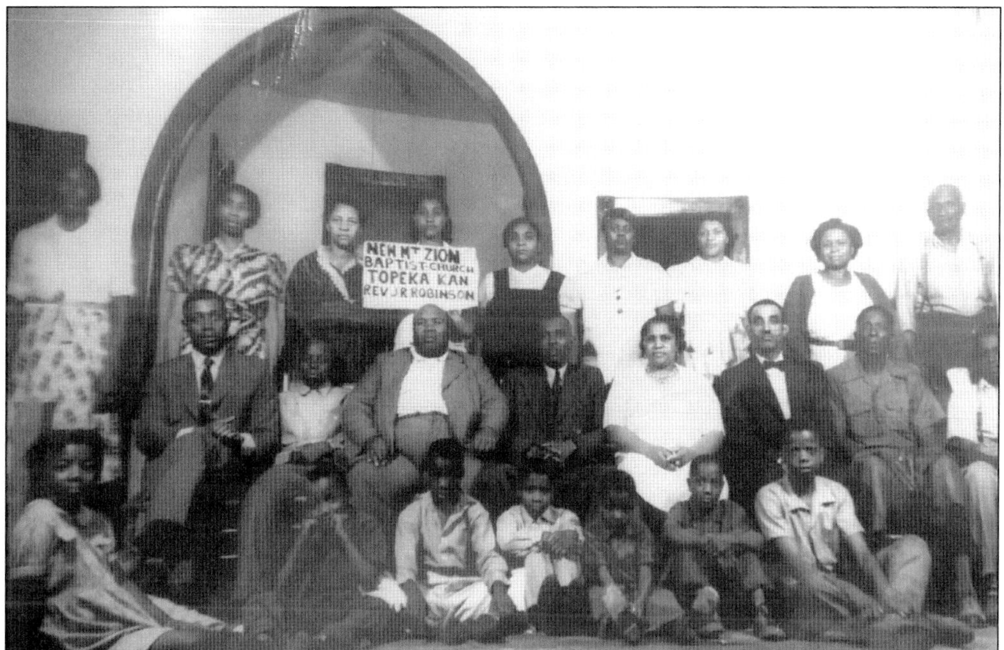

NEW MOUNT ZION CHURCH MEMBERS. This photograph of the New Mount Zion members is from the late 1930s. Pictured here are, from left to right, (first row) Ollie Ruth Grubb, Raymond Cole, three unidentified children, Calvin Grubb, and Clarence Henderson; (second row) Willie Cole, ? Grubb, Andrew Grubb, Rev. J.R. Robinson, Leola Robinson, Mrs. Woodall, Son Johnson, and Wilmur Henderson; (third row) Maddie Low, Carrie Williams, Zeda Smith, Zelma McDonald, Gladys Woodall, Ida Johnson, Bettey McKay, unidentified, and John Irving. (Courtesy of Leola Montgomery.)

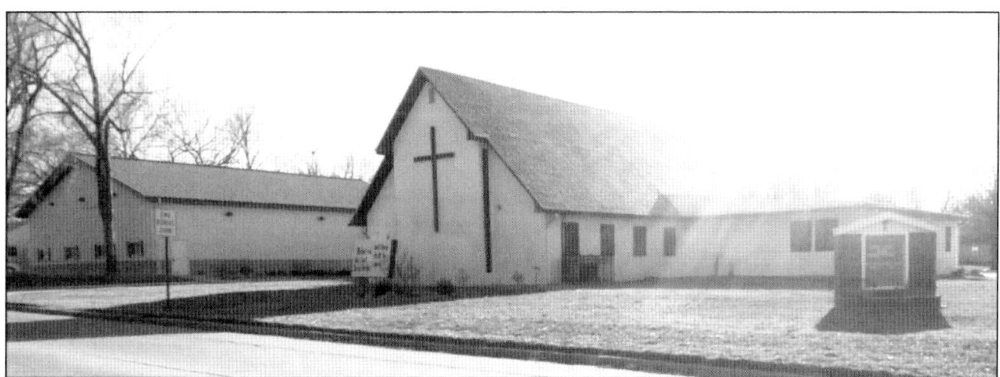

NEW MOUNT ZION MISSIONARY BAPTIST CHURCH. In 1923, New Mount Zion was organized at First and Adams Streets by a group of 15 men and women under Rev. John Cox. A building was purchased, and the church was moved to 214 SE Madison Street. In 1962, it moved to 214 SE Fourteenth Street, and its current building at 2901 SE Indiana Avenue was purchased in 1981 from the Highland Park Assembly of God Church. (Photograph by the author.)

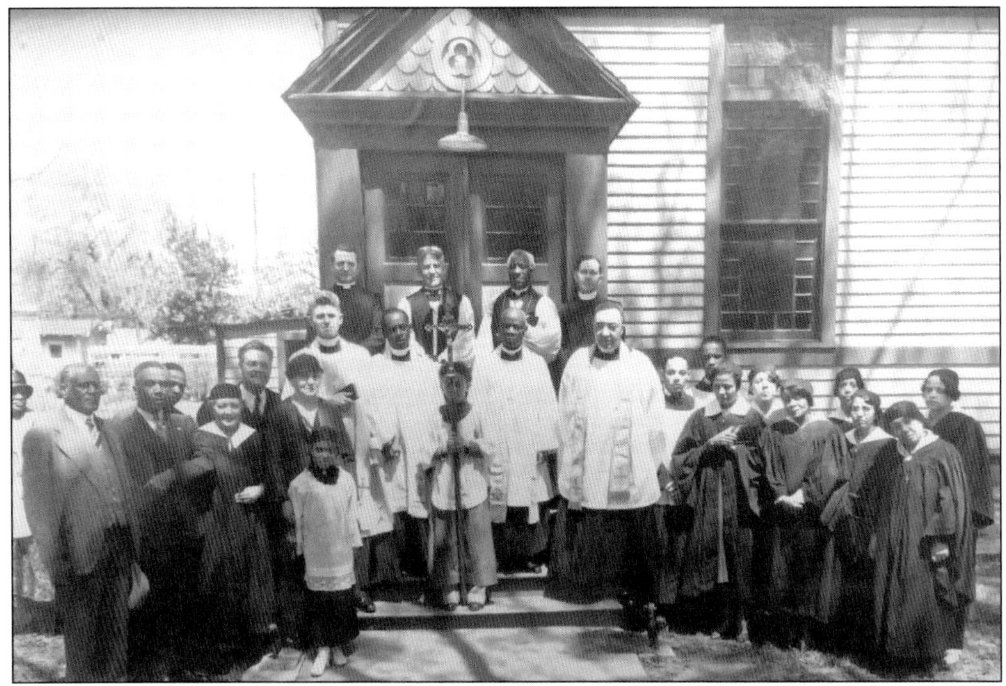

St. Simon's Episcopal Church. Founded in 1885, St. Simon's was originally called Church of St. Simon the Cyrenian. It started in the law office of James Guy at 413 Kansas Avenue and then moved to Seventh Street and Western Avenue. Dr. Thaddeus P. Martin and A.M. Thomas were members and part of its lay leadership. In this photograph, members attend the ordination of Fr. M.R. Hogarth at the church's 915 West Tenth Street location. Once affiliated with Grace Cathedral, St. Simon's no longer exists. (Courtesy of KHS.)

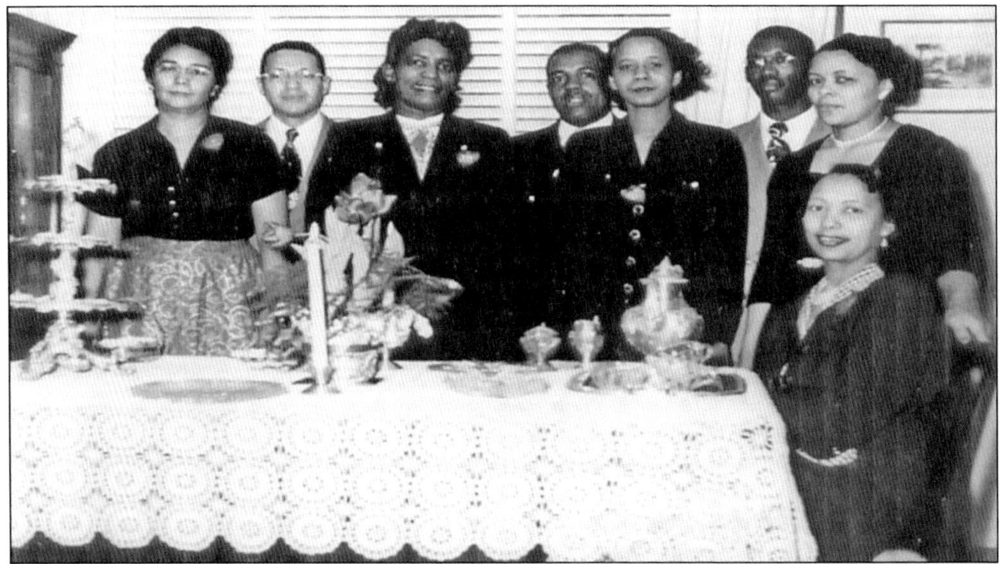

St. John AME Usher Board, 1948. Members of the usher board meet in the home of one of its members. Pictured here are, from left to right, Lucinda and Alvin Todd, Iva Blount, Wilber Davis, Nyda Woods, August Jackson Sr., Ida Sheffield-Norman, and Mildred Davis. (Courtesy of Maxine Dawson.)

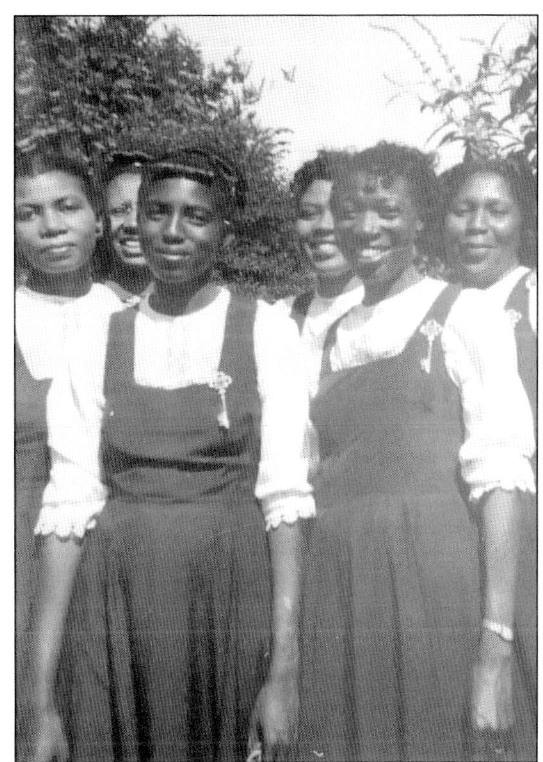

KEYS OF ZION GIRLS' SEXTET. The Keys of Zion was one of many gospel singing groups in Topeka. The sextet, formed in 1948 and managed by Oliver Brown, performed in many Kansas towns and in Kansas City, Missouri. All but one singer was a member of St. John AME Church. Pictured are, from left to right, Leola Brown (Montgomery), Louberta Williams, Lola Bell Smith, Harriet Robinson, Evelyn Davis, and Ardenia Brown (the lone member from Second Baptist Church). (Courtesy of Leola Montgomery.)

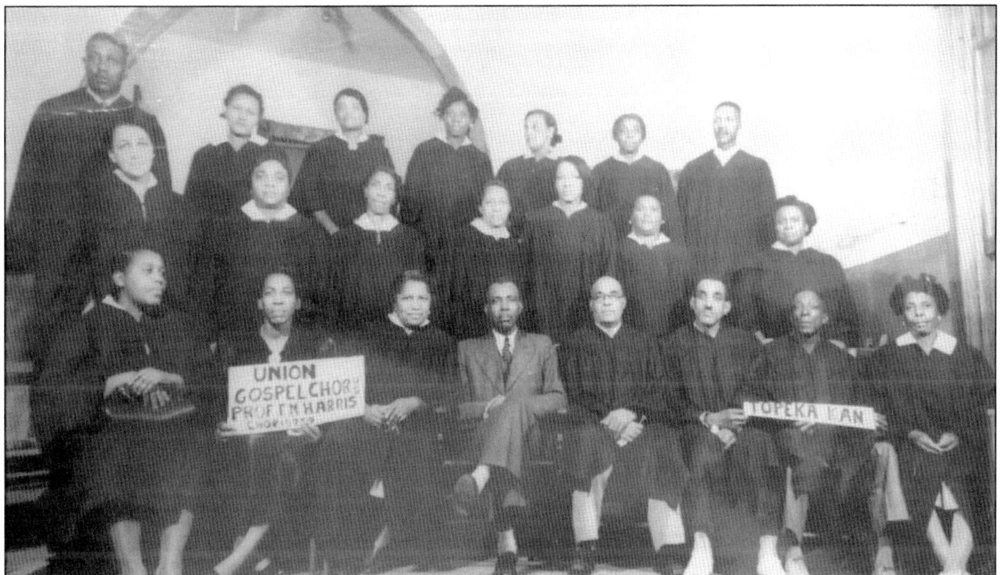

UNION GOSPEL CHOIR, 1940S. The Union Gospel Choir, under the direction of Rev. J.R. Robinson, performed for many audiences in Topeka, throughout Kansas, and in Missouri. Pictured are, from left to right, (first row) Mrs. Smith, Ida Harris, Leola Robinson, Rev. J.R. Robinson, Frank Harris, Mr. Woodall, Son Johnson, and Ella Dunn; (second row) Allison ?, Gladys Woodall, Carrie Williams, Zeda Smith, Edna Carson, and two unidentified women; (third row) Willie Cole, Mary ?, Pearl ?, Christine Mitchell, Evelyn Knight, Maddie Low, and George Smith. (Courtesy of Leola Montgomery.)

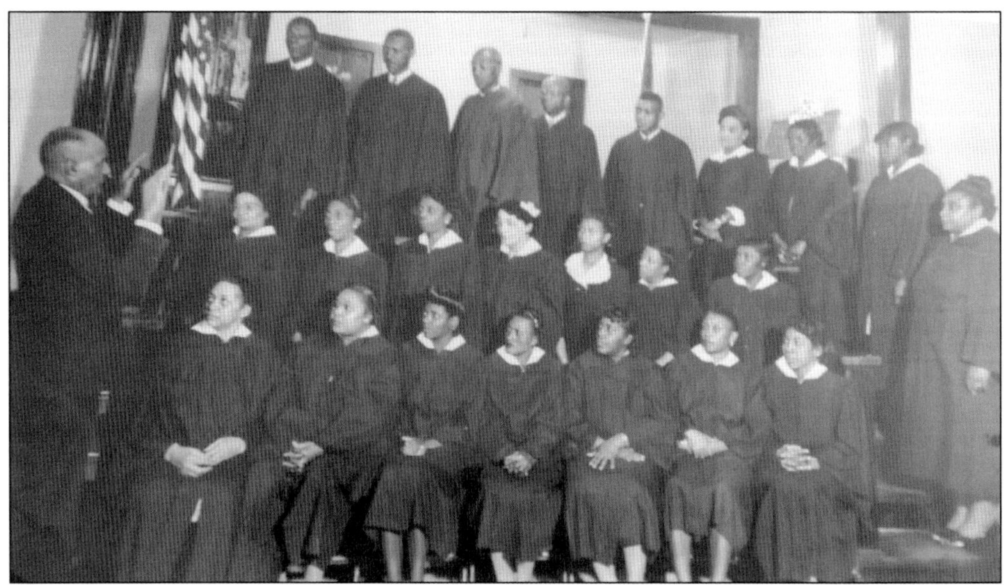

All City Gospel Choir, 1938. The All City Gospel Choir performed over much of eastern Kansas and Missouri. The congregations represented included Mount Carmel Missionary Baptist, Antioch Missionary Baptist, and New Mount Zion Baptist Churches. Frank Harris, pictured on the left, was the musical director. Also pictured are, from left to right, (first row) unidentified, Rosabell Jefferson, Christine Mitchell, Mary ?, Mrs. Smith, Rosie Hawkins, and Ida Harris; (second row) Pearl ?, Carrie Williams, Ella Dunn, unidentified, Leola Williams, Creola Rhodes, and Mattie Low; (third row) Son Johnson, Mr. Smith, Jack Jefferson, Ed Williams, Willie Cole, Ida Knight, unidentified, Leanna Grubbs, and Gladys Woodall. (Courtesy of Leola Montgomery.)

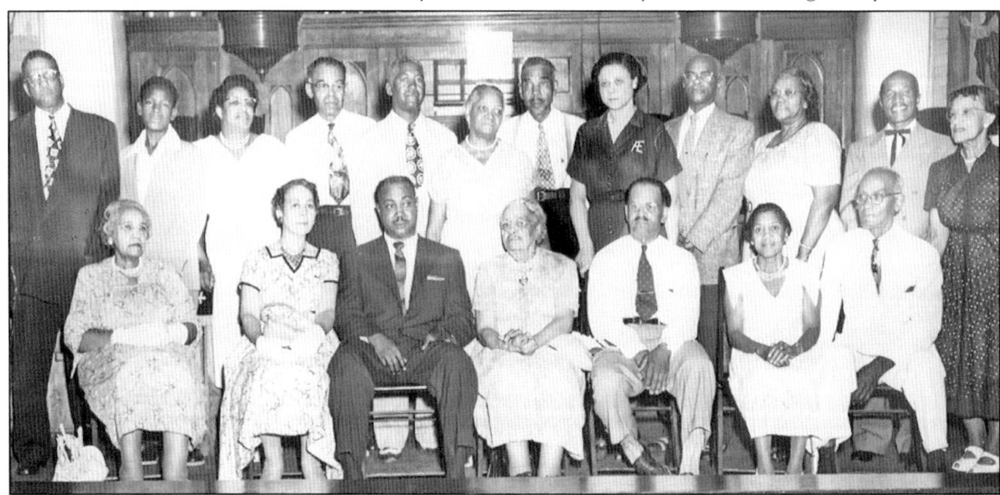

St. John AME Roundabout Club. The Roundabout Club of St. John AME was a social club for adults in the congregation. Members who appear in this photograph from the 1940s are, from left to right, (first row) Irene Booker, Minnie Mims, unidentified man, Lizzie Buckner, Arthur Newman, Ethel Washington, and Amos Booker; (second row) Mr. Schultz, grandson of Virginia Newman, Virginia Newman, William Newman, Alonzo Tyler, Bessie Bennett, Parker Weddington, Pearl Bowser, S. Newt Bowser, Jessie Tyler, Samuel Washington, and Esther Fisher. This picture also shows the pipe organ that was later removed when the church was remodeled. (Courtesy of Maxine Dawson.)

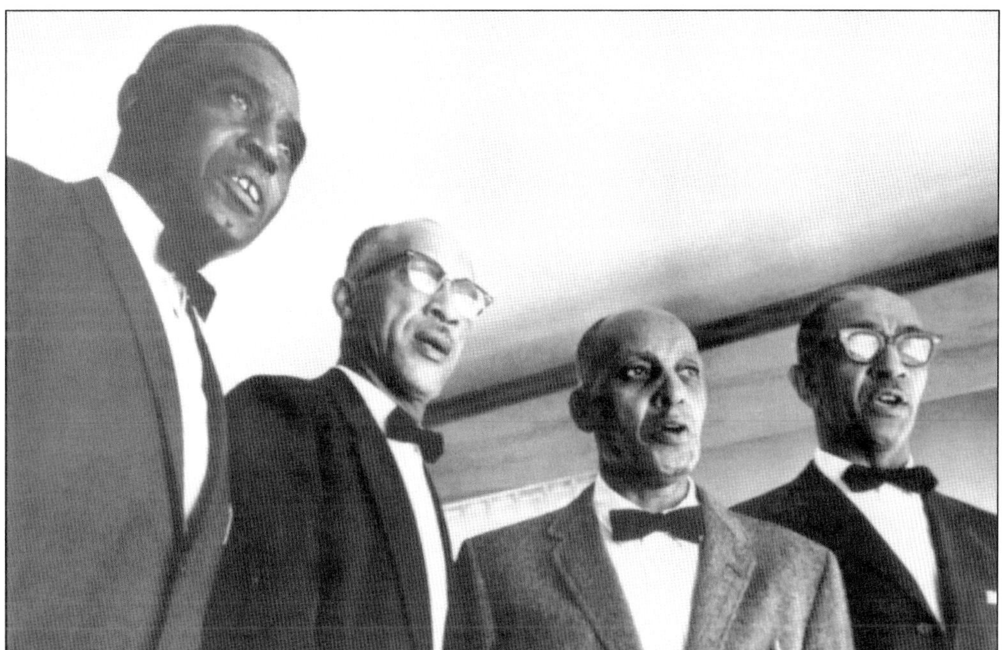

THE GOSPEL FOUR. Topeka's black male quartet, the Gospel Four, was like many of the popular gospel singing groups of their time. They performed for many audiences as a group throughout the 1920s and 1930s. They are, from left to right, Leo Anderson, Fred Redmon, Oscar Lewis, and Sheldon Sudduth. (Courtesy of TSCPL.)

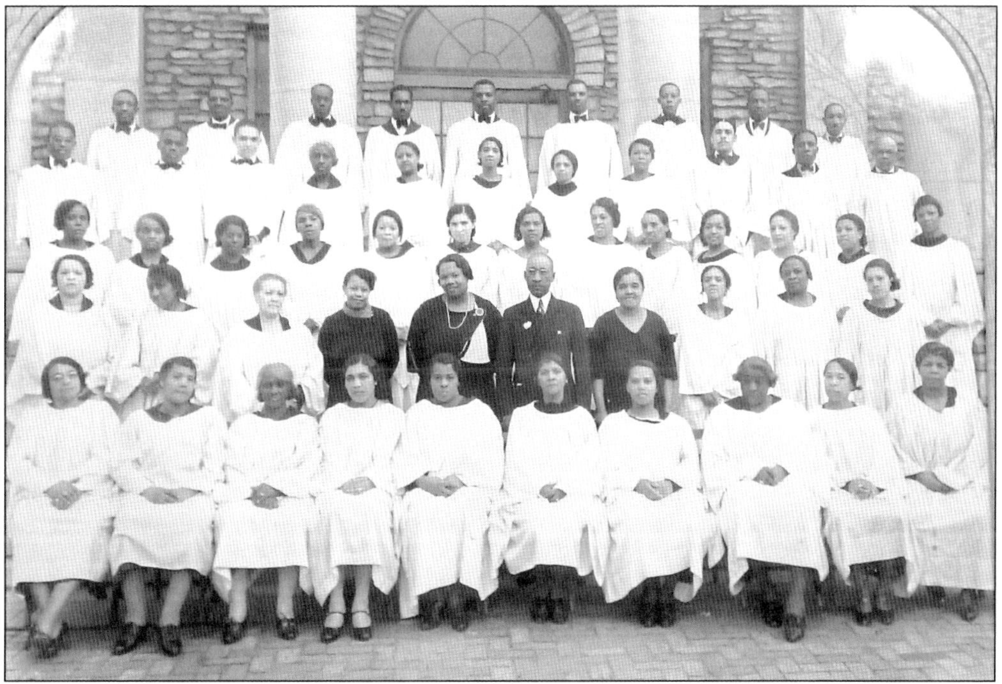

NEGRO FESTIVAL CHOIR. This very popular Topeka choir, which was organized and led by Ben and Emma Gaines of Gaines & Sons Mortuary, performed in many cities on the eastern border of Kansas. In 1940, the group performed at the Municipal Auditorium. (Courtesy of KHS.)

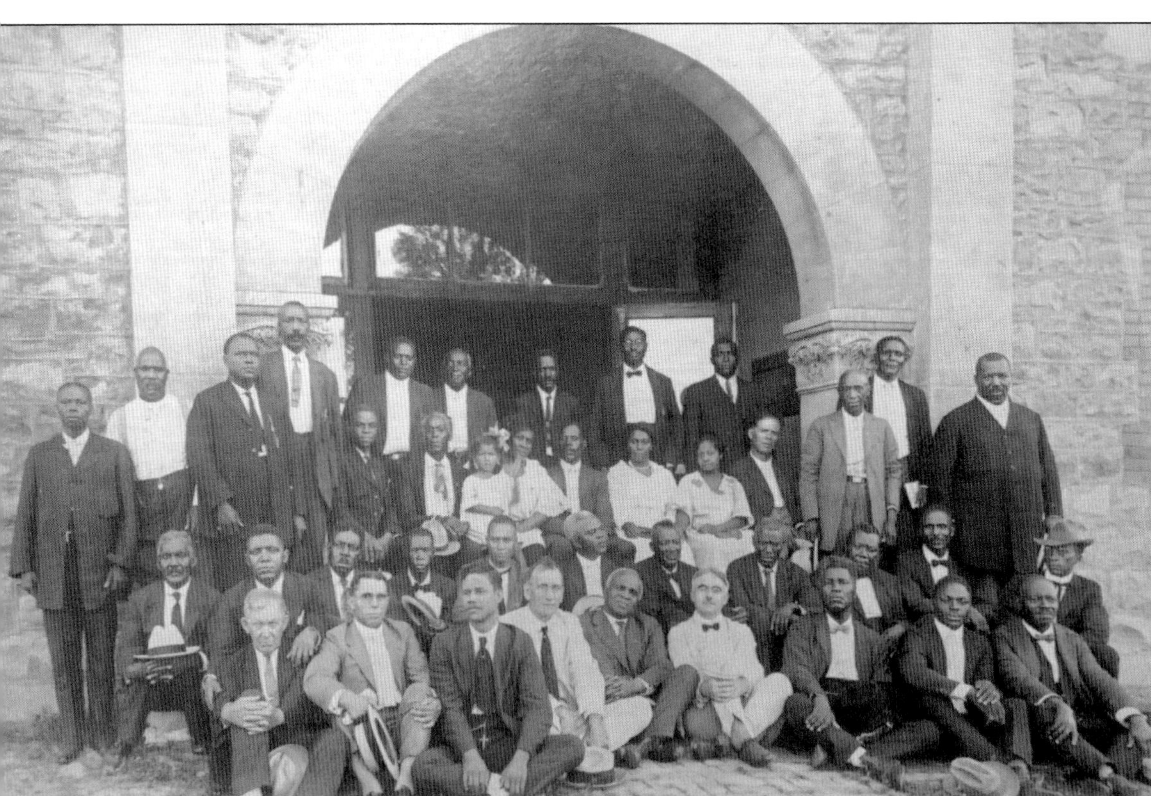

Central Baptist Theological Seminary. The Central Baptist Theological Seminary, pictured here, was established in 1921 and was located just east of Topeka on Victory Highway (now known as Highway 40), opposite Kansas Vocational School (KVS). This photograph was taken in front of the KVS Administration Building. Under the leadership of Dean Enos Larkin Scrugg, the seminary gave a complete course in theology and taught special preparation in other church work. The eight-month terms began in October and ended in May of each year. In 1928, there were 24 students enrolled. (Courtesy of KHS.)

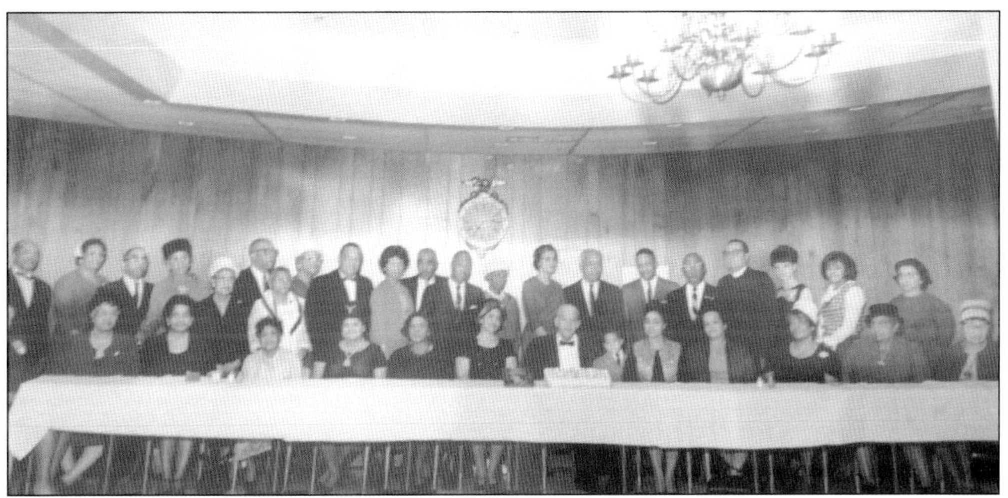

Banquet Honoring Dr. E. Louis Ransom. Dr. E. Louis Ransom was a great community leader. In 1962, he was honored with a banquet in recognition of his work with the NAACP and his support of the community. Guests at the banquet included, from left to right, (first row) ? Jones, Matilda Jamison, Gladys Tyler, Ethel Washington, two unidentified, Mabel Warren, Mrs. Ransom, Dr. E. Louis Ransom, their grandson James and daughter Ethel Woodson, unidentified, and Bessie Hickman; (second row) Sam Washington, ? Newman, Mr. and Mrs. Brown, Hester Fisher, Royal Tyler, Mrs. Woods, Vassie Gardenhire, Rev. Brown (Second Baptist Church), Leola Brown, Parker Weddington, Glenda Warren, Mary Weddington, Mrs. Ransom, Payne Ransom, Jimmy Woodson, Mr. Jenkins, Rev. Acres, ? Acres, Sharon Woodson, and Mary Blackwell. (Courtesy of TSCPL.)

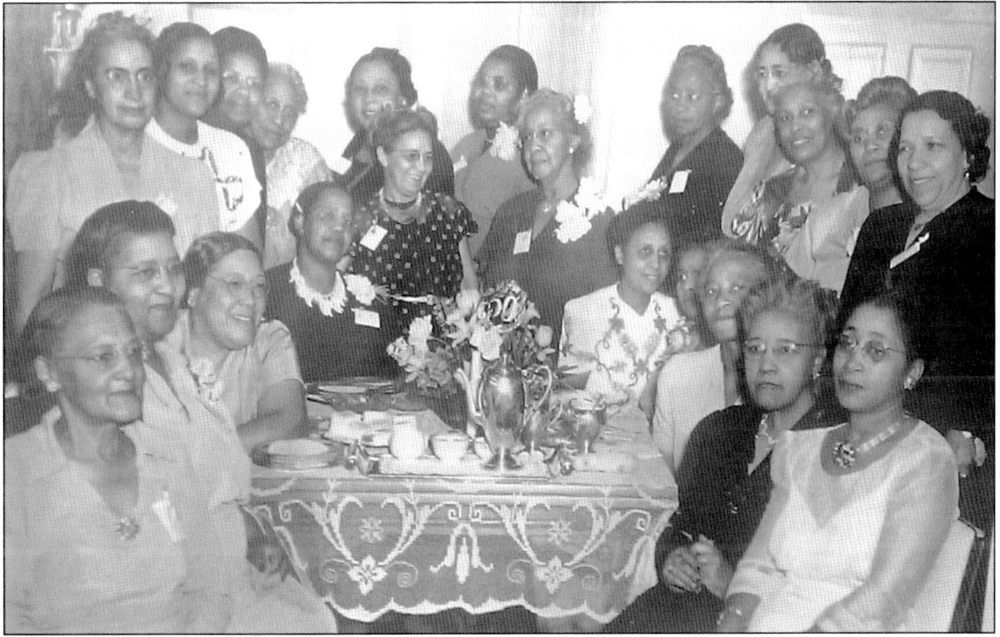

Ne Plus Ultra Colored Women's Club. Organized on February 17, 1899, by Cassie Fox, this club aimed to develop a spirit of unity and goodwill among the African American women of Topeka so that various human needs and problems could be met intelligently. Their activities in the service of this purpose included the sale of their art and fine needlework and the study of literature. This photograph shows the women during one of their meetings in 1929. (Courtesy of KHS.)

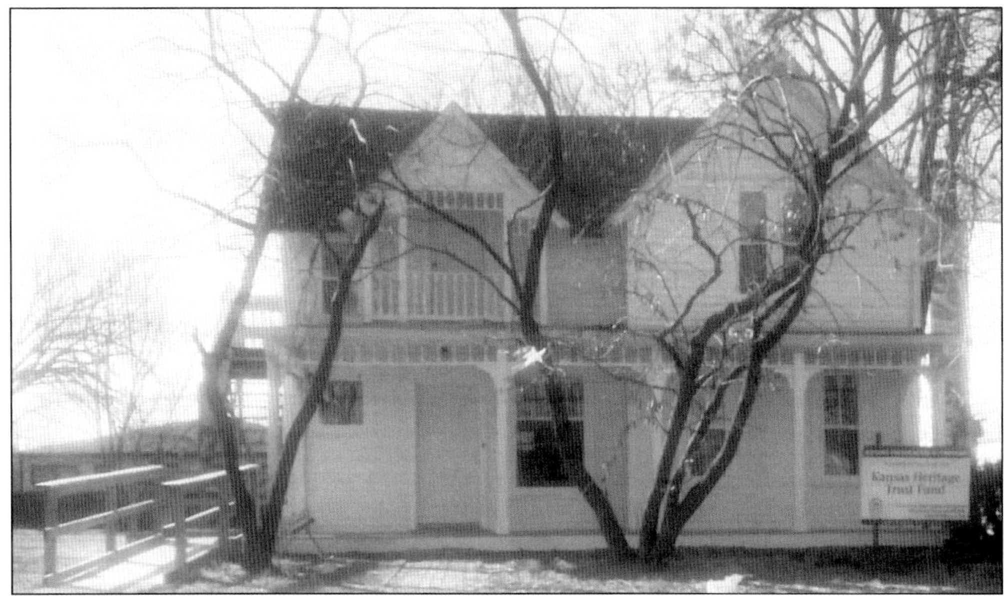

COLORED WOMEN'S CLUB HOUSE. The first Colored Women's Clubs in the nation began as early as the 1830s. In 1899, the first Colored Women's Clubs began to form in Topeka. One year later, in 1900, there were seven such organizations, including the Oak Leaf Art, Dumas, Oriental, Golden Rod, Rose Bud, and St. Elmo Clubs. In 1917, these groups banded together to create the Topeka Council of Colored Women's Clubs and then joined the Kansas Association of Colored Women's Clubs (KACWC). Together, the women served their community and supported their race through self-improvement, art, and literacy projects. The Topeka clubs held meetings at churches and members' homes until 1931, when they bought this building at 1149 SW Lincoln Street. (Courtesy of the author.)

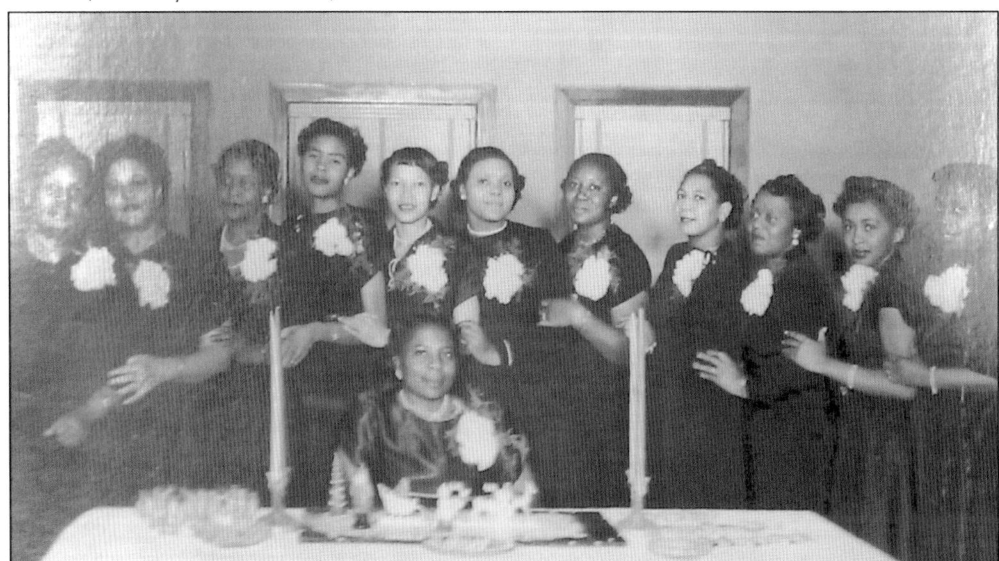

KACWC 20TH CENTURY MOTHER'S TEA. During the 1920s, the Kansas Association of Colored Women's Clubs created the nation's first junior club for girls. The club members worked with young girls to teach them leadership skills. This photograph shows the new generation of young Colored Women's Club members participating in the Mother's Tea. (Courtesy of KHS.)

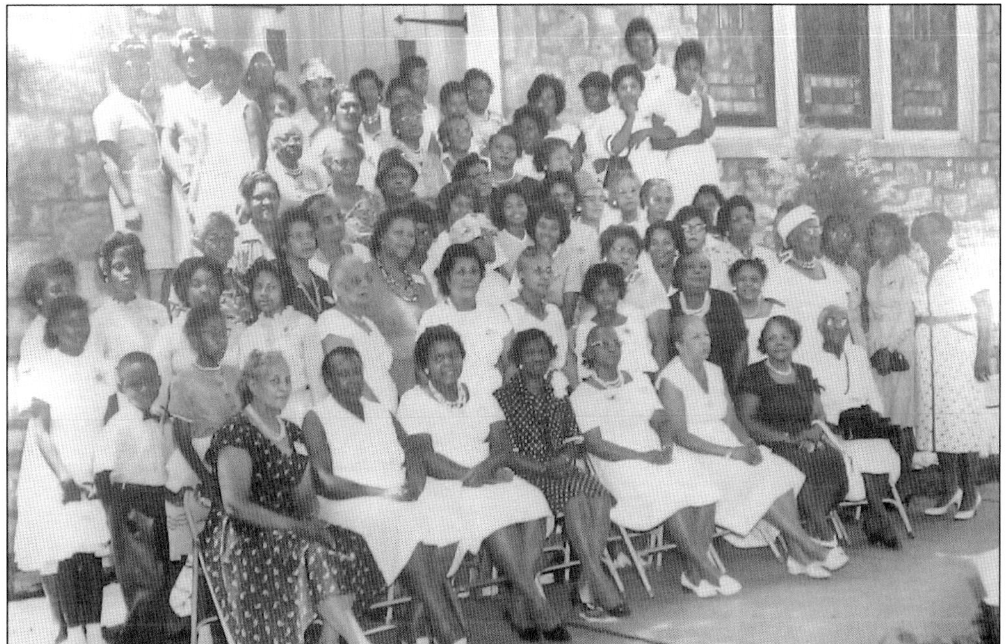

KACWC Federation Conference. Each year, the Kansas Association of Colored Women's Clubs held an annual conference, which was hosted by members in one of the cities in Kansas where clubs existed. In 1948, it was held in Topeka at St. John AME Church. This group photograph includes many women from Topeka and neighboring cities as far as Atchison and Parsons. (Courtesy of KSCOLL.)

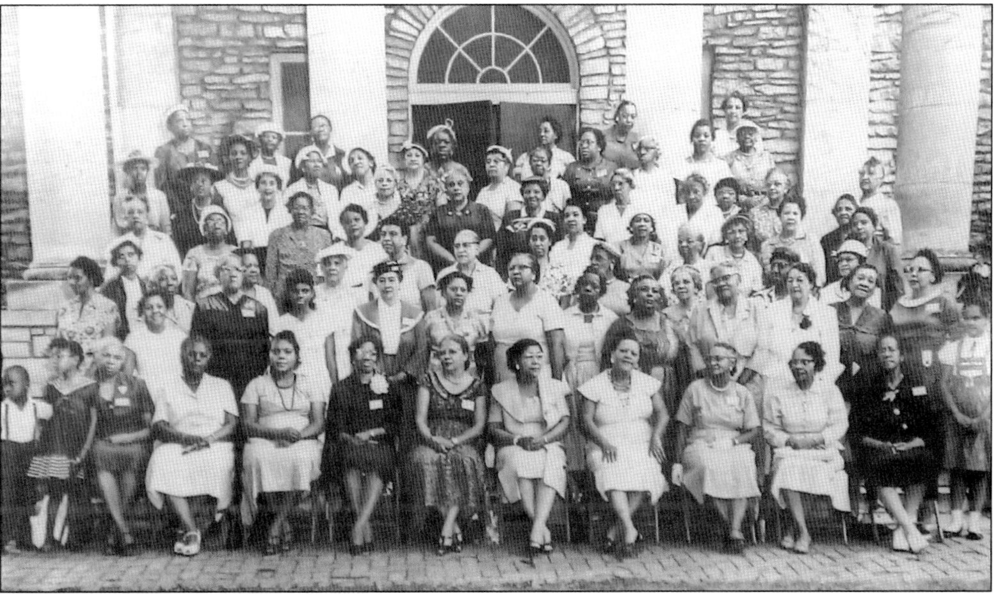

KACWC, Shiloh Baptist Church, 1962. In 1962, the annual Kansas Association of Colored Women's Clubs meeting was again hosted by the Topeka Council of Colored Women's Clubs, this time at the Shiloh Baptist Church. It was attended by many of the Topeka women from the various churches around the city. The major topic for the period from 1959 to 1962 was "Public Health and Hygiene." (Courtesy of KSCOLL.)

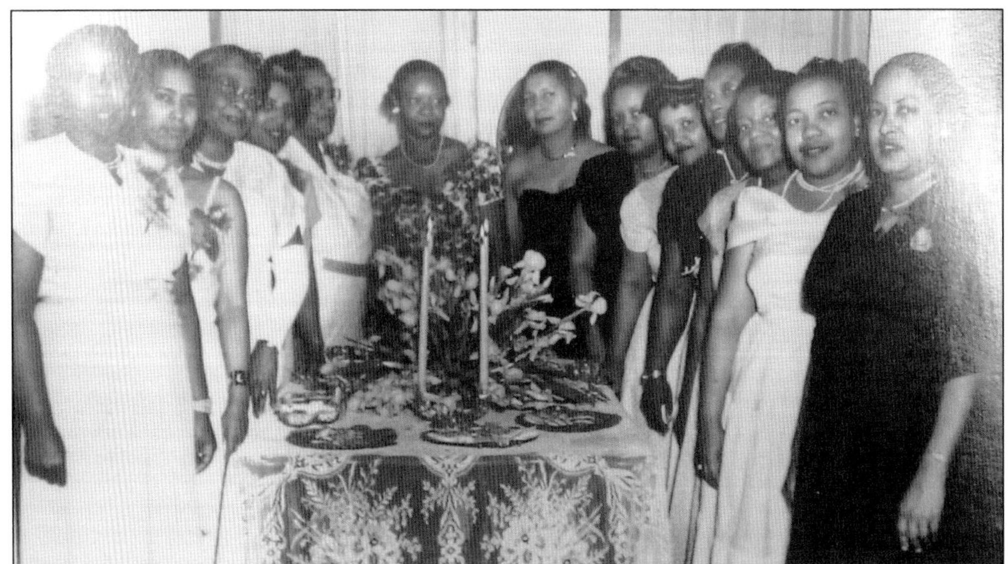

Stella Puella Art and Literary Colored Women's Club, 1949. The Stella Puella Colored Women's Club met in Topeka in 1949. Many of the women in this photograph were from Second Baptist Church. The Stella Puella Club chose art and charity as its main themes, and it made and sold various art pieces to fund charitable activities. (Courtesy of KSCOLL.)

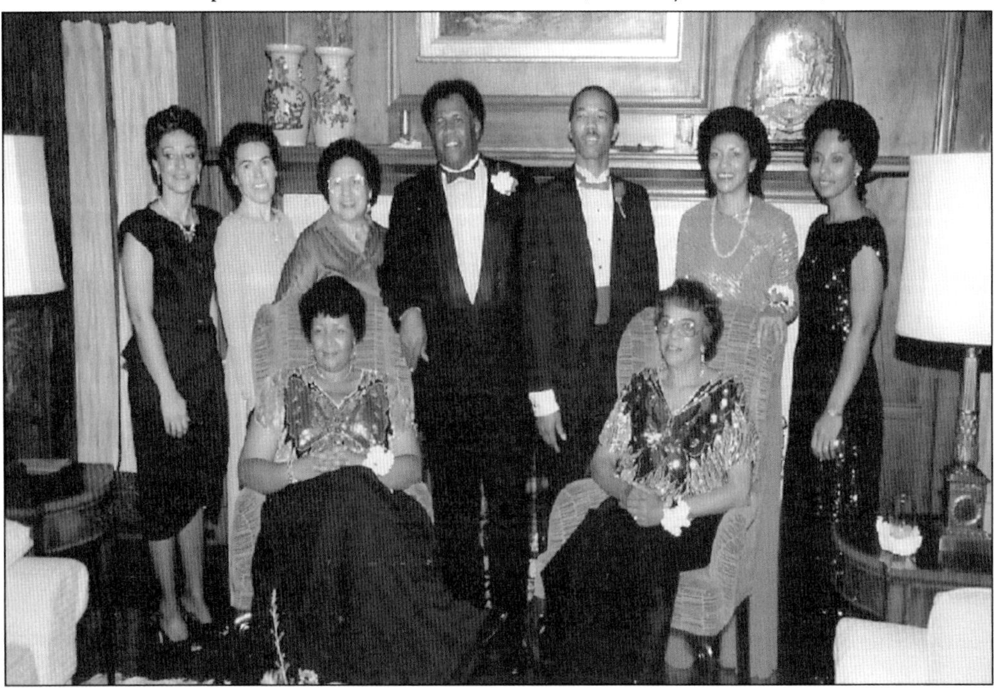

Living the Dream Committee, 1990. Living the Dream, Inc., was chartered as a nonprofit, community-based organization in 1985 by Robert Bugg. Its mission is to serve as a multicultural citizens' group to help preserve the legacy and example of the late Dr. Martin Luther King Jr. Members plan ceremonies and programs in conjunction with the Martin Luther King holiday enacted by the US Congress. In 2007, the Living the Dream Foundation was established to provide scholarships to local high school students. (Courtesy of KSCOLL.)

TOPEKA CHAPTER

OF

Link's Inc.

PRESENTS

"Showers of Loveliness"

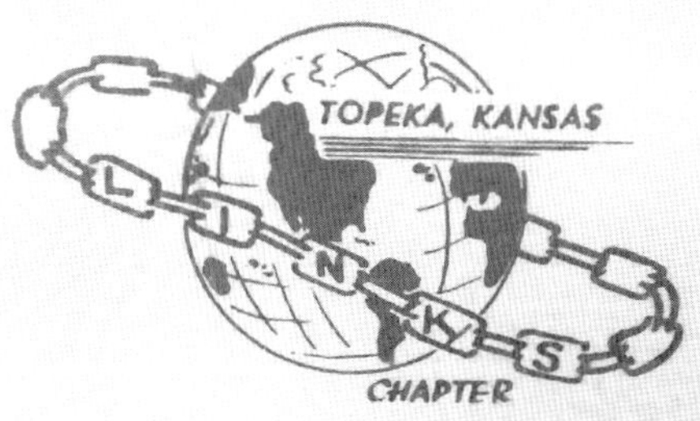

1968 Debutante Ball

500 ROOM

HOWARD JOHNSON MOTOR LODGE

Topeka, Kansas

SATURDAY, APRIL TWENTY-SEVEN

Nineteen Hundred Sixty Eight

Links Debutante Ball Program, 1968. Topeka Links, Inc., was formed in November 1958 to meet the new needs of black women. The organization's aim was to provide social, charitable, and intercultural activities for women. Like the earlier Colored Women's Clubs, Links members worked to help their communities and families. The charter members included Carrie Coleman, Jean Ann Price, Gladys DePriest, Annette Rease, Mary E. Gaines, Lucinda Todd, Evelyn Harper, Dimple Watkins, Dorothea Harris, Joy Williams, Oletha Jenkins, Ethel Woodson, and Arbeecher Kerford. Pictured here is the 1968 program for the annual debutante ball. (Courtesy of KSCOLL.)

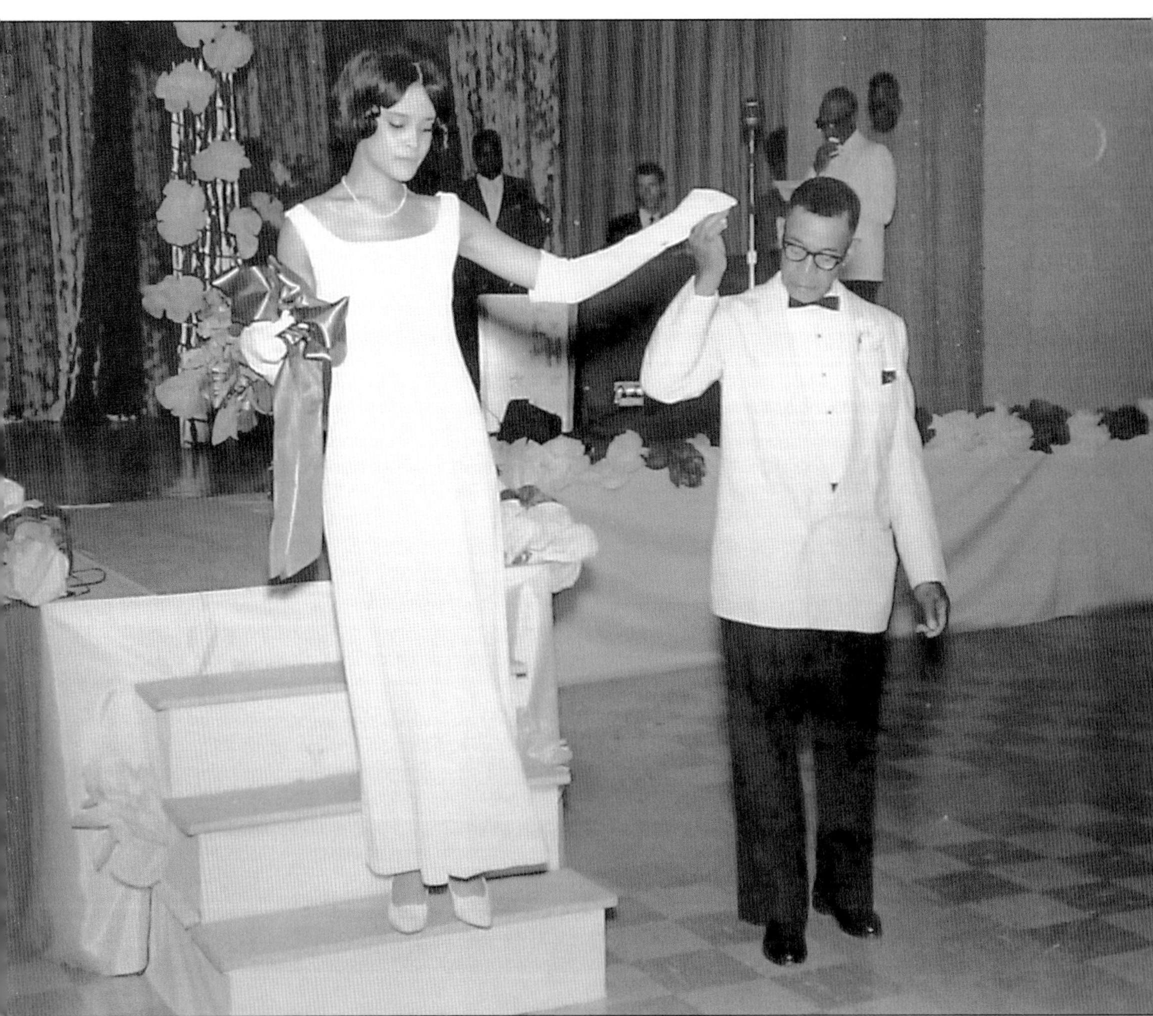

LINKS DEBUTANTE BALL, 1958. Links has provided scholarships for black youth and focused on teaching them leadership skills. The club sponsored talent shows, art exhibitions, public forums, and debutante balls. This photograph shows Nancy Todd and her father, Alvin Todd, at the 1958 debutante ball. Some of the recent programs and initiatives sponsored by the Topeka Chapter of Links include a black history program, Positive Image Award, annual fashion show, African-American Read-In, Links to a Bright Beginning program, Linkages to Life Donor Program, and the International Black Doll Project. (Courtesy of KSCOLL.)

Three

Education
Topeka's Focus

Education has been a core value of African Americans in Topeka ever since the earliest years of Kansas statehood. From the earliest schools for black children prior to the 1879 Exodus and the first black kindergarten started by Charles Sheldon to the groundbreaking *Brown v. Board of Education of Topeka* desegregation decision of 1954 and the subsequent magnet schools, education has been a significant part of Topeka's African American history.

Eager for advancement and empowerment after slavery, African Americans in Topeka took advantage of every opportunity to educate themselves and their youth. The first school for the education of black children in Topeka opened in 1867 on Sixth Street, between Kansas Avenue and Quincy Street. In 1868, it had 113 children. Due to overcrowding, the board of education rented a church building to accommodate 60 additional black students.

Topeka schools were only segregated at the elementary level. Classes in the junior and senior high schools were integrated, though extracurricular activities were not. The first reported black graduates from Topeka High School were Harriet E. Freeman and Ann Schumacher, members of the class of 1882. In 1884, Edmond Adams became the first black male student to graduate from Topeka High. In the 1886–1887 school year, 10 black students qualified to attend Topeka High School, and seven graduated.

The fight for educational excellence, equity, and freedom in Topeka began early. In 1894, the black community fought the board of education and won the right to have black teachers for their black children. In 1903, William Reynolds sued the school board over the separation of children by race in some of the city's schools; he lost his case. The fight for an adequate education for African American children continued until the *Brown v. Board of Education of Topeka* decision of 1954.

The images in this chapter illustrate the history of education for African Americans in Topeka from post-slavery days to the modern era.

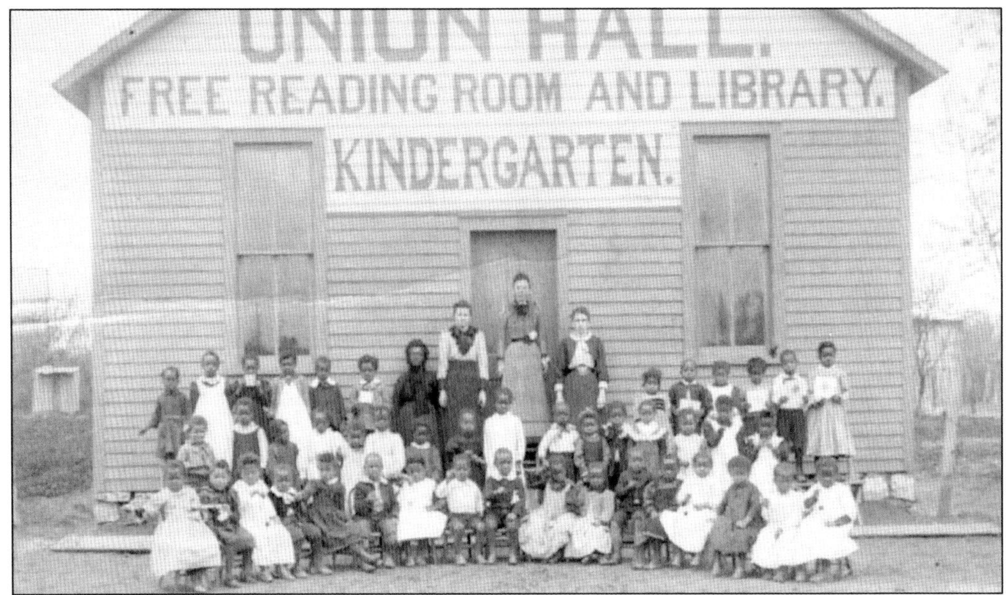

TENNESSEE TOWN KINDERGARTEN. In 1893, the Tennessee Town Kindergarten was started for the African American children of the community. It was sponsored by Central Congregational Church under the leadership of its pastor, Dr. Charles Sheldon. This kindergarten was the first of its kind west of the Mississippi River. In this photograph, the kindergarten students and teachers stand in front of their makeshift school building. The adults are, from left to right, Mother Ransom, Margaret Adams, Miss Doolittle, and Nettie Miller. (Courtesy of KHS.)

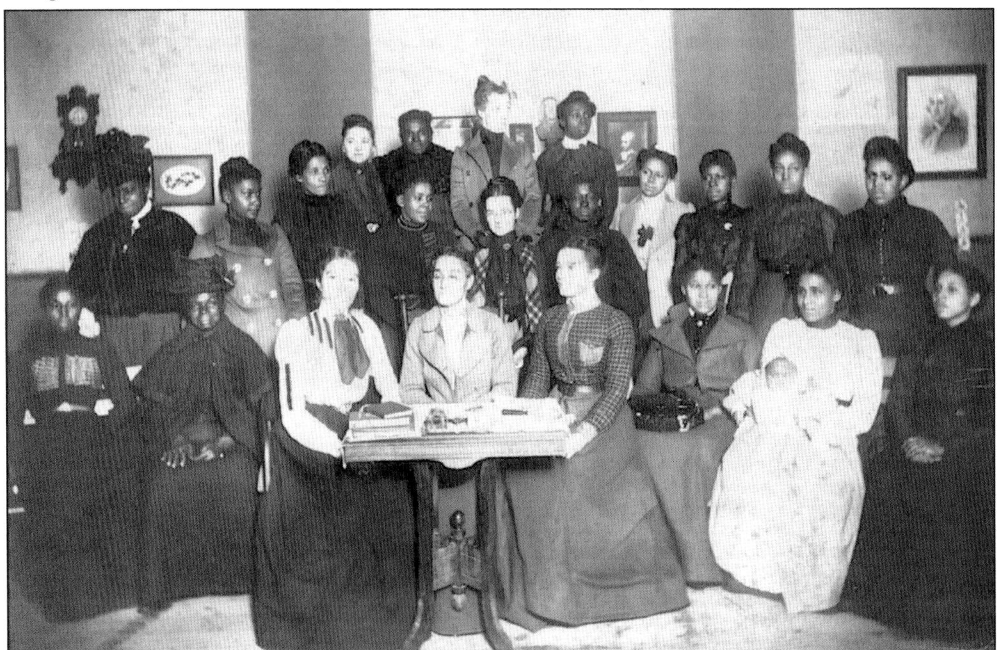

SHELDON MOTHERS' MEETING. This photograph shows mothers of some of the Sheldon Kindergarten students in a meeting with their children's teachers at the school. The mothers were supportive of their children and the teachers who taught them. This early picture of a parent-teacher meeting is dated between 1893 and 1899. (Courtesy of KHS.)

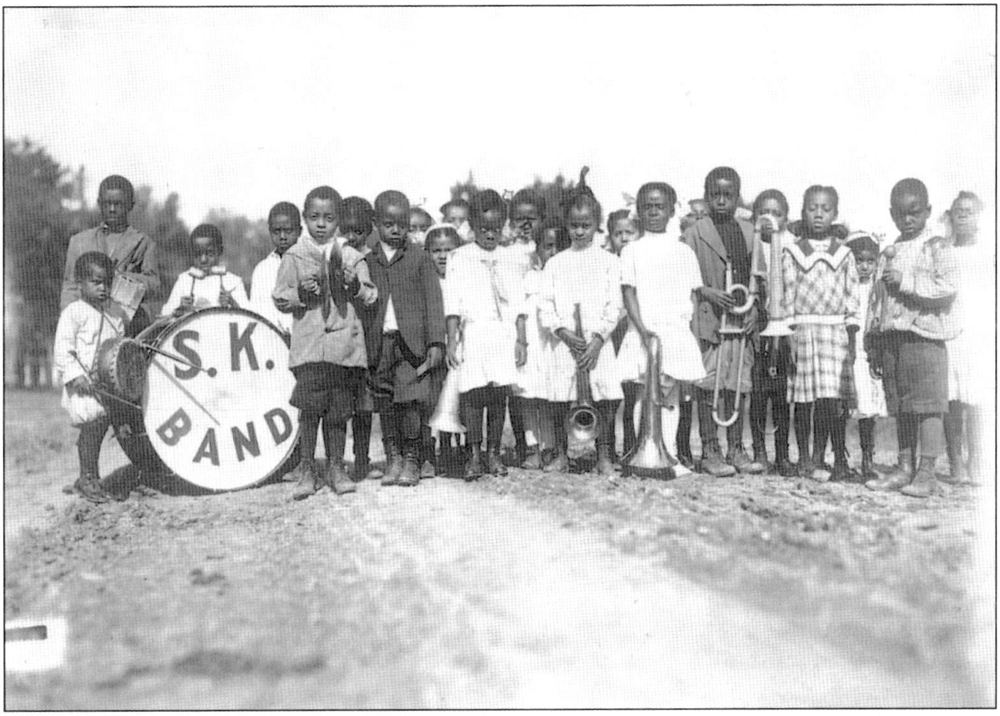

TENNESSEE TOWN KINDERGARTEN BAND. Many of the newly arrived residents of Tennessee Town were poor and needed support from the community. Dr. Charles Sheldon and his Central Congregational Church aided the families of Exodusters. In this photograph, the members of the children's band from the Sheldon Kindergarten are shown with their instruments. (Courtesy of KHS.)

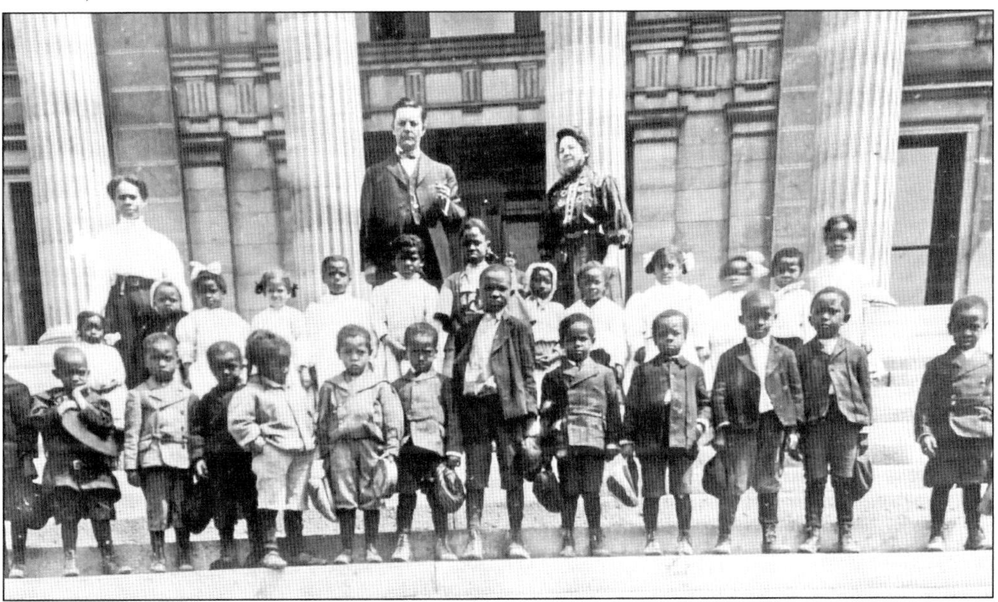

TENNESSEE TOWN KINDERGARTEN VISITS THE STATEHOUSE. The Tennessee Town Kindergarten children took a field trip to the Kansas State Capitol. Rev. Charles Sheldon is pictured here with them and their teachers on the statehouse steps. (Courtesy of KHS.)

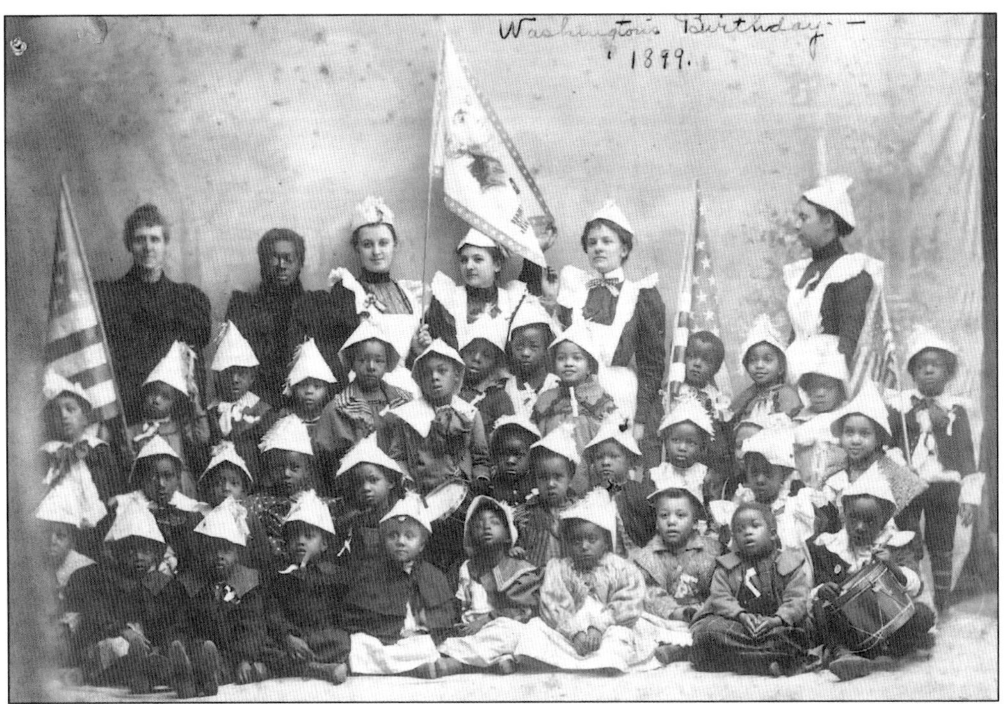

TENNESSEE TOWN SHELDON KINDERGARTEN, 1899. The kindergarten children celebrated the birthday of George Washington, the first president of the United States. The teacher and students posed for this image wearing paper hats. (Courtesy of KHS.)

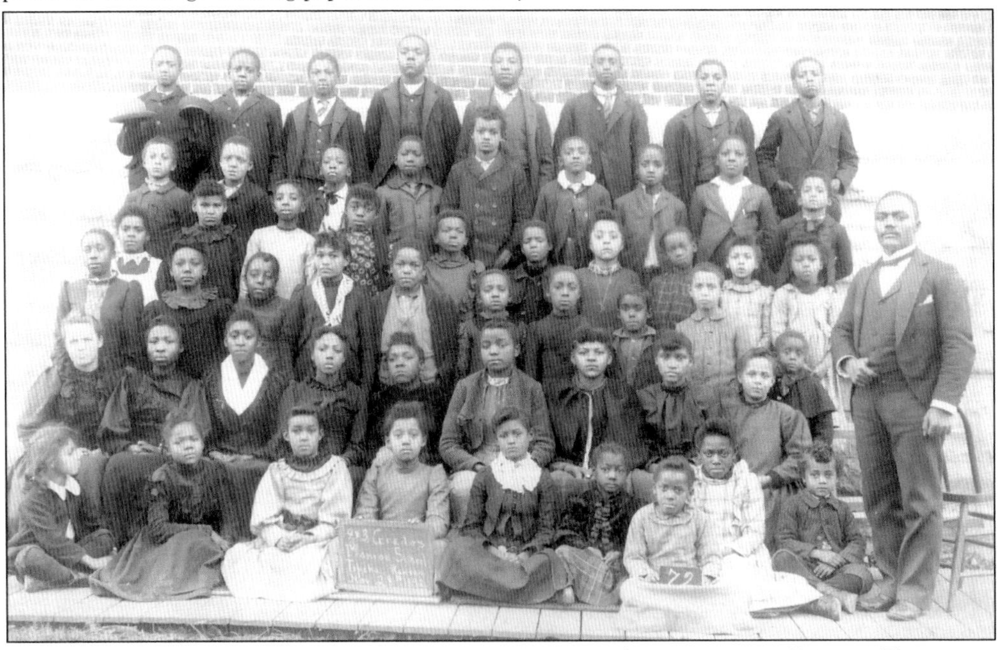

MONROE ELEMENTARY SCHOOL THIRD AND FOURTH GRADES. This 1892 image of Monroe Elementary School students is one of the earliest photographs of any of Topeka's black elementary schools. The students are shown here with their teacher, Fred Roundtree, standing in front of the school building at Fifteenth and Monroe Streets. (Courtesy of KSCOLL.)

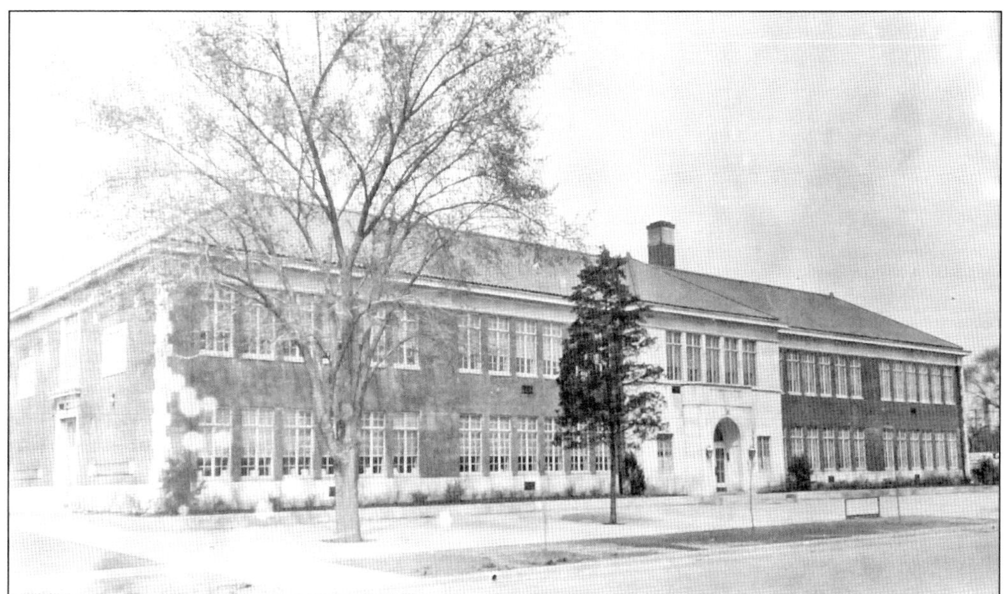

MONROE ELEMENTARY SCHOOL. Completed in 1927, the new Monroe Elementary School building was constructed on the lot adjacent to the old one. It was one of the four segregated black schools in Topeka when the *Brown v Board of Education of Topeka* lawsuit was filed in 1951. In 1992, the school was designated a National Historic Landmark. In 2004, it was dedicated as a National Site, part of the National Park Service. Its mission is to educate the public about the case and the struggle for civil rights. (Courtesy of KHS.)

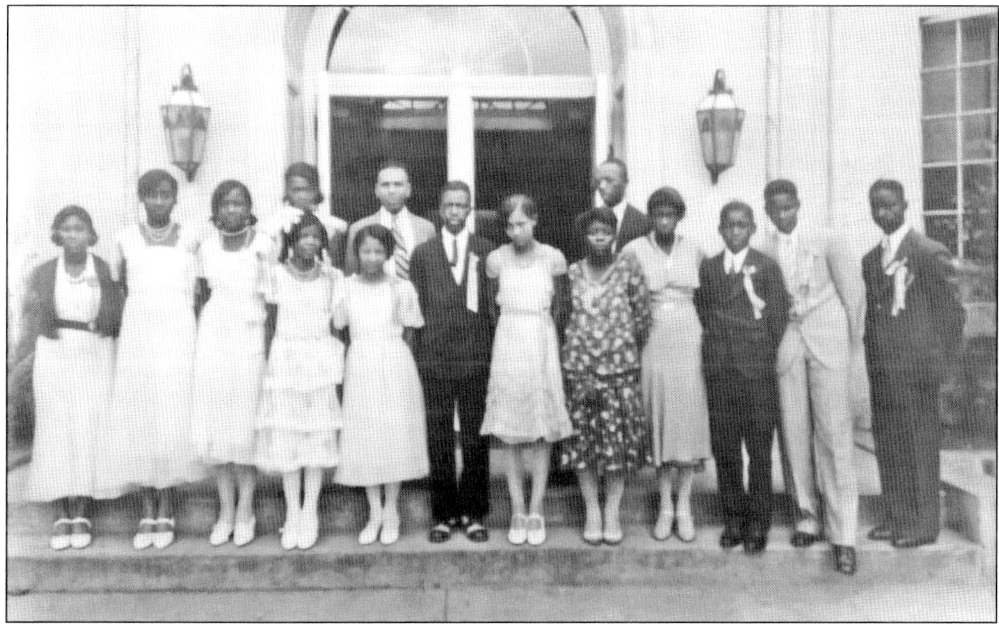

MONROE ELEMENTARY SCHOOL EIGHTH-GRADE GRADUATES. While white students in Topeka went to junior high schools for seventh and eighth grades, black students remained in elementary schools for those grades and only attended integrated junior high schools for ninth grade. In this photograph, Henrietta Sheppard Cox (first row, fifth from left) is shown during her eighth-grade graduation from Monroe School in 1932. (Courtesy of KSCOLL.)

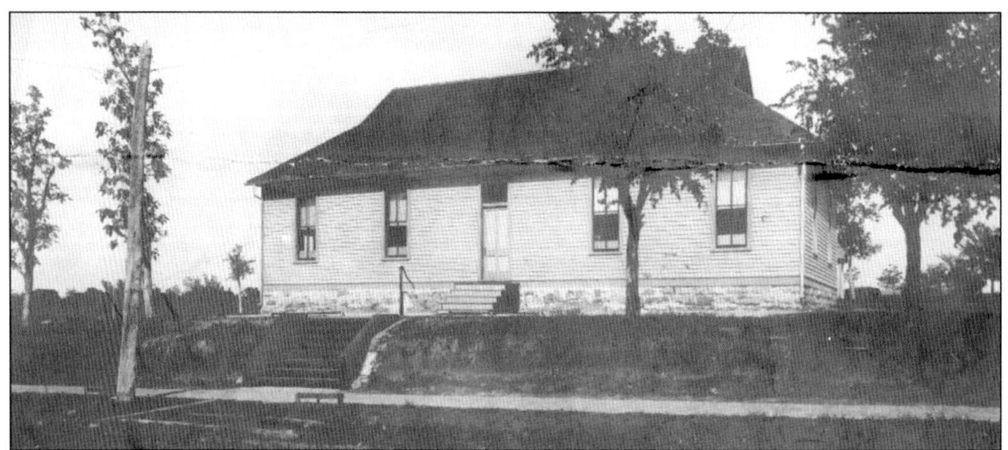

DOUGLAS ELEMENTARY SCHOOL. Douglas Elementary School was located on Polk Street between Third and Fourth Streets. This photograph, which shows the substandard conditions of this old, two-room school for blacks, was submitted to the Kansas Supreme Court in 1903 as Exhibit A in *William Reynolds v. The Board of Education of the City of Topeka*. Reynolds, a black parent, lost his lawsuit, which was the first court case from Topeka to challenge the constitutionality of segregation laws in Kansas. (Courtesy of KSCOLL.)

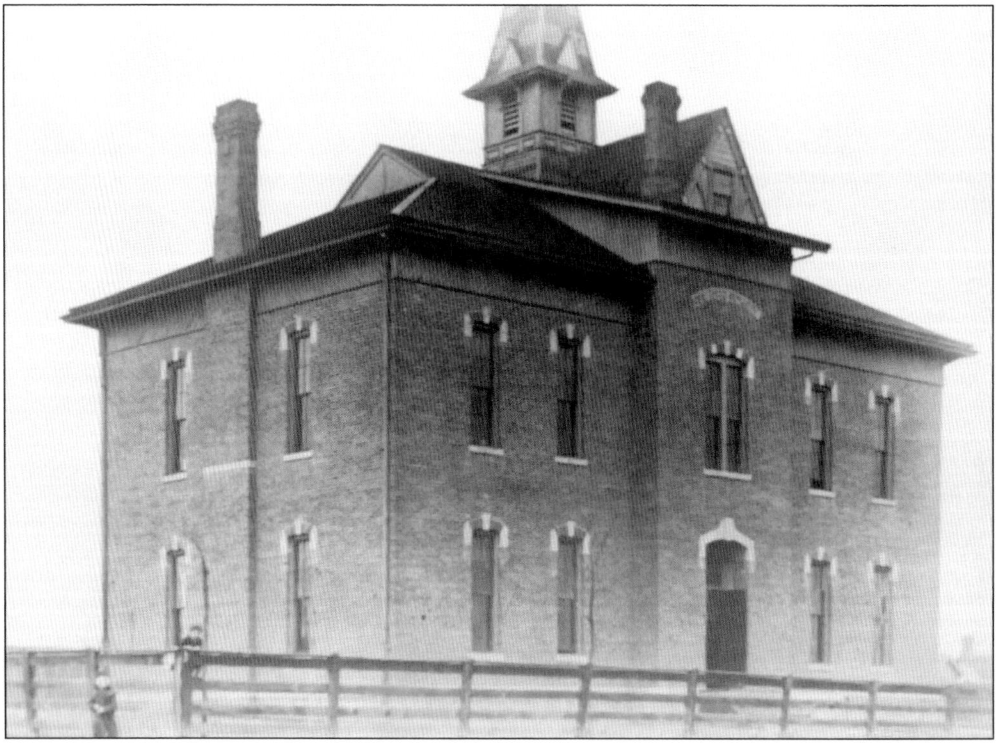

OLD SUMNER ELEMENTARY SCHOOL. The original Sumner School, pictured here, was a two-story brick building used by African American students until 1885. After it burned, it was replaced by a two-room, one-story frame building that could not hold all of the black students. Many of the students had to be sent to other black schools. Sumner was damaged in 1898 by strong winds and was rebuilt in 1901. However, the new, two-story brick building, which had eight classrooms, was not used for black children; it became a school for white children instead. (Courtesy of KHS.)

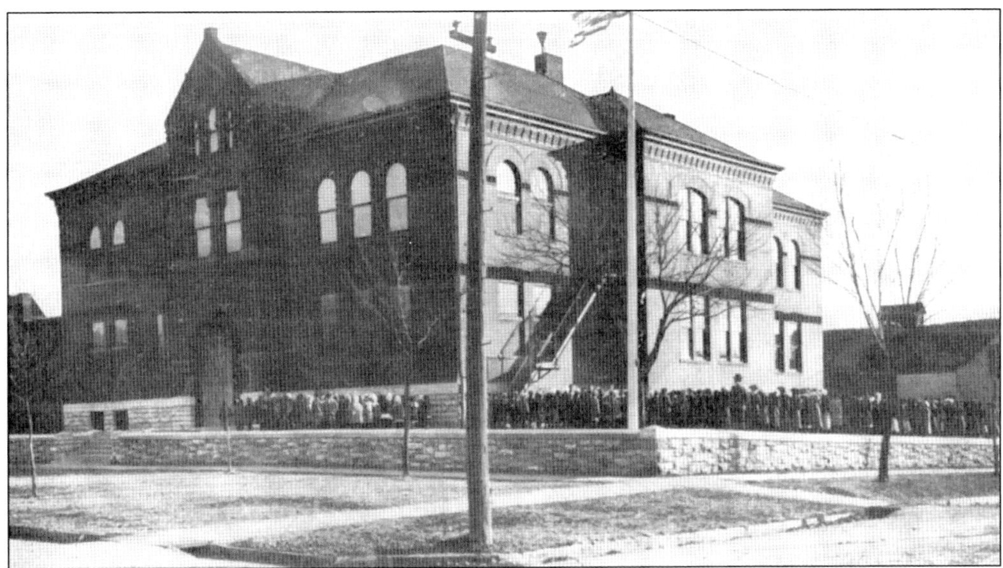

Sumner School. In 1901, the new two-story brick Sumner building—the third constructed at the corner of Fourth Street and Western Avenue—had eight classrooms. It was used for some of the first junior high students in the city before it was damaged by fire in 1915. The walls became structurally unsound, and the top floor was removed. (Courtesy of KHS.)

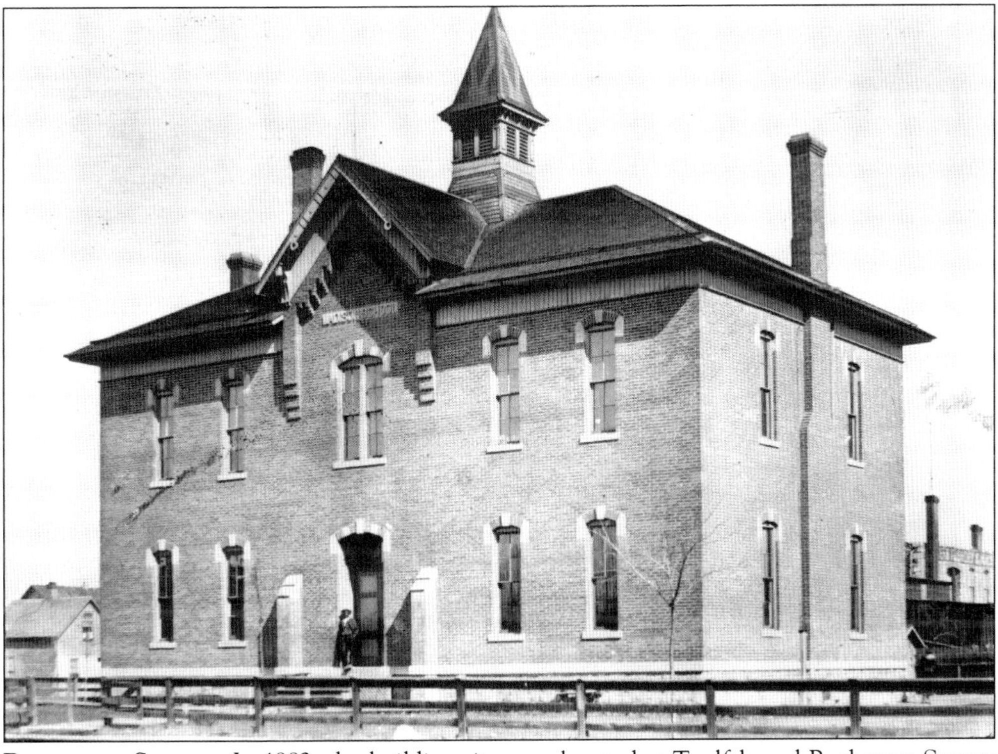

Buchanan School. In 1882, the building site now located at Twelfth and Buchanan Streets was purchased for a new school for black children, and Buchanan was erected in 1885. In 1920, the Sheldon Kindergarten was relocated to Buchanan School due to its location in the middle of Tennessee Town. (Courtesy of KHS.)

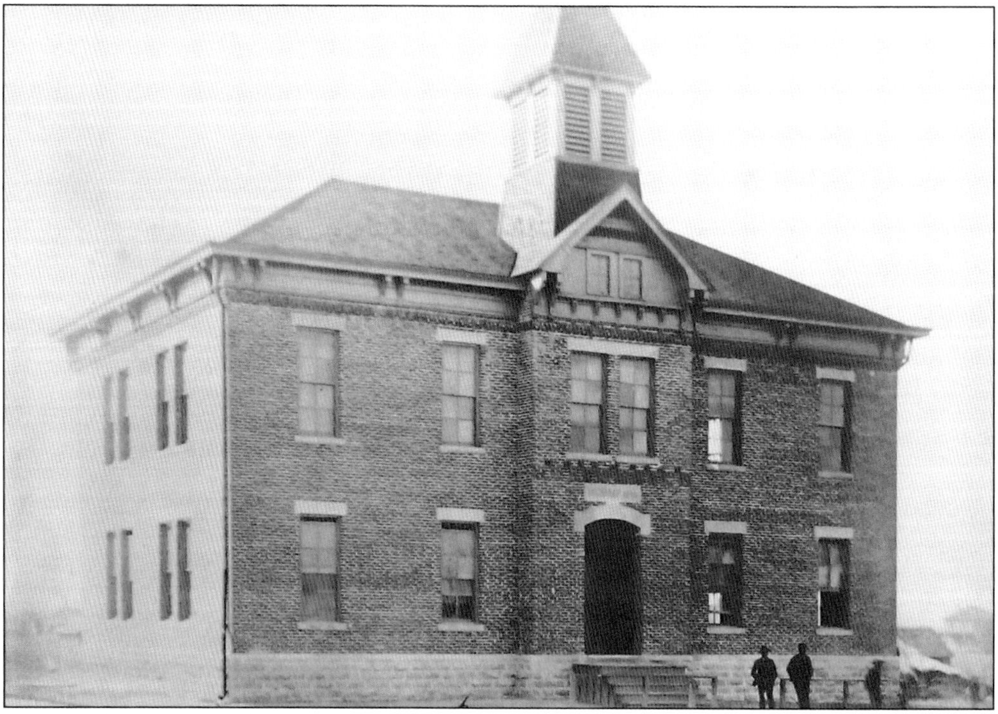

Madison Elementary School. Madison was another one of the black elementary schools. In 1886, it had the highest enrollment of all the black schools: 346 students. In 1915, it was closed, and the students were bussed across town to the Buchanan School. (Courtesy of KHS.)

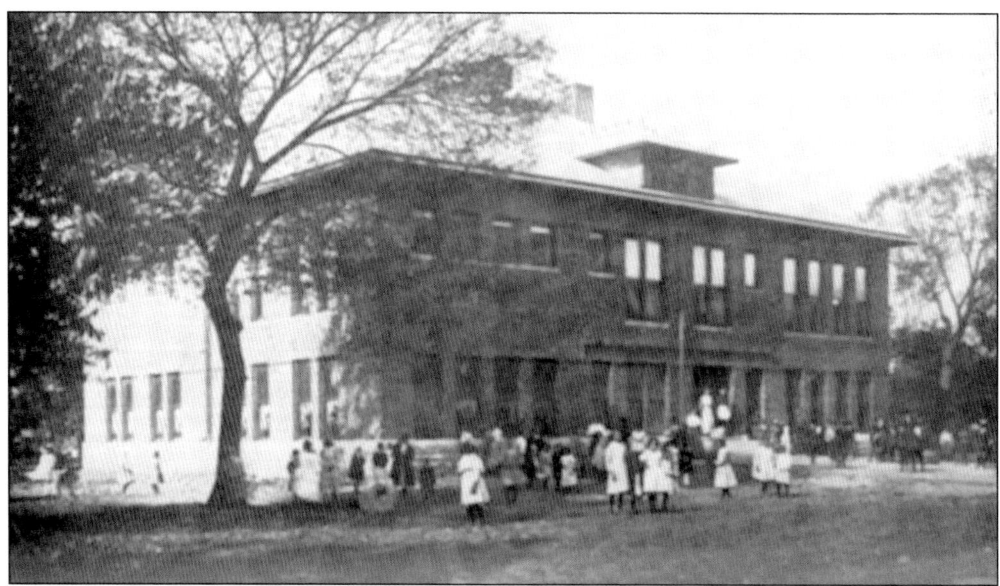

McKinley Elementary School. The McKinley School, located at 925 NW Taylor Street, was one of the four black elementary schools in Topeka when the *Brown v. Board of Education of Topeka* suit was filed. This photograph of the two-story brick structure shows a group of African American students participating in playground activities. The photograph appeared in the Topeka Public Schools Annual Report. (Courtesy of KHS.)

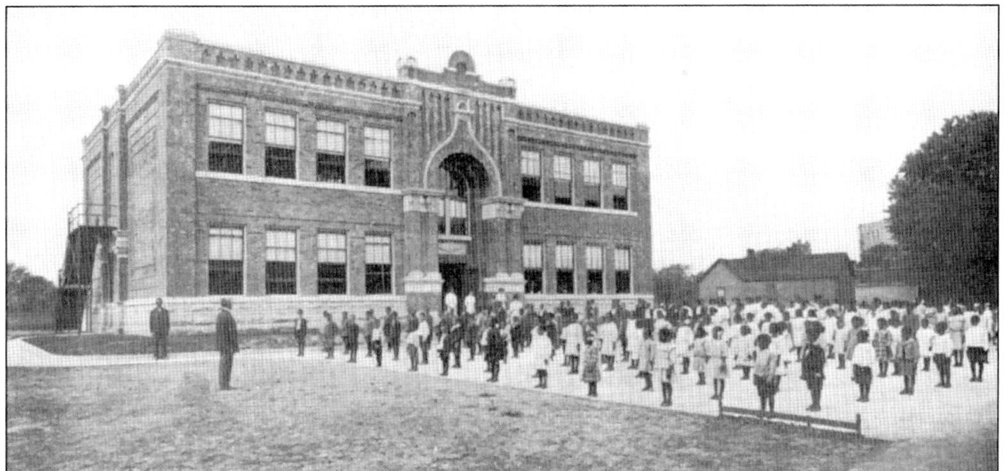

Washington Elementary School. Located near Tenth Avenue and Washington Street, the Washington School building underwent several changes. In 1904, the old Nickel Plate School building (located at Second and Buchanan Streets) was moved to the Washington School grounds at Eleventh and Washington Streets. In 1910, a new school building was built, and in 1926, it was remodeled, then used for black children. Washington was one of the four black elementary schools in Topeka when the US Supreme Court ruled in 1954 that segregated schools were unconstitutional. (Courtesy of KHS.)

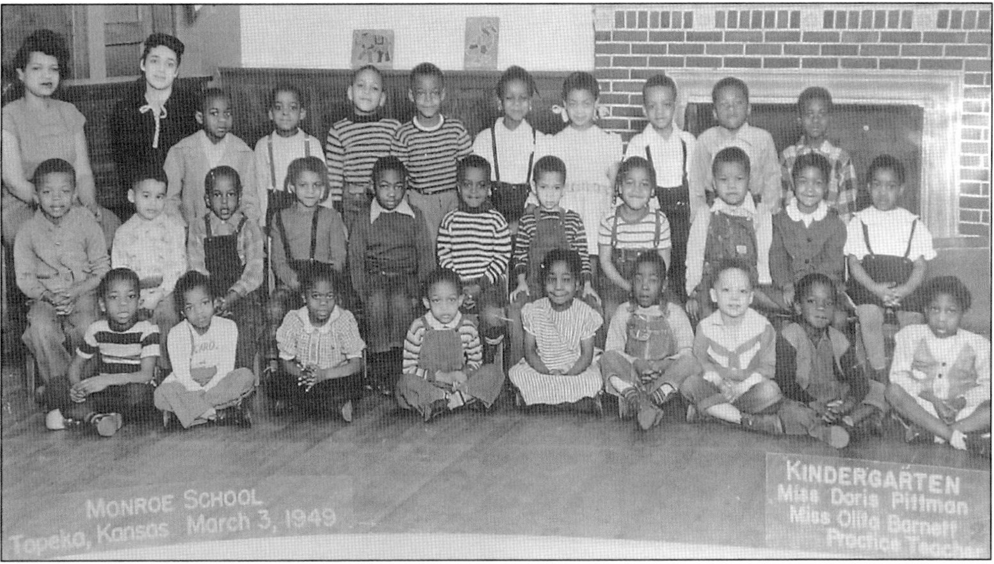

Kindergarten Students at Monroe School. The 1949 Monroe kindergarten class included Linda Brown, whose father, Oliver Brown, was the lead plaintiff in the *Brown v. Board of Education of Topeka* case. Linda still lives in Topeka and remembers most of her classmates. Miss Pittman is seated in the back to the far left beside an unidentified teacher's assistant. The students pictured are, from left to right, (first row) unidentified, Carol Hutton, Shirley Gentry, Virginia Bell, Fanny ?, Willie Cole, unidentified, Robert Warren, and Genevie Sims; (second row) Gregory Phillips, Dwight Saten, William Benson, Dale McKay, Bernard Hurd, Tommy Grisham, ? Turner, unidentified, Verdell Bugg, unidentified, and Barbara Richardson; (third row) Curtis Gentry, Phil Carper, Jimmy Parks, ? Jackson, Lois Henderson, Linda Brown, Vernon Turner, and two unidentified boys. (Courtesy of KHS.)

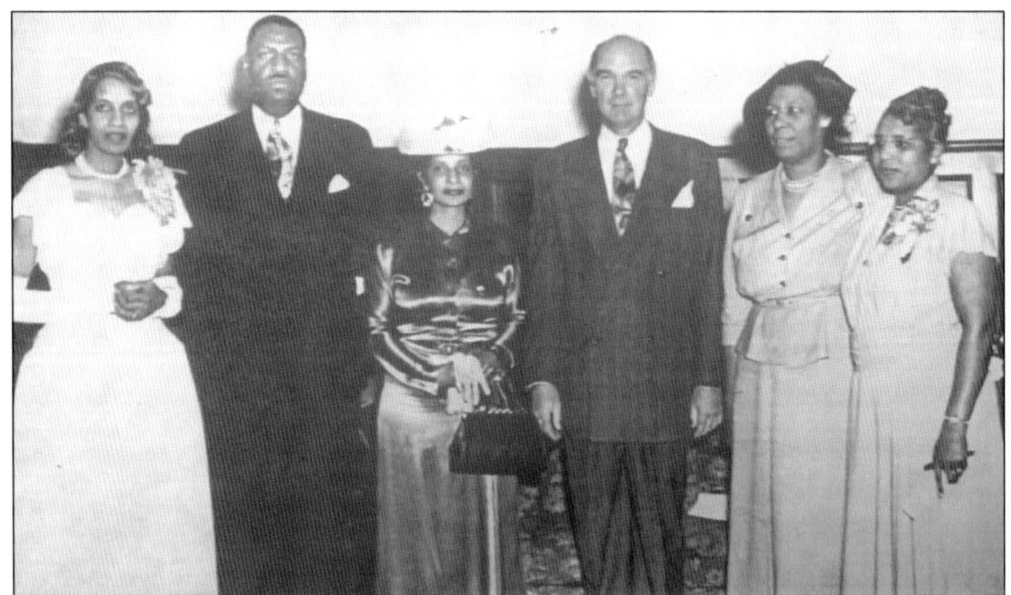

Harrison Caldwell. Harrison Caldwell, a native of Fort Scott, Kansas, came to Topeka in 1941. He received his associate's and master's degrees from Kansas State Teaching College in Pittsburg, Kansas. In 1941, he became the superintendent of the four African American elementary schools in Topeka: Buchanan, Monroe, McKinley, and Washington. At that time, he oversaw 27 teachers and between 800 and 900 students. The school administrators pictured here are, from left to right, Juanita Frazier, black schools superintendent Harrison Caldwell, Geraldine Harmon, Topeka Public Schools superintendent Kenneth McFarland, Tracy Mitchell, and Pearl Anderson. (Courtesy of Marie Carter.)

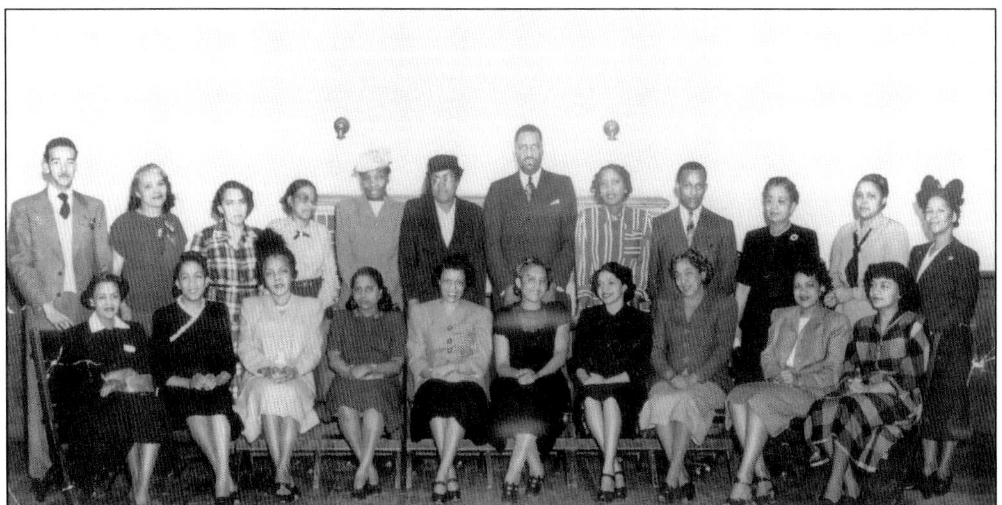

Teachers from Black Elementary Schools, 1949. The teachers of the four black elementary schools—Buchanan, McKinley, Monroe, and Washington—posed for this photograph, the only one of its kind. They are, from left to right, (first row) Katherine King, Dorothy Bradshaw, Mildred North, Geraldine Gilliam, Minerva Washington, Ada Eggleston, Barbara Ross, Dorothy Crawford, Doris Love, and Julia Patterson; (second row) Merrill Ross, Myrtle Starnes, Edna Vance, Fannie Patton, Mamie Williams, Eva Walker, Harrison Caldwell, Ethel Barbour, J.B. Holland, Mary B. Hill, Ida Norman (school nurse), and Althea McBrier. (Courtesy of Dr. Robert McFrazier.)

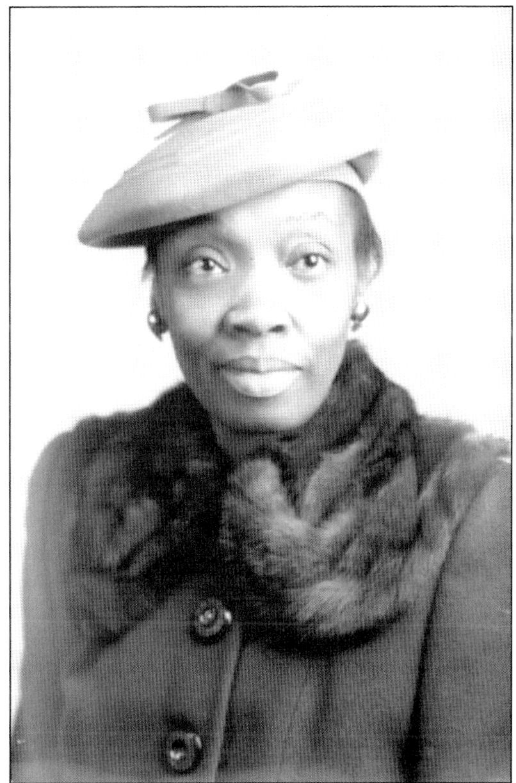

Mamie Luella Williams. This portrait of Mamie Luella Williams was taken between 1915 and 1919. Williams taught at Washington and Monroe Elementary Schools and was also a principal at Washington Elementary. Because of her contributions to the education of children in Topeka, one of the city's desegregated magnet schools was named after her. (Courtesy of KHS.)

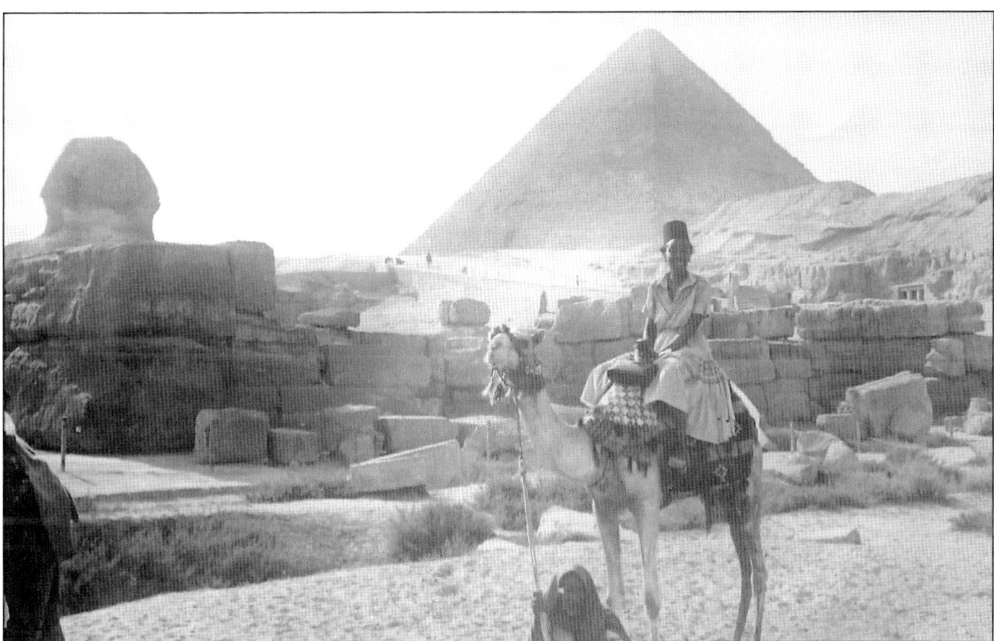

Mamie Williams in Egypt. Mamie Williams traveled the world. Here, she is seen riding a camel by the Great Pyramids in Egypt. In 1956, she also traveled to India, Japan, Hawaii, and West Africa. Her travels helped her to teach her students about blacks around the world and to write and edit curricula for the black elementary schools. (Courtesy of KHS.)

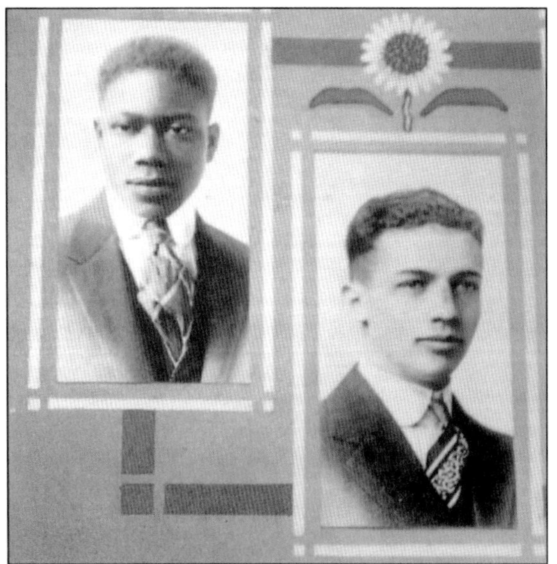

AARON DOUGLAS. Born in Topeka in 1899, Aaron Douglas is pictured above on the left as one of the 1917 graduates of Topeka High. The school hailed him as "one of the most talented artists." In high school, he contributed to several yearbook covers. Intending to ultimately pursue an art career in Paris, he moved to Harlem in June 1925. He soon won a scholarship to study with German illustrator Winold Reiss, who encouraged Douglas to look to his African ancestry for artistic inspiration. (Courtesy of TSCPL.)

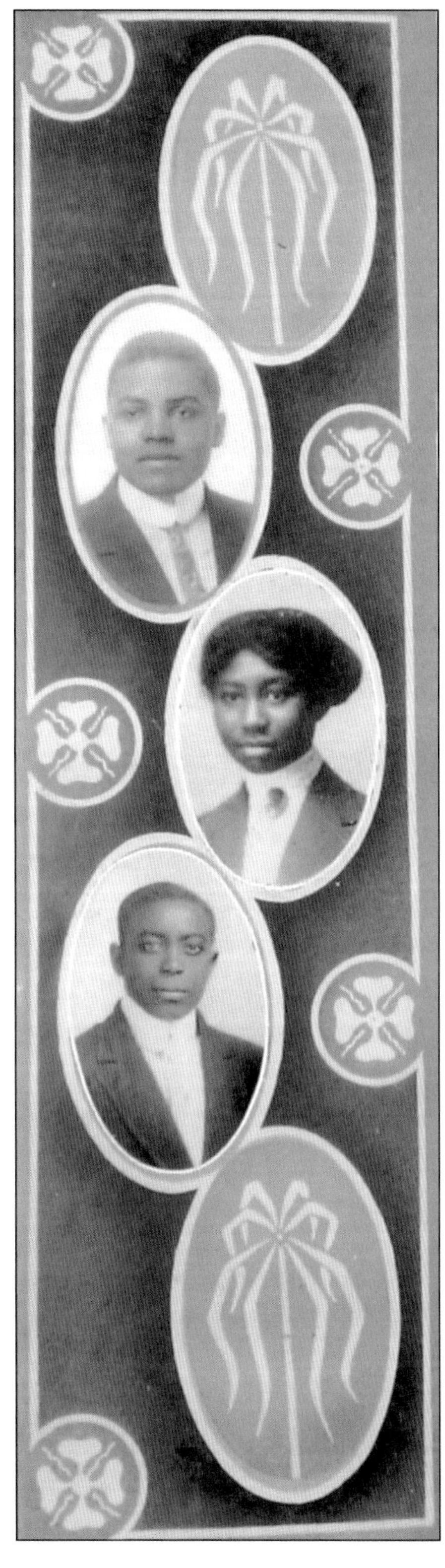

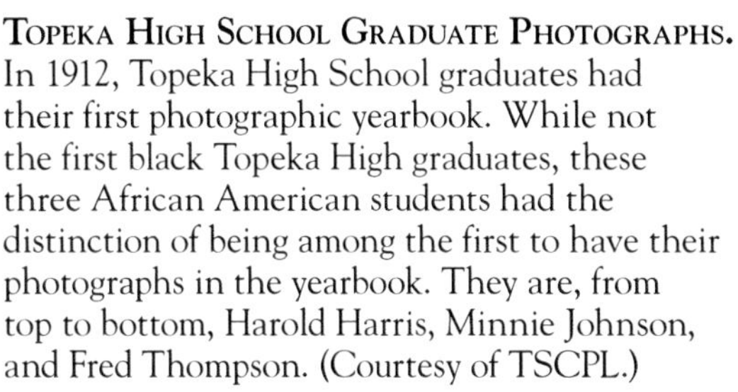

TOPEKA HIGH SCHOOL GRADUATE PHOTOGRAPHS. In 1912, Topeka High School graduates had their first photographic yearbook. While not the first black Topeka High graduates, these three African American students had the distinction of being among the first to have their photographs in the yearbook. They are, from top to bottom, Harold Harris, Minnie Johnson, and Fred Thompson. (Courtesy of TSCPL.)

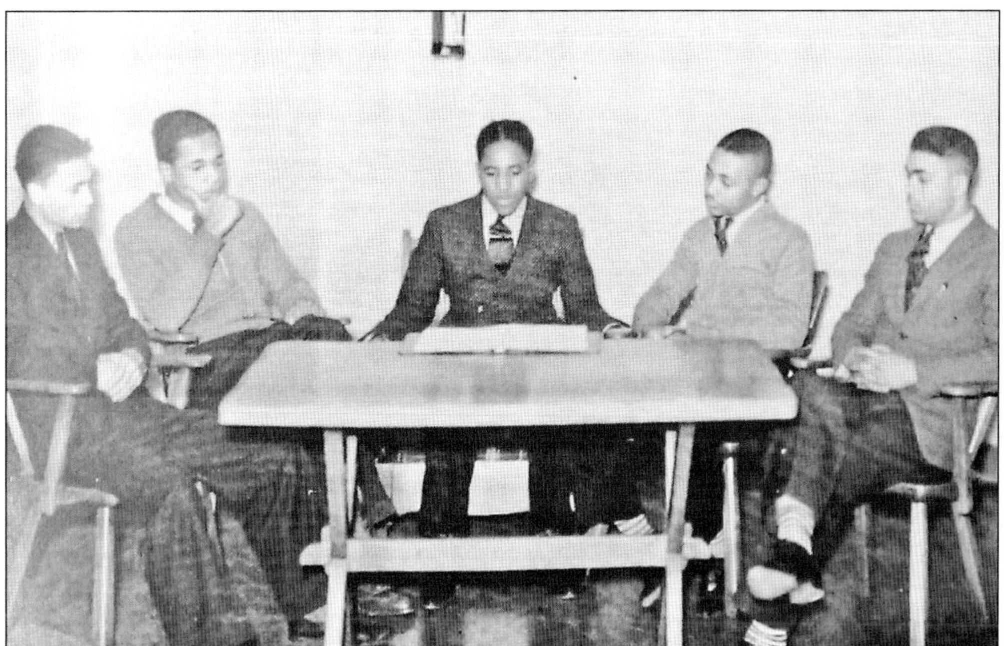

Topeka High School Booker T Boys Officers. The Topeka High School Booker T Boys social club for African American young men participated in many activities as a group. In this 1939 photograph, they plan their social events. From left to right, they are Abercrombie Napue, treasurer; John J. Scott, chief executive; Robert Gatewood, president; Druis Moss, secretary; and Oliver Brown, vice president. (Courtesy of TSCPL.)

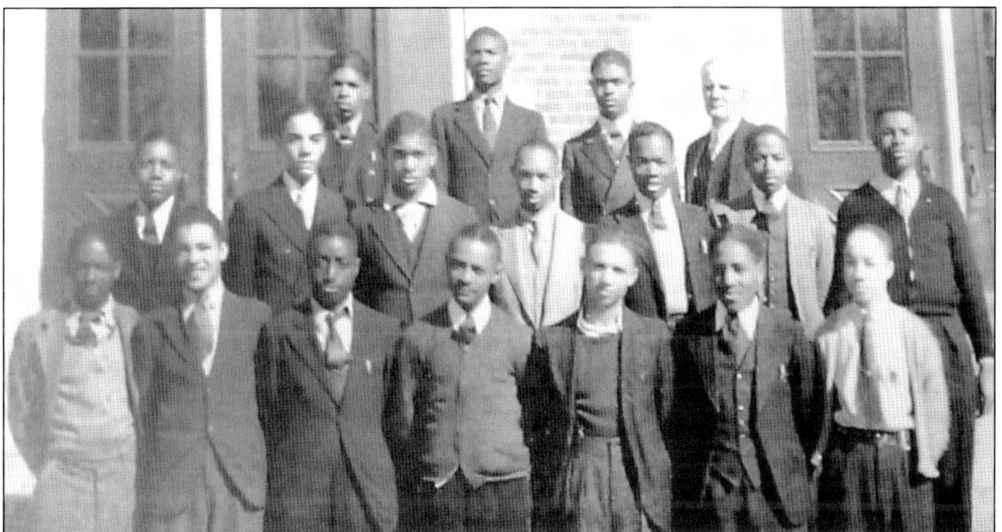

Topeka High School Booker T Boys Club. The Booker T Boys was a social club for African American young men, many of whom remained friends for their entire lives. The group is seen in this 1940 image from the Topeka High School yearbook. Most of those pictured here were identified only by their last names in the yearbook. From left to right are (first row) King, A. Moss, McConnell, D. Moss, Napue, Gatewood, and Jones; (second row) Murray, Burke, Nicholson, Morgan, Fisher, Carl Williams, and Scott; (third row) Charles Williams, Moore, Brown, and Mr. Dice. (Courtesy of TSCPL.)

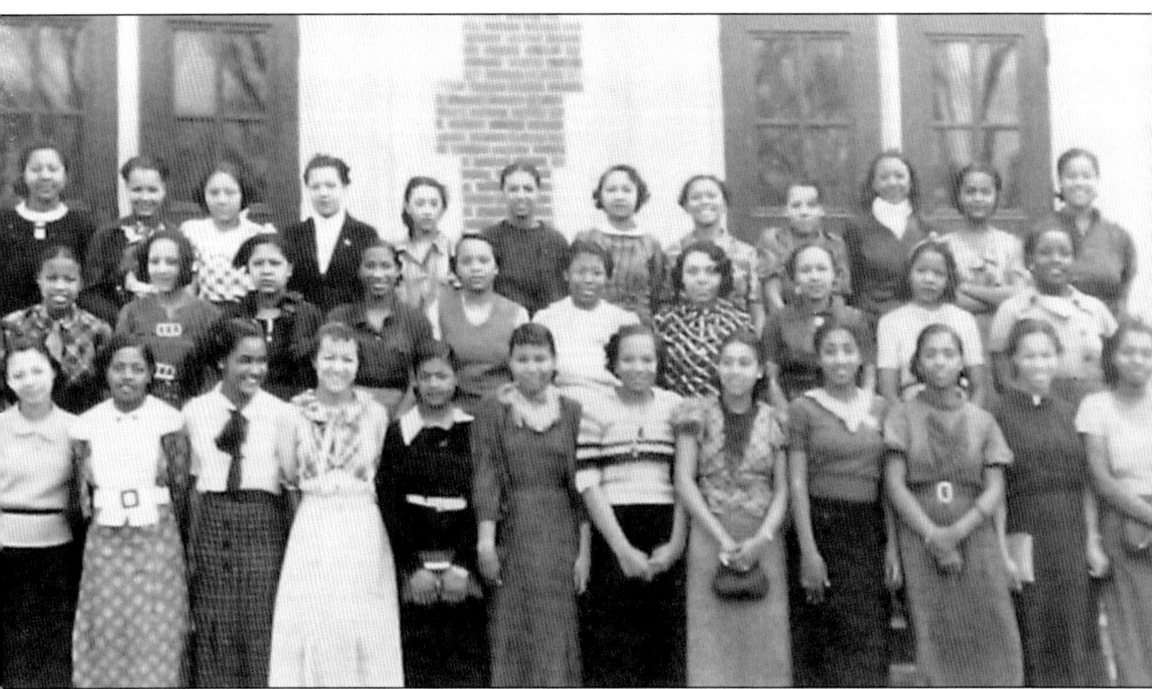

PHYLLIS WHEATLEY GIRLS' RESERVES. This Topeka High club began in 1923. It was originally called the Colored Girls' Reserves Club but changed its name in 1924. Members learned homemaking skills, such as cooking and sewing. Identified only by their last names, the girls pictured here are, from left to right, (first row) Sheppard, Watson, Jones, Smith, Watson, Duke, Hickman, Simms, Atkinson, Riley, Rainy, and Bailey; (second row) Clark, Ross, Oliver, Harris, Hickman, Johnson, Turner, Taylor, Carter, and Graves; (third row) Carney, Williams, Osborne, Evans, Sadler, James, Thompson, Hall, Davis, King, Bass, and Sayles. (Courtesy of TSCPL.)

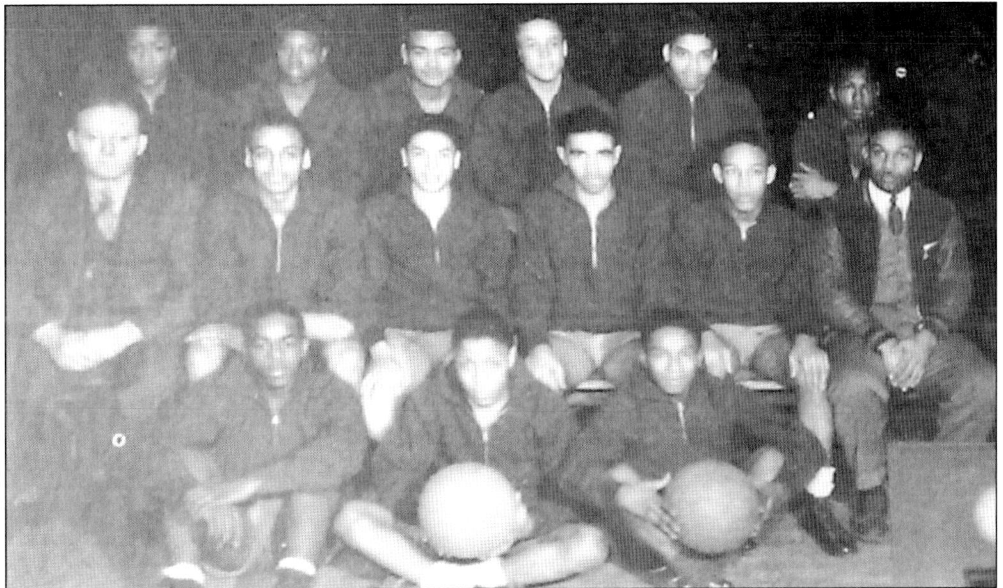

Topeka High School Ramblers. Topeka High's black basketball team, the Ramblers, was regarded as one of the finest "colored" teams in the state. Led by coach Lloyd Kistler, this team had eight wins and five losses in 1939. Pictured are, from left to right, (first row) Lenard Johnson, Sheridan Parks, and Thayer Phillips; (second row) coach Lloyd Kistler, Robert Reed, Irving Burton, Stewart Newman, Joseph Wright, and coach Jim Parks; (third row) Sherman Parks, Charles Kendricks, Delma Williams, Howard Hurst, Forrest Slaughter, and Oliver Brown. (Courtesy of TSCPL.)

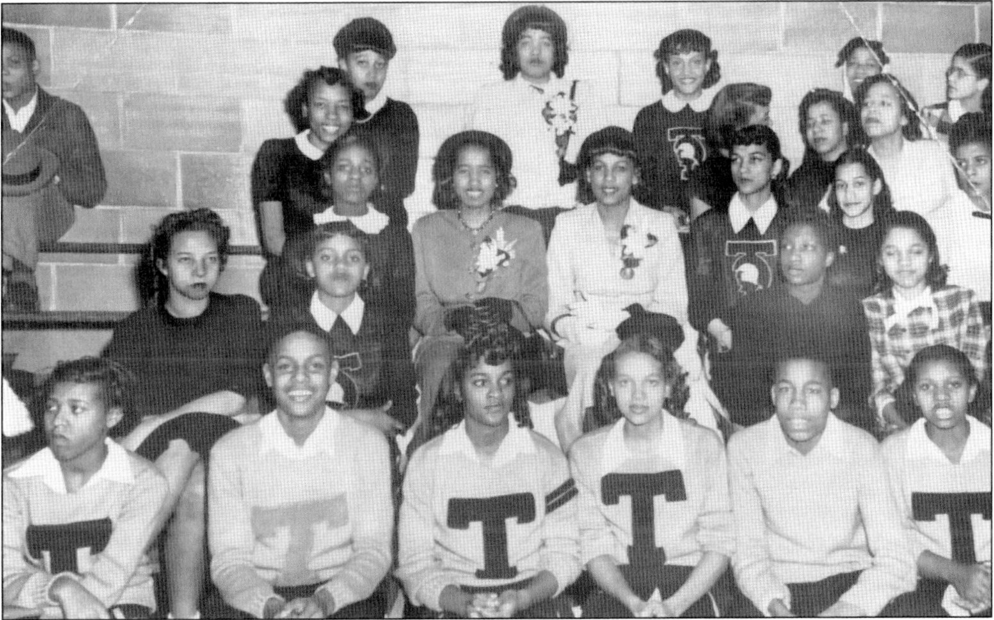

Ramblers Cheerleaders. Prior to 1954, during segregation, Topeka High School had separate sports teams and separate cheerleaders. All of the school's extracurricular activities were separate. The Topeka High School Ramblers all-black basketball team and cheerleaders were two of the black community's best assets. This 1932 photograph shows the cheerleaders on the sidelines at a basketball game. (Courtesy of KSCOLL.)

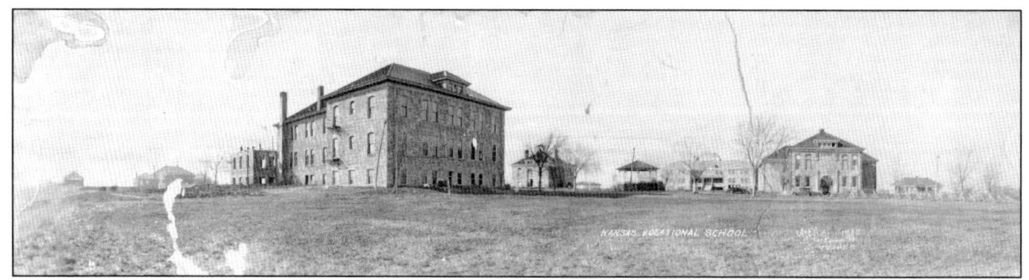

KANSAS TECHNICAL INSTITUTE. The Kansas Technical Institute (KTI) was founded in 1895 by Dr. Edward Stevens and Izie Beddick and was originally named the Kansas Industrial & Educational Institute. First located on Washington Street, it moved to Second Street and Kansas Avenue in 1896, then Eighteenth Street and Kansas Avenue in 1898. The school was finally moved in 1903 to a 110-acre lot purchased in East Topeka. Supported by state funding and private donations, KTI was considered to be much like the famous Tuskegee Institute, since, in 1900, it was placed under its direction. The Topeka school served blacks from all over Kansas and the United States until it closed in 1955 after the State of Kansas stopped funding it following the *Brown* decision. A women's prison now stands on the site. (Courtesy of KHS.)

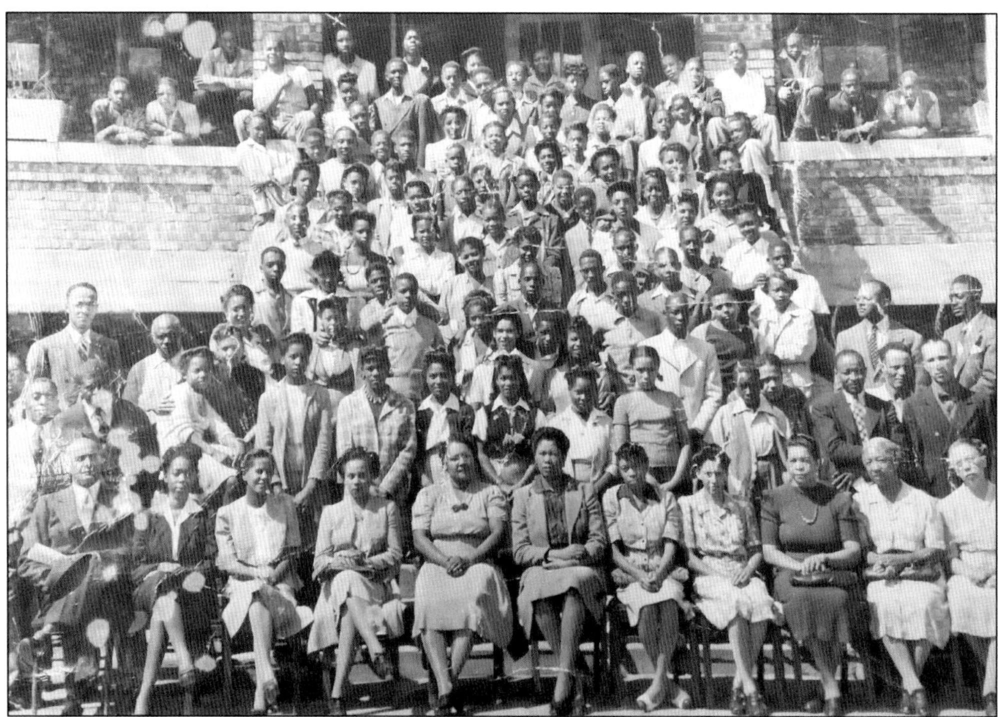

KANSAS TECHNICAL INSTITUTE STAFF AND STUDENTS. Originally called Kansas Industrial and Educational Institute, the school's name was changed several times: to Kansas Vocational School, Kansas Vocational Institute, and finally, Kansas Technical Institute. Students came from across the country to attend the school, which was a must-see for all tourists to Topeka. The staff and students of KTI were proud of their school. Their school mascot, a buffalo they lovingly called "Old Buff," is now in Cushinberry Park. The park, which is located at Fifteenth and Jefferson Streets, is dedicated to Grant Cushinberry, a local African American philanthropist. (Courtesy of KSCOLL.)

KTI **Baptist Summer Assembly.** During the summer, KTI offered credit and noncredit Bible classes for Baptist churches. This poster advertised the summer training in 1946 and listed the many ministers and laypersons who participated in teaching the classes. It includes images of the principal, Herman T. Jones, and KTI buildings, including the academic building, the girls' dormitory, the boys' trade building, the boys' dormitory, and the hospital. (Courtesy of KSCOLL.)

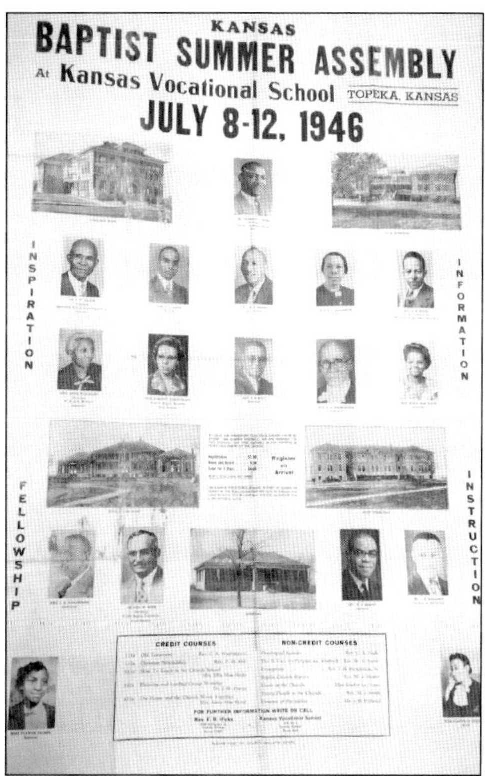

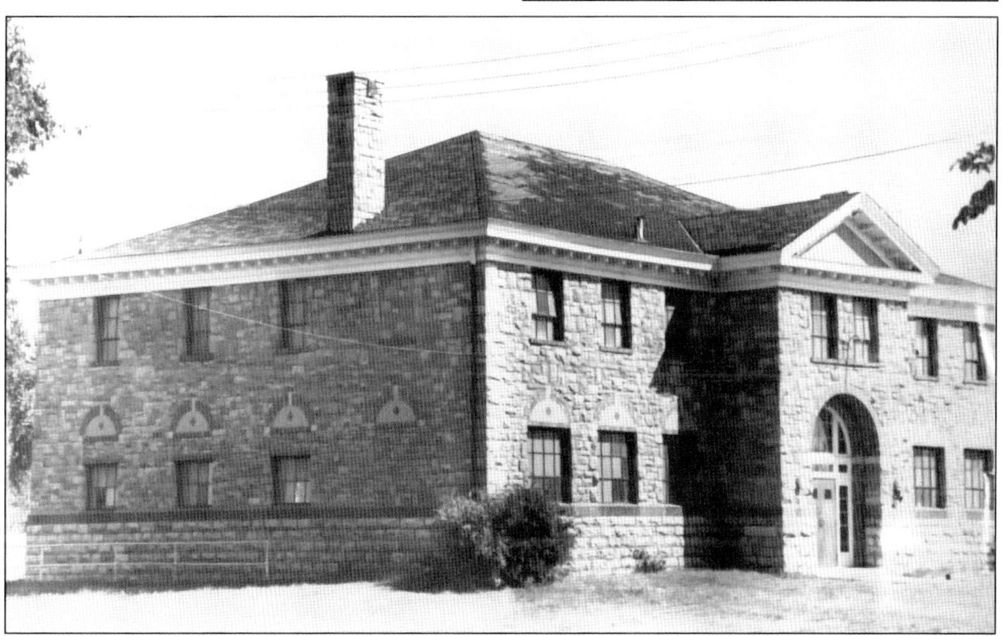

Bradford Miller Hall. The Kansas Technical Institute provided vocational, technical, and commercial curricula to young men and women in the 11th and 12th grades and the first and second years of college. Youths ages 16 and older could apply for admission. Bradford Miller Hall was a two-story building containing offices, classrooms, the music department, a library, and an auditorium with a stage. (Courtesy of KSCOLL.)

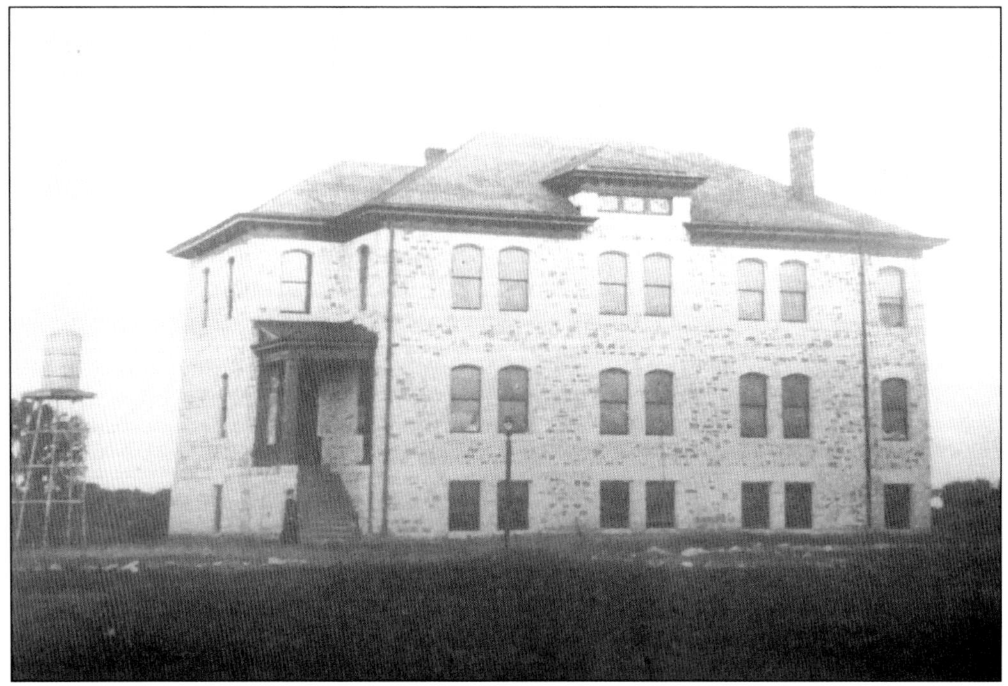

Girls' Dormitory. J.B. Larimer Hall, the girls' dormitory, was one structure built on the campus of the Kansas Vocational Institute. Constructed in 1907 and paid for by the State of Kansas and Andrew Carnegie, it was a three-story building designed to accommodate 125 young women. It included a large kitchen, dining hall, and laundry room. The girls' dormitory was the site of many functions, including the conventions of the Kansas Women's Club. (Courtesy of KSCOLL.)

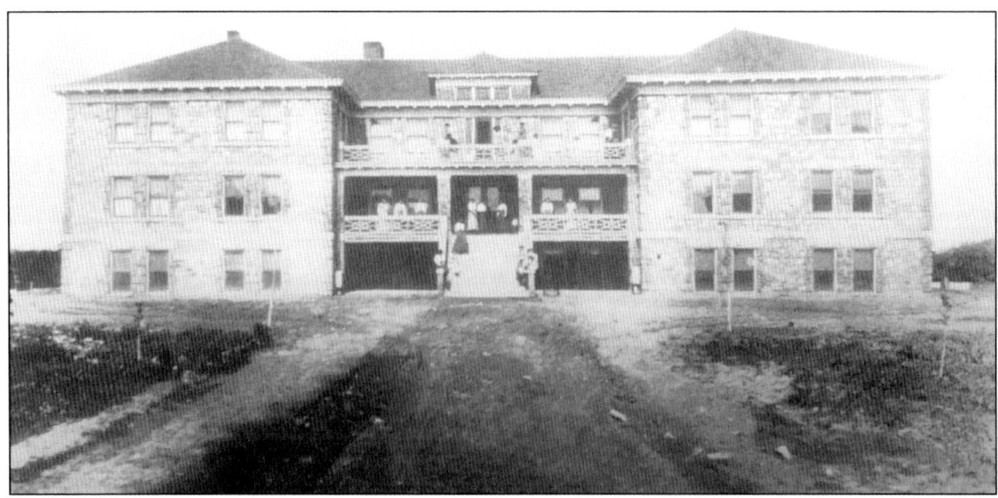

Boys' Dormitory. Howland Hall, the boys' dormitory, was a three-story stone building with a basement. The first floor of this building had a gym and a study hall. Dorm rooms were on the second and third floors. In addition to football and basketball, the boys at KTI also participated in the band and glee club. (Courtesy of KSCOLL.)

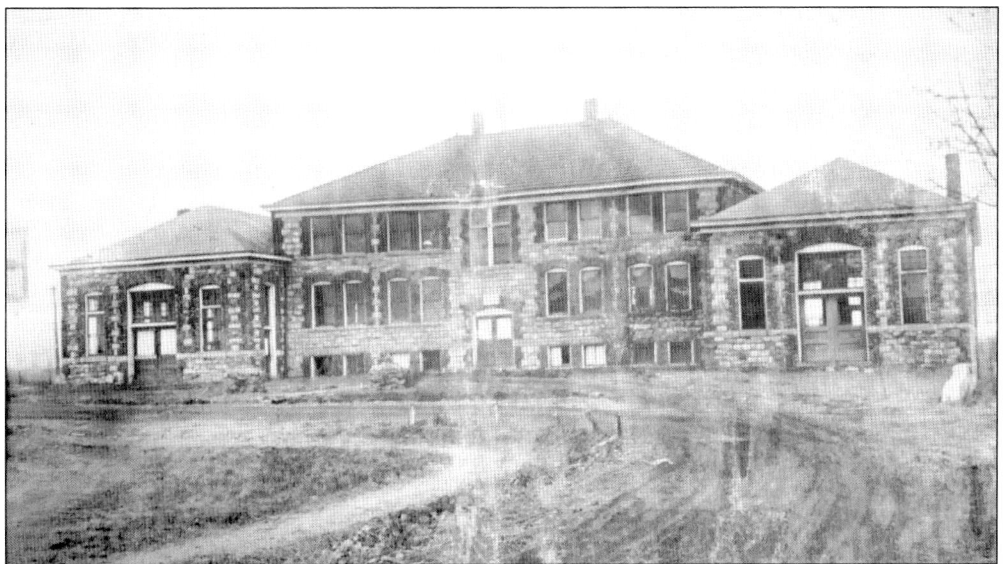

Boys' Trade Center. The boys' trade center housed male-specific trades and activities. The courses were approved by the Veterans Administration and accredited by the Kansas Board of Education. Some of the courses that were offered included agriculture, carpentry, tailoring, printing, auto mechanics, blacksmithing, military service, and ROTC. (Courtesy of KSCOLL.)

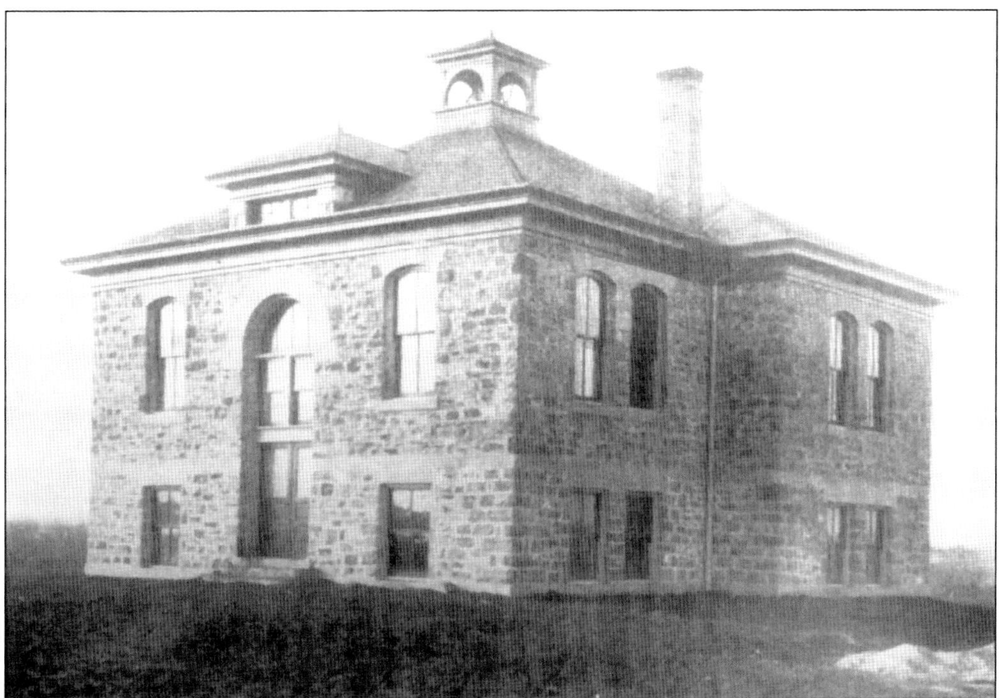

Girls' Trade Center. The girls' trade center was built in 1907, along with the girls' dormitory. The courses offered for girls included nursing, music, domestic arts and sciences (such as sewing and cooking), and millinery. Girls also participated in the girls' basketball team and glee club. (Courtesy of KSCOLL.)

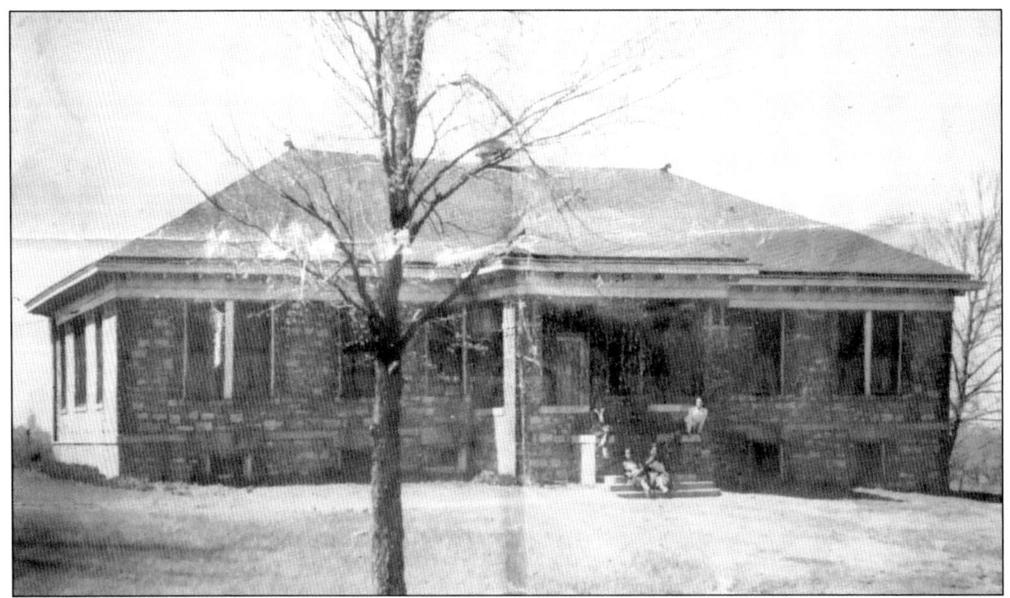

Kansas Technical Institute Hospital. The Nellie Johns Hospital on the KTI campus was an integral part of the education of nursing students. This then-modern facility, which had space for 30 patients, gave the students hands-on work experience. The nursing program lasted two years and nine months and included one year of nursing experience, which was required before a nurse could work in a hospital. Students ranged in age from 16 to 30 years old. (Courtesy of KHS.)

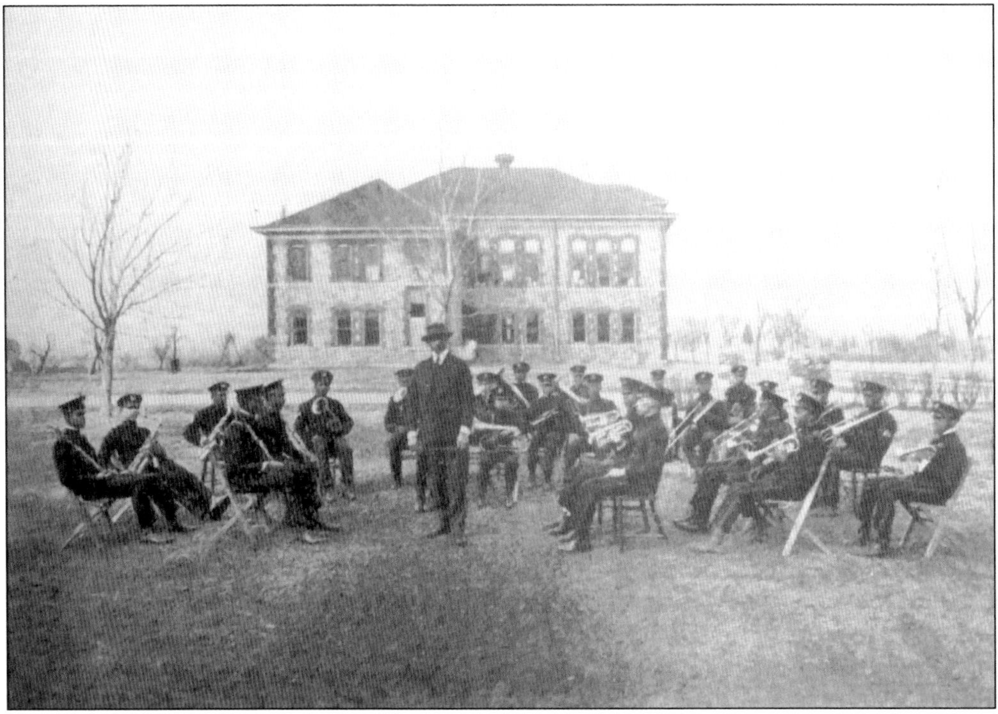

Kansas Technical Institute Band. This photograph shows the band practicing outside the academic building. The 25-piece ensemble was an important part of the school and offered students with musical ability the opportunity to develop their talents. (Courtesy of KSCOLL.)

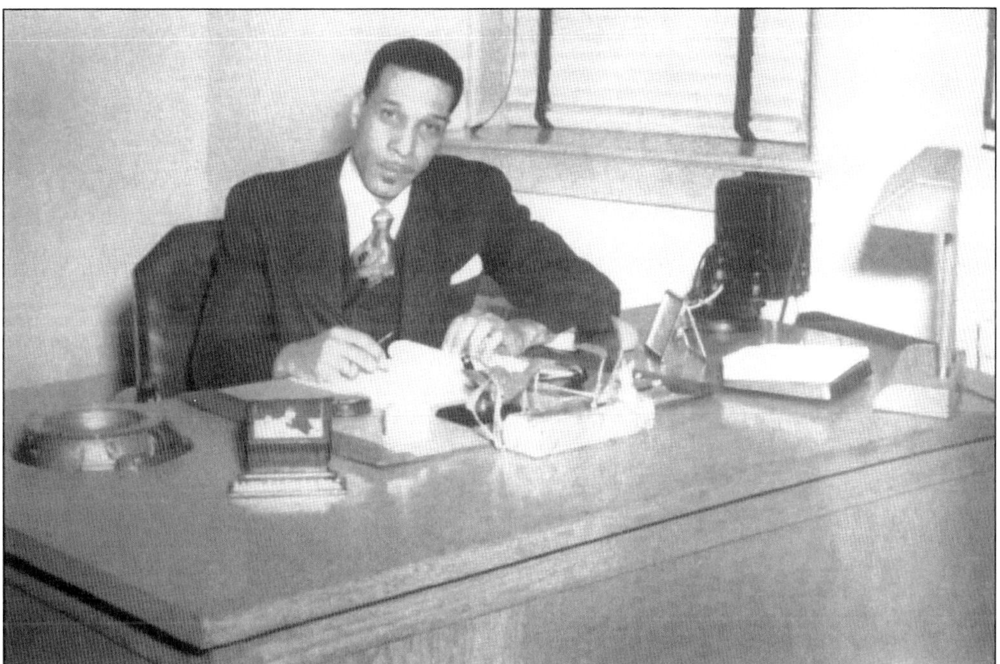

Dr. G. Robert Cotton. In 1947, Dr. G. Robert Cotton became the president of the Kansas Vocational Institute. During his tenure, the school was reorganized, and the name was changed to the Kansas Technical Institute. Dr. Cotton served until 1954, a year before the school was closed. (Courtesy of KSCOLL.)

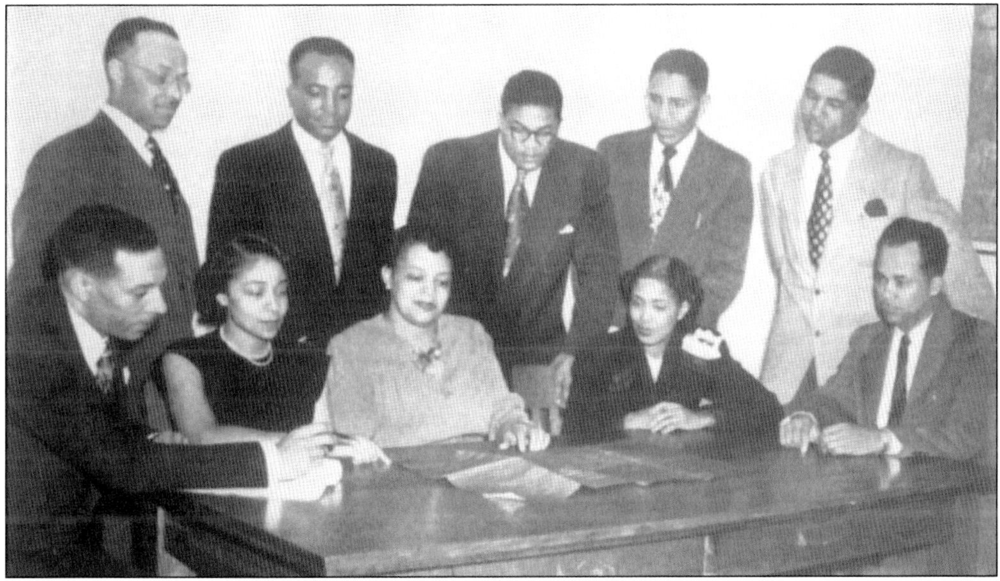

KTI Administrative Council. The KTI administrators included, from left to right, (first row) Dr. G. Robert Cotton, president; Wilnetta Jones, nurse; Anita Burney, cafeteria worker; Ernestine Hayes Smith, counselor; and Horace Murdock, business manager; (second row) Vance J. Williams, registrar and evening school director; John E. Scott, librarian and public relations director; Richard Mack, athletic director; Thomas Willard, counselor; and David Ware, superintendent of buildings and ground. (Courtesy of KSCOLL.)

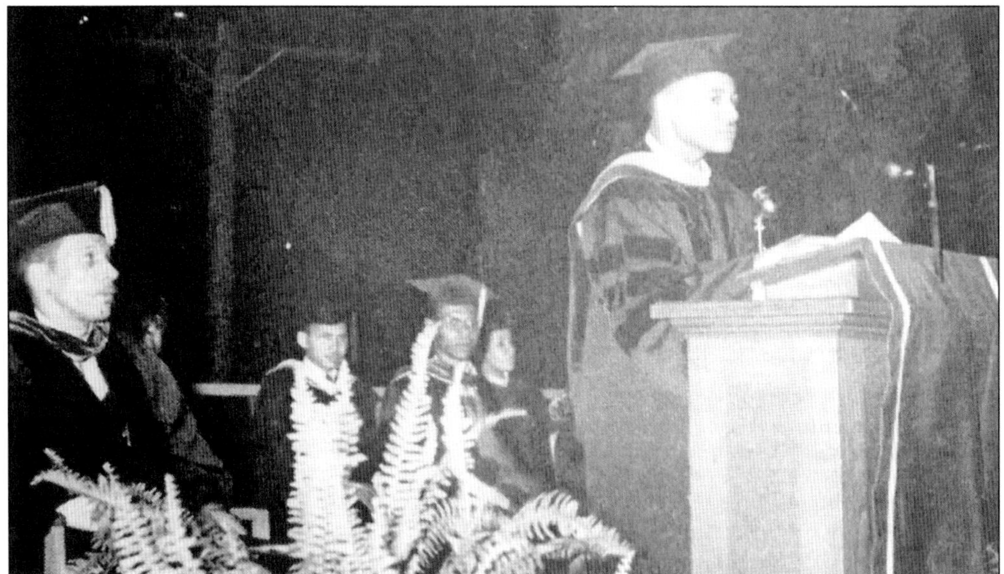

54TH KTI COMMENCEMENT ADDRESS. In this photograph, John Sengstacke, the editor/publisher of the *Chicago Defender* and president of the National Negro Publishers Association, gives the commencement address to KTI graduates. Sengstacke was the nephew of the newspaper's founding editor/publisher, Robert S. Abbott. The *Defender*, which began in 1905, was the nation's most influential black weekly newspaper and the first to have a readership of over 100,000 per week. (Courtesy of KHS.)

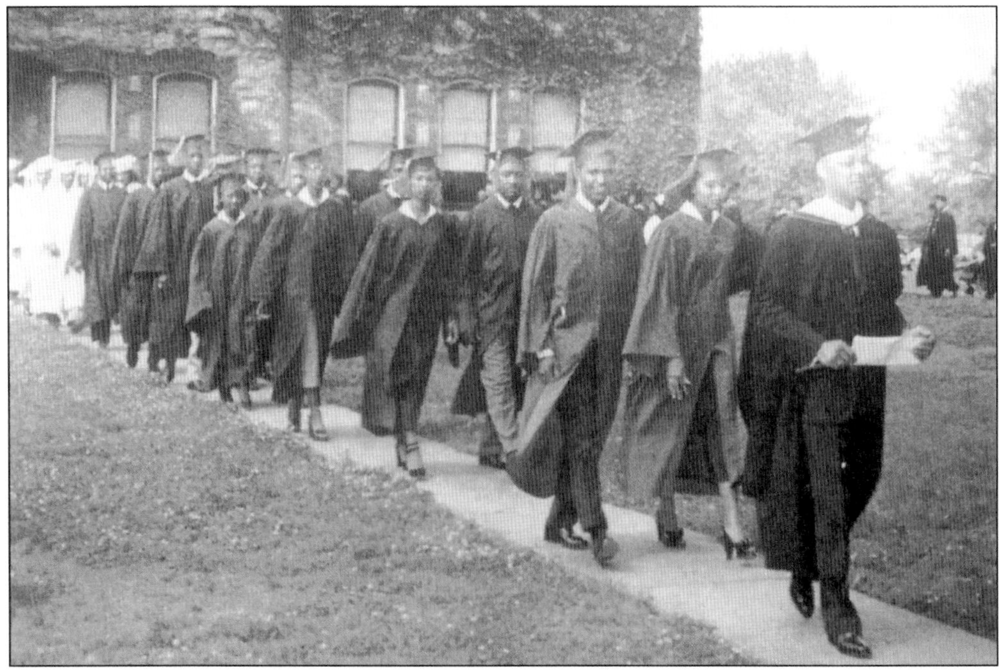

KANSAS VOCATIONAL INSTITUTE GRADUATION, 1949. In this photograph, men and women of the Kansas Vocational Institute's class of 1949 follow one of their instructors in the graduation procession on campus. Behind the regular classmen are the nurses in white caps and gowns and other graduating students. (Courtesy of KSCOLL.)

Dr. Marvin Edwards. In 1985, at the age of 41, Dr. Marvin Edwards became the first black man to serve as the superintendent of Topeka Public Schools. After three rounds of rigorous interviews, Edwards was chosen as the best candidate. A *Topeka Capital-Journal* news article in 1985 stated that he received the position on his own merits and not because of his race. Edwards was educated in Chicago, where he received his bachelor's and master's degrees. He served as superintendent in Topeka for three years and, during his tenure, established the Topeka Public Schools Foundation. (Courtesy of Topeka Public Schools.)

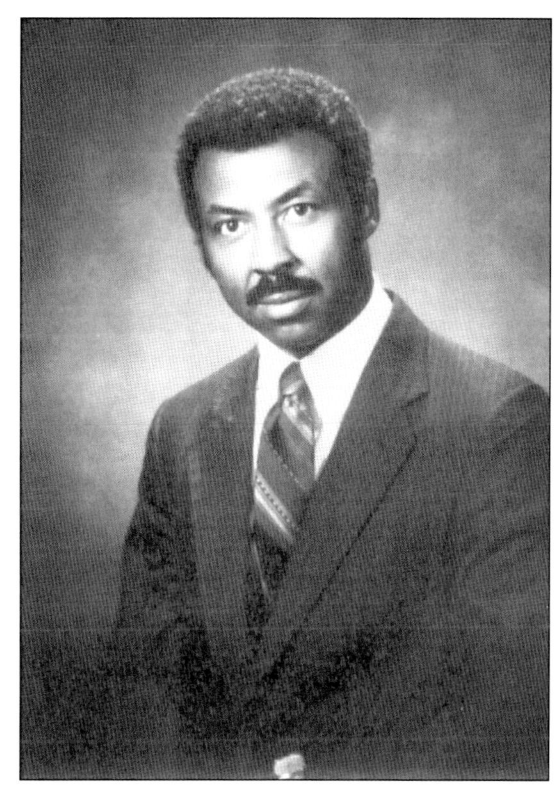

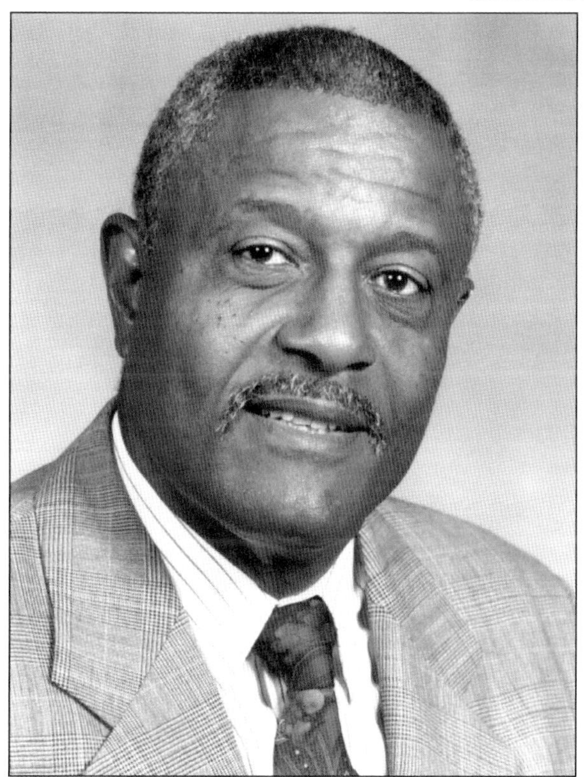

Dr. Robert McFrazier. Affectionately known as "Mac" at the Topeka Public Schools' administration building, Dr. McFrazier was the second African American to serve as the district's superintendent, a position he filled from 1999 to 2003. Under his leadership, Topeka schools made significant gains in student achievement, and the district's new Hummer Sports Park was constructed. As an administrator in the district prior to becoming superintendent, McFrazier help to craft the district's 1994 desegregation plan following the case known as *Brown v. Board III*. (Courtesy of Topeka Public Schools.)

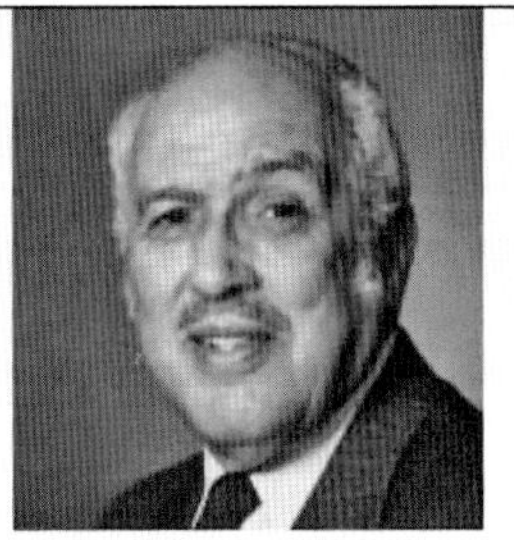

Onan Burnett

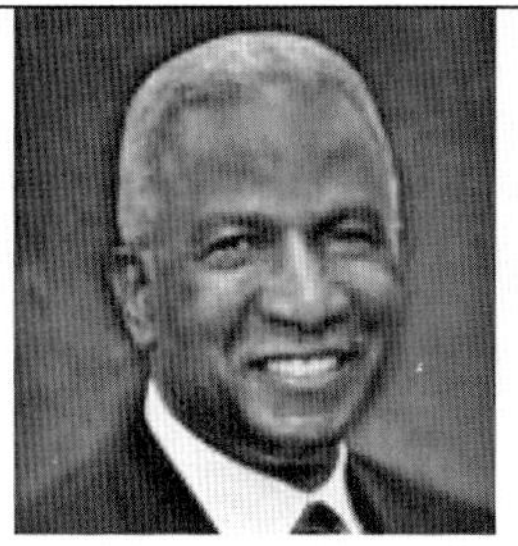

Dr. Ronald Epps

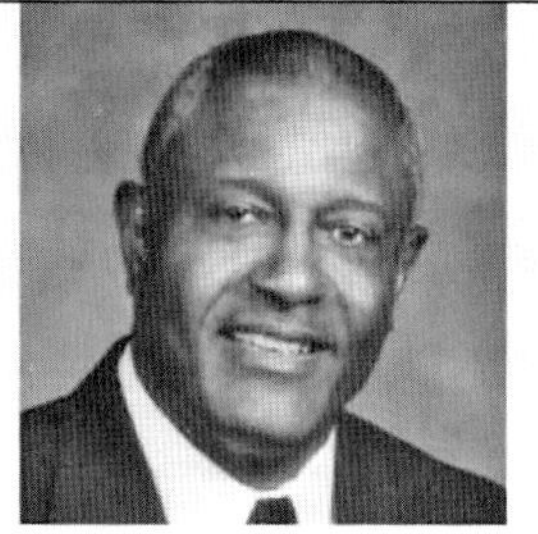

Dr. Robert McFrazier

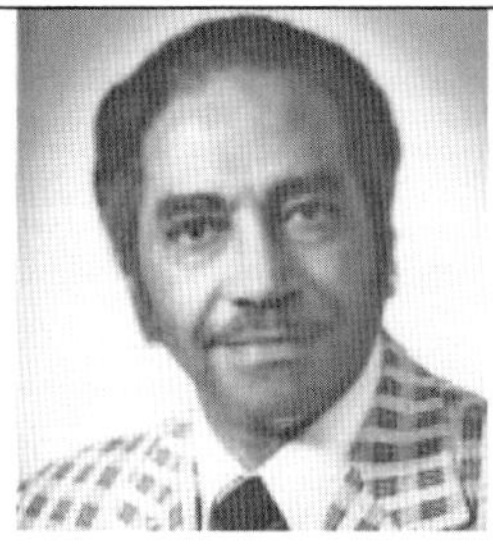

Forest Slaughter,

Theresa Counts,

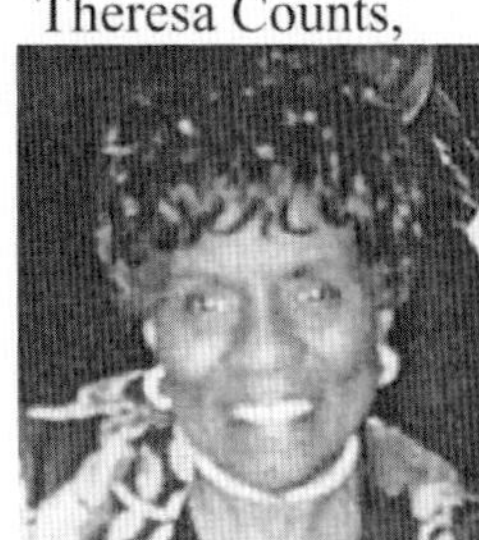

Ernest Hodison,

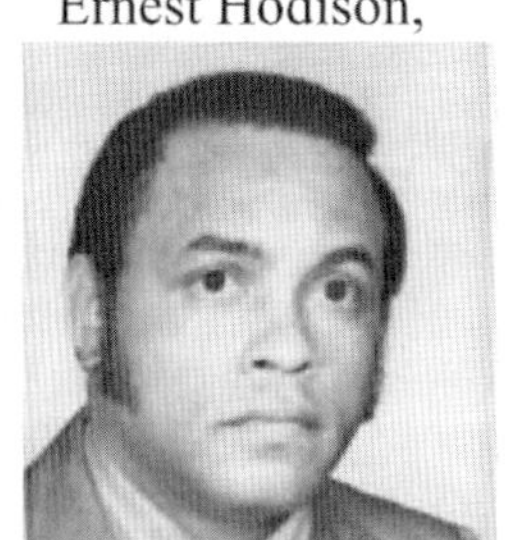

Merrill Ross,

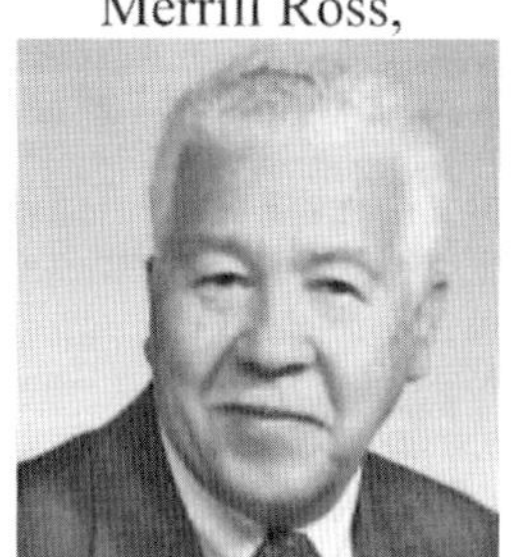

Winfred Tidwell

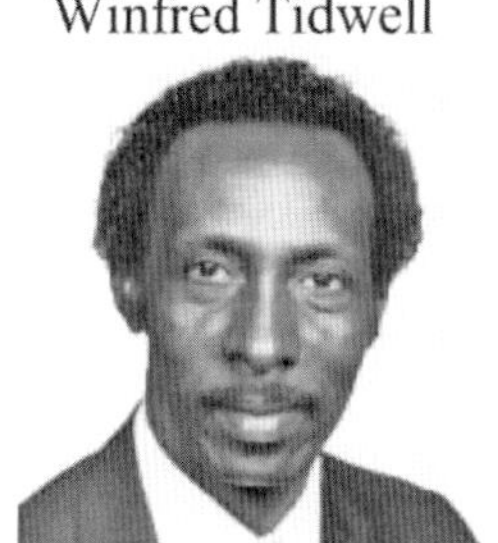

FOUNDING MEMBERS OF THE KANSAS ALLIANCE OF BLACK SCHOOL EDUCATORS (KABSE). The KABSE is an affiliate of the National Alliance of Black School Educators (NABSE). The charter members of KABSE met initially in 1983 in the home of Merrill Ross. Dr. Ronald Epps served as the unofficial leader, and Theresa Counts served as the note taker. The primary focus was to discuss concerns and challenges they faced as African American administrators. In November 1983, Dr. Ronald Epps and Onan Burnett presented the idea of becoming an affiliate of NABSE to their group of African American administrators and officially formed KA-NABSE in the 1984–1985 academic school year. The Topeka Alliance of Black School Educators (TABSE) is a strong supporter of the annual KABSE conference. (Courtesy of KABSE.)

Four

Black Economic Development Building a Community

Before the civil rights marches of the 1960s, Jim Crow laws throughout the United States limited where many blacks could live and travel, the businesses they could enter, and the associations they could have. In Kansas—and in Topeka specifically—life was different than in the South, where laws were much more restrictive. However, the laws that kept some segregation in force in Topeka had the positive effect of building and strengthening the black community. Though blacks still mingled with whites, there were many services that they provided for themselves: grocery stores, barber and beauty shops, car repair shops, and recreation and entertainment venues. Within Topeka, there was a large community of African Americans that worked together, served each other, and socialized.

Blacks in Topeka could and did work among whites, but only in limited ways. Many worked in traditional servant and laborer jobs. In fact, the Santa Fe Railroad employed many blacks as laborers, and it also employed some as porters and cooks. Education was the key to advancement, and many African Americans took advantage of opportunities to learn so that they could improve their skills and their lives.

Topeka was home to black doctors and lawyers, as well as to teachers, dentists, other business owners, and politicians. The people who were able to do well for themselves professionally and financially were generally the major forces in their community. They were active in society and made an impact on the experiences of their peers. They banded together to right the wrongs, lift one another up, and enjoy the lifestyles they worked hard to achieve. They also enjoyed many social gatherings together.

Fred M. Stonestreet. G. W. Hamilton.

Stonestreet & Hamilton,

Successors to J. M. Knight.

Undertakers and Embalmers.

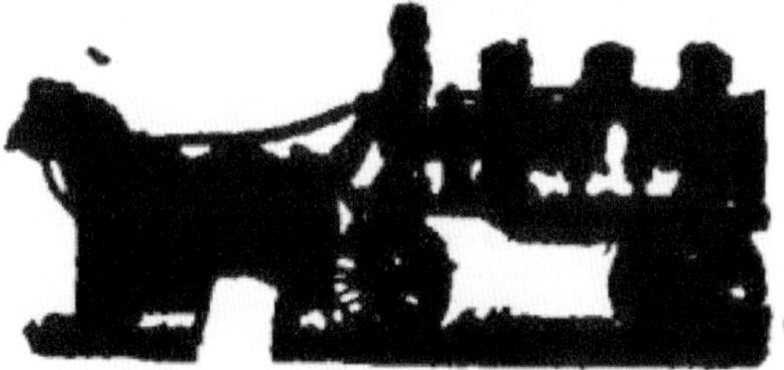

We carry one of the finest lines of Undertaking goods in Topeka.

Corner 7th and Quincy Sts. Topeka, Kansas.

STONESTREET & SONS MORTUARY. Fred Stonestreet came to Topeka in 1862. He worked at the statehouse, became marshal of Topeka, and was the city's first black fireman. In 1903, he bought an established undertaking company from F.W. Knight and went into business with G.W. Hamilton to form Stonestreet & Hamilton Undertakers and Embalmers, located at Seventh and Quincy Streets. By 1909, Stonestreet broke with Hamilton, and he soon afterwards became a partner with Ben Gaines. Later, he formed Stonestreet & Sons at 636 Quincy Street with his son Wilbur and son-in-law Henry Carper. (Courtesy of the *Plaindealer*.)

HENRY CARPER. Henry Carper was born in Topeka and attended local schools. This photograph comes from his 1923 graduation from the Cincinnati School of Embalming. Carper married Harriett Stonestreet, the daughter of the local undertaker, and joined his father-in-law, Fred Stonestreet, in his undertaking business. (Courtesy of KSCOLL.)

Gaines & Son Funeral Home

OUR MOTTO: SERVICE

Phone 24008 **Day or Night**

AMBULANCE SERVICE

E. E. Bufford—Mortician **1182 Buchanan St.**

GAINES & SON FUNERAL HOME. In 1910, Ben and Emma Gaines joined Fred Stonestreet as partners in the funeral home business. By 1927, the Gaineses had their own funeral home at 305 Kansas Avenue. When their son Benjamin later joined the family business, its name was changed to Gaines & Son Funeral Home. Gaines & Son, which later moved to 1182 Buchanan Street, was a well-respected establishment for many years. (Courtesy of the *Plaindealer*.)

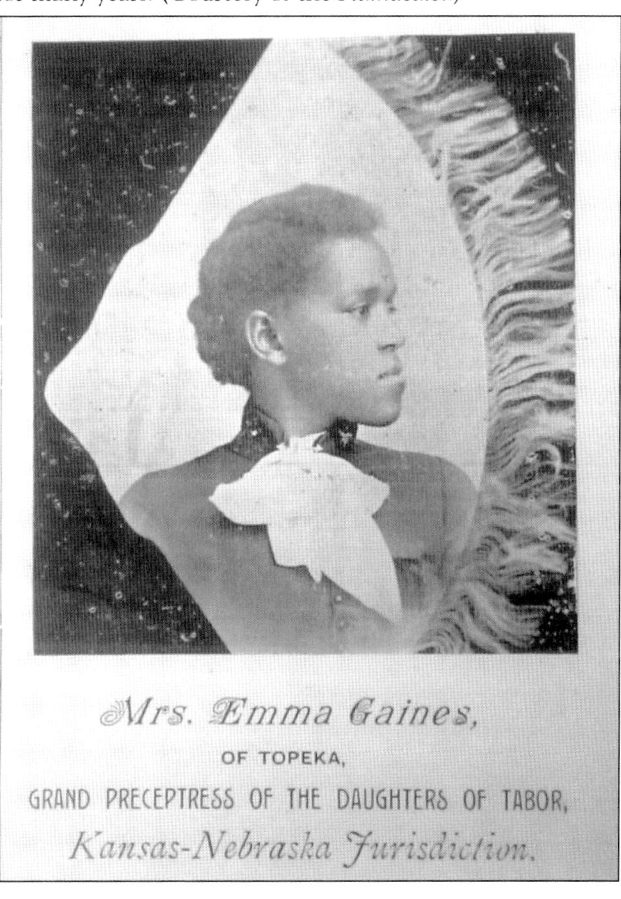

EMMA GAINES. Some of the earliest businesses in Topeka were actually owned by women. Emma Gaines was the wife of mortician Ben Gaines. This is an advertisement from the *Blade*, a black newspaper from Parsons, Kansas. Emma Gaines took out this notice listing herself as the "Grand Preceptress of the Daughters of Tabor" over Kansas and Nebraska. She was a prominent member of the community and held high positions at Shiloh Baptist Church and in many lodges and women's clubs. (Courtesy of TSCPL.)

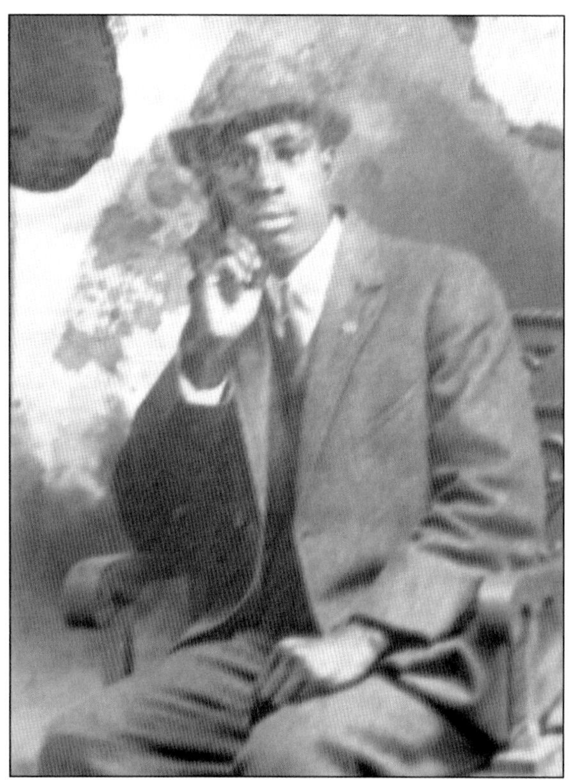

Elisha Scott Sr. An attorney and counselor at law, Elisha Scott Sr. was one of the Midwest's most prominent and experienced lawyers. He was educated at the Kansas Vocational School (later called the Kansas Technical Institute) and, in 1916, graduated from the Washburn College School of Law. He defended the well-known riot cases of Tulsa, Oklahoma, and Coffeyville, Kansas, and some of the notable Indian and oil cases from all parts of Oklahoma and Kansas and throughout the Southwest. Scott was well known for his efficiency and shrewdness as a lawyer. A resident of Topeka since the late 1890s, he owned a beautiful home at 1139 Lane Street and had his law office at 410 South Kansas Avenue. He was the father of three sons: John, Charles, and Elisha Jr., who joined his law practice. Scott also served in the military and was commissioned a captain in World War I. (Courtesy of KSCOLL.)

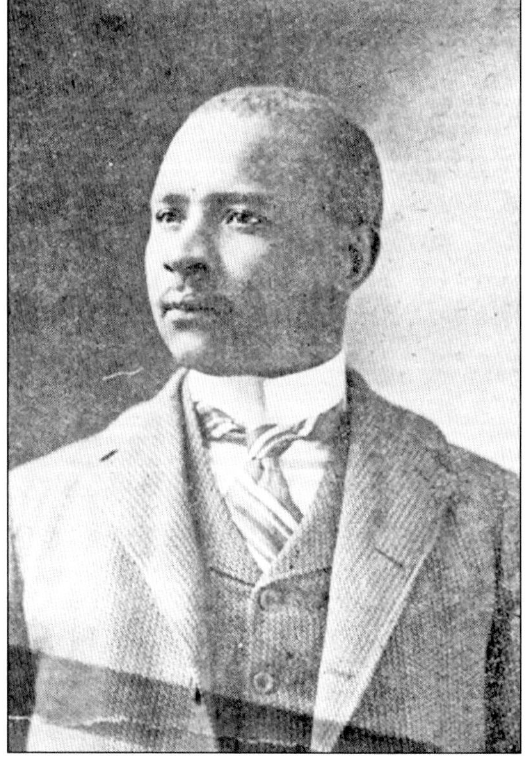

Nick Chiles. Nick Chiles was born in South Carolina and moved to Topeka in 1886. He owned several businesses, including the Chiles Hotel and the *Plaindealer* between 112 and 118 SE Seventh Street. He was involved in many organizations and was well respected in the community. In 1898, he bought the *Topeka Call* and changed the name to the *Plaindealer*. That newspaper ran from January 1899 to November 1958. The *Plaindealer*, located also at the Seventh Street addresses, was said to be the most successful and longest running African American newspaper in Kansas and one of the most influential in the nation. (Courtesy of KHS.)

A.M. Thomas. A graduate of the University of Michigan, A.M. Thomas practiced law in Topeka from 1889 until well into the 1940s. His law offices were located at 415 and 431 Kansas Avenue. A successful lawyer, he was once partners with James H. Guy and W.A. Price. Thomas served as attorney for the Topeka branch of the NAACP when it was founded in March 1913. Along with Elisha Scott and James Guy, he served as an attorney in Topeka for many years. He attended the Church of St. Simon the Cyrenian, where he served as clerk and treasurer. (Courtesy of KHS.)

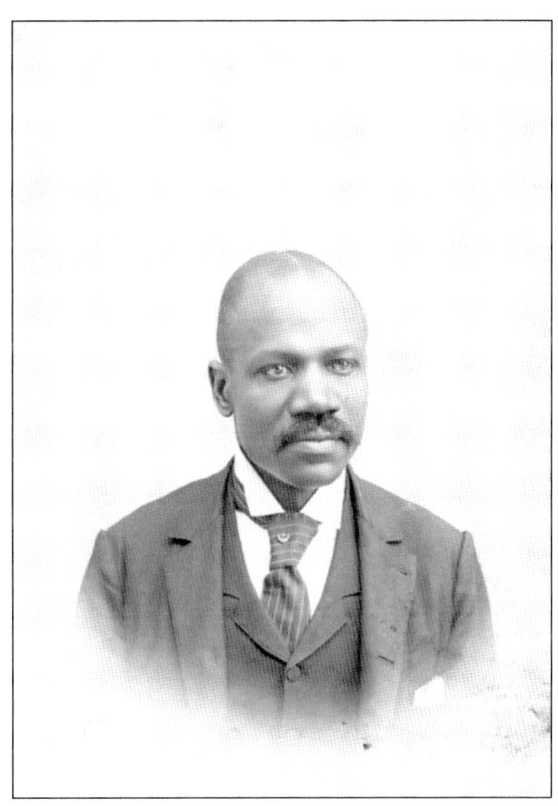

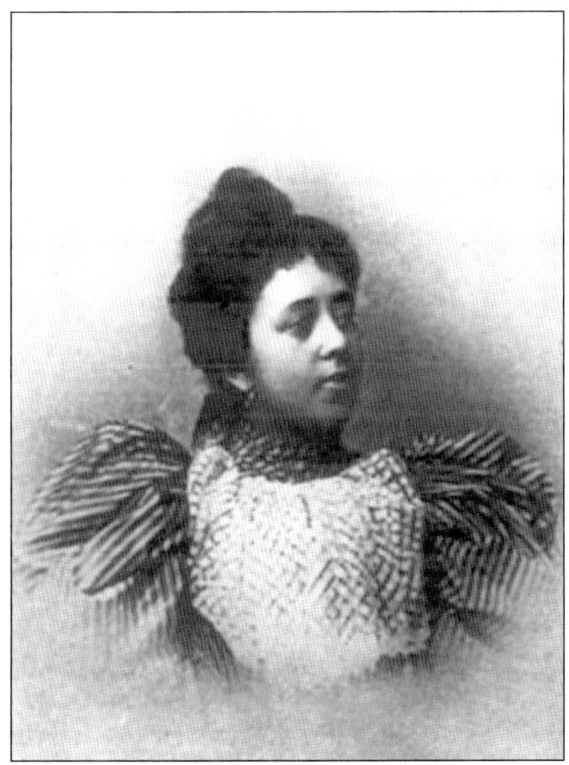

Lutie Lytle. Born in 1871, Lutie Lytle was raised in Topeka's Tennessee Town and graduated from Topeka High School. Realizing that education would free her from the problems of her parents' generation, she earned a law degree and became the first woman and first African American to pass the bar in Kansas and Tennessee. At that time, she was one of only three black women attorneys in the country. She later became a popular public speaker. (Courtesy of KHS.)

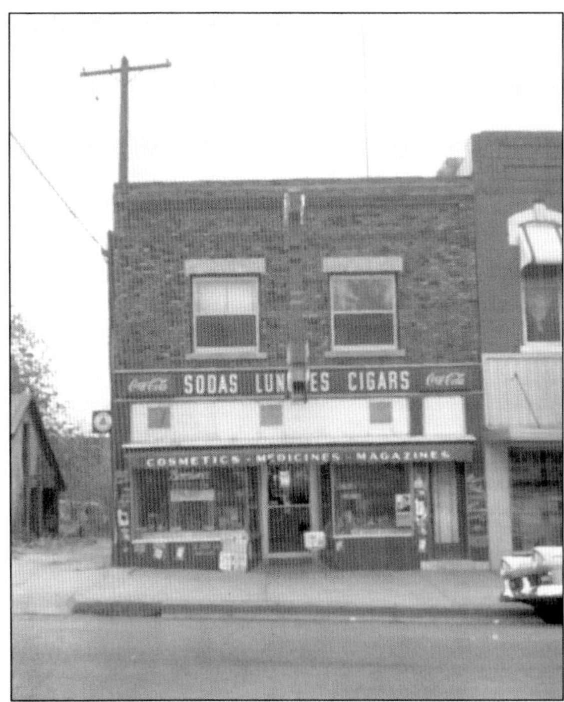

LYTLE'S DRUG STORE. Located on East Fourth Street between Quincy Street and Kansas Avenue, Lytle's Drug Store was torn down as part of the urban renewal project between 1961 and 1963. It was said to be owned by Charles Lytle, son of John R. Lytle and brother of Lutie Lytle. The drugstore had a lunch counter where sodas and ice cream were served, and in the window was a welcome sign that read, "We serve everybody." (Courtesy of KHS.)

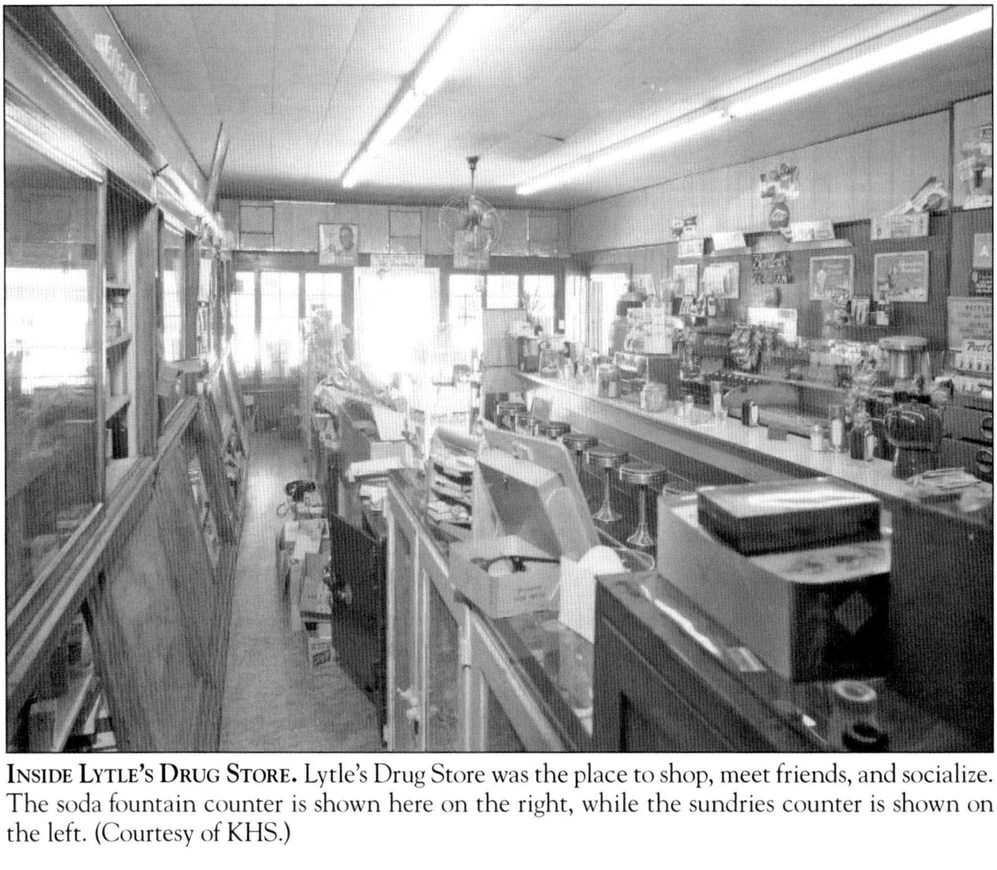

INSIDE LYTLE'S DRUG STORE. Lytle's Drug Store was the place to shop, meet friends, and socialize. The soda fountain counter is shown here on the right, while the sundries counter is shown on the left. (Courtesy of KHS.)

Police Officers. African Americans have worked for the police department since shortly after the Civil War. This 1890 photograph of the Topeka Police Department shows four black officers. In the bottom row are G.R. Smith (far left), Abe Henderson (second from left), Richard Boyd (a guard, second from right), and M.C. Simpson (far right). (Courtesy of TSCPL.)

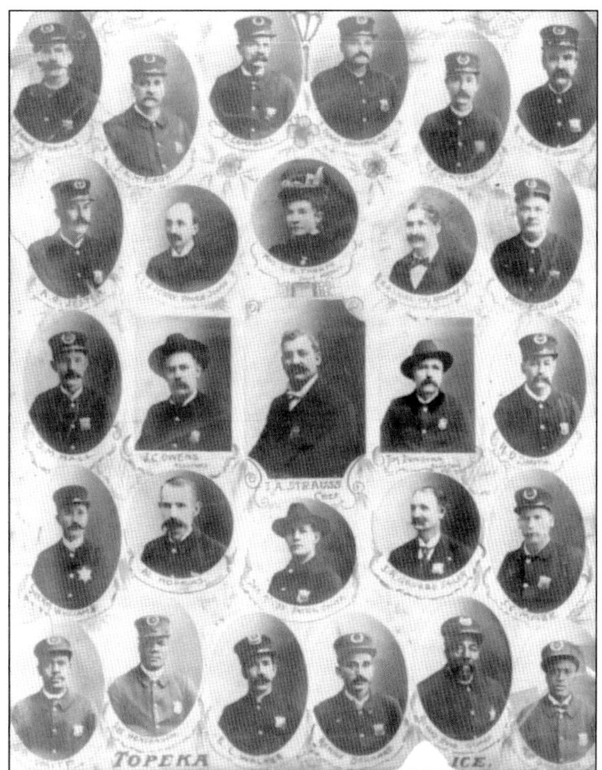

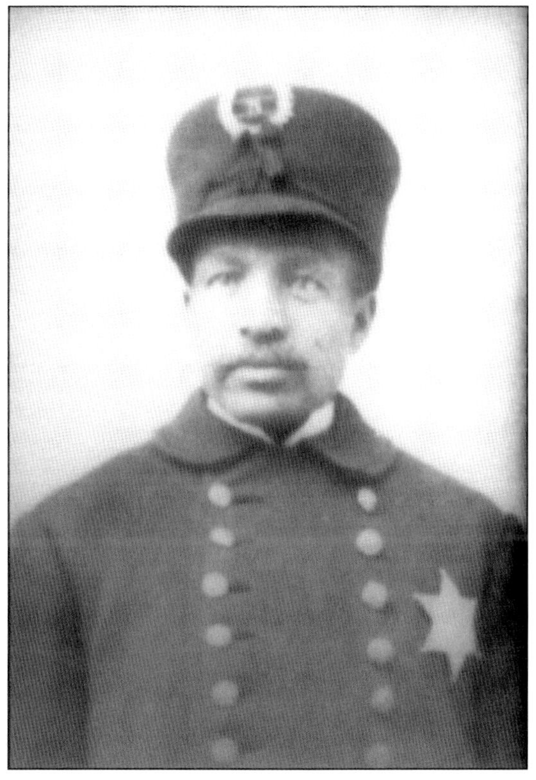

John R. Lytle. Lytle was a respected businessman who owned and operated a barbershop at 326 Kansas Avenue for many years. He was a longtime member of St. John AME Church, one of the major institutional pillars of the black community, and was active in several fraternal organizations. Lytle also served on the Topeka Police Department. In 1897, he was nominated for a political office by the Republican Party but was not elected. (Courtesy of KHS.)

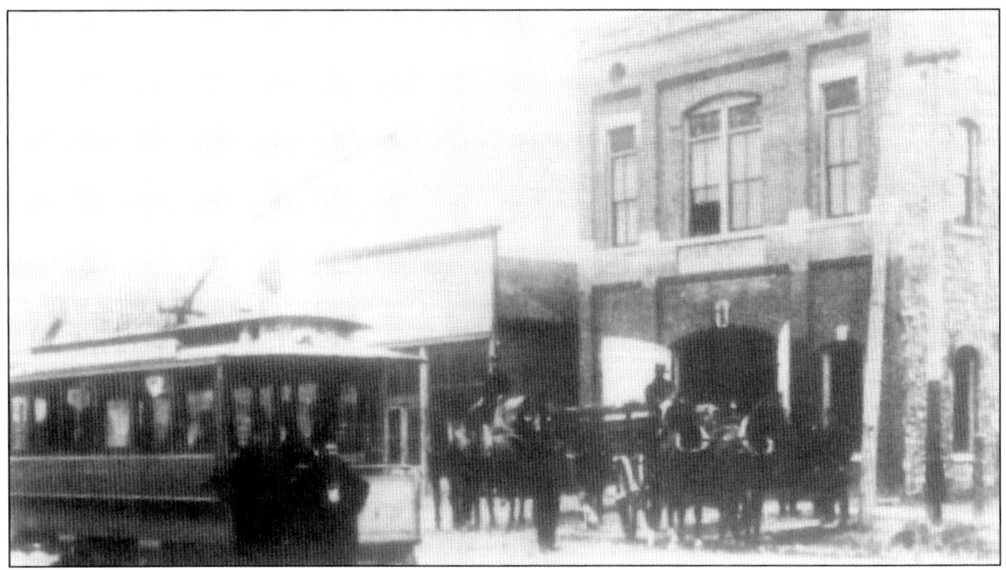

Fire Station No. 3. This was the first all-black fire station in Kansas and possibly the nation. The building, located at 318 Jefferson Street, was torn down in 1963, and a new building was put in its place. This photograph shows the horse-drawn fire wagon that was used in the early days of Topeka. (Courtesy of KHS.)

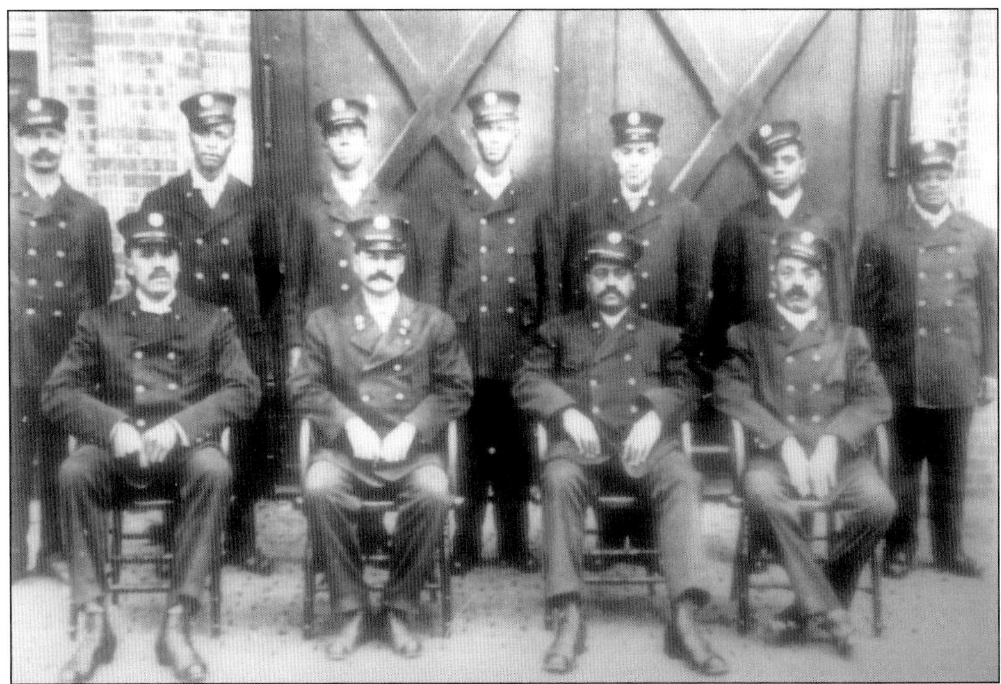

Fire Station No. 3 Firemen. Seen in this 1915 photograph of the firemen at this all-black station are, from left to right, (first row) J. Watson, Capt. Louis Knott, Lt. James W. Washington, and horseman Silas Brown; (second row) John H. Rhodes, William M. Hatcher, Samuel J. McCombs, William M. Frazier, ? Clark, Tom Forte, and ? Miles. (Courtesy of KHS.)

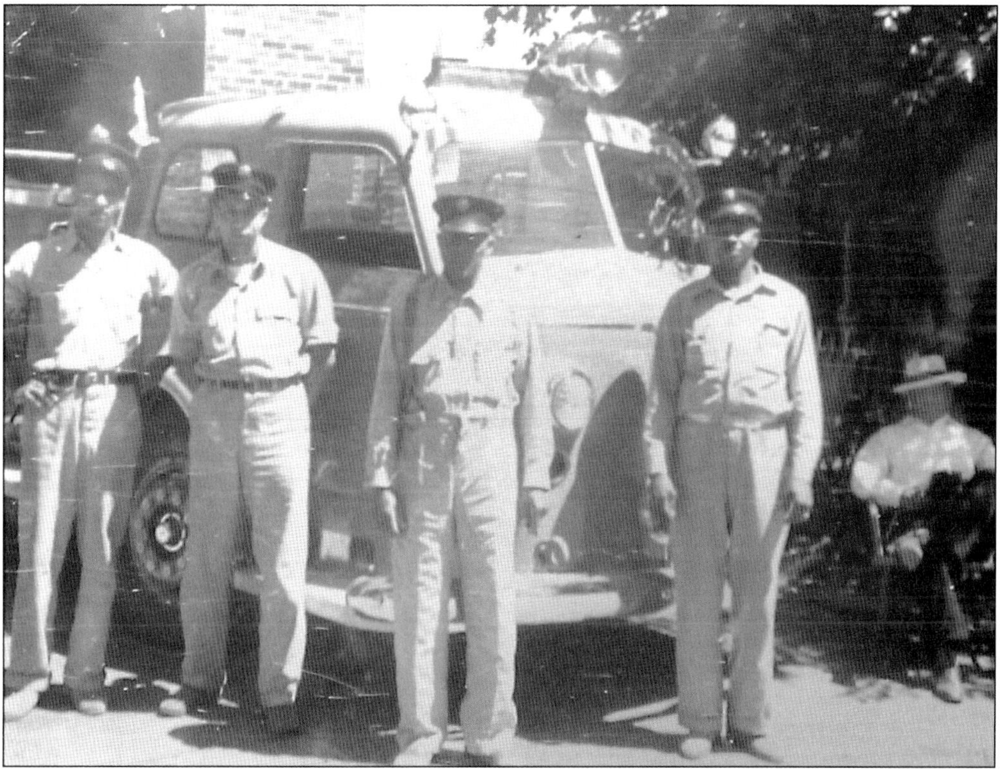

Fire Station No. 3. The all-black Fire Station No. 3 was built in 1882 at 318 SE Jefferson Street. The oldest station in Topeka, it was the first in Kansas (and possibly in the United States) to be manned entirely by blacks. In this photograph, taken in the 1950s or 1960s at the current location, are, from left to right, Albert Evans, Leslie E. Newman, Orville "Buck" Benny, and Theodore "Ted" Jones. (Courtesy of KHS.)

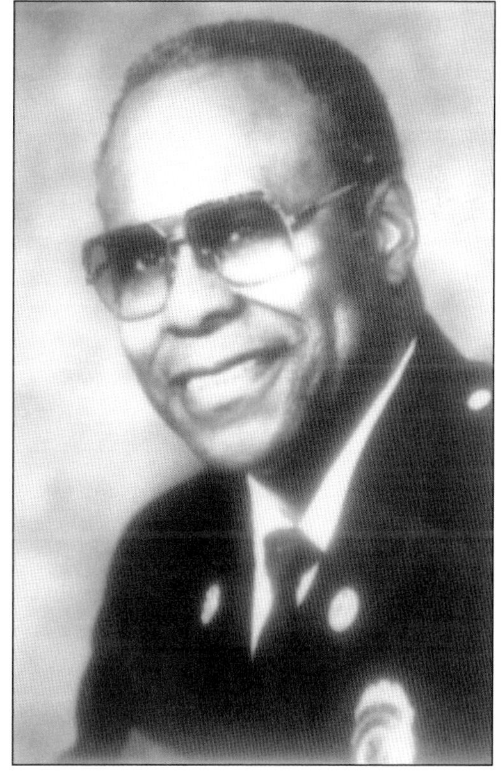

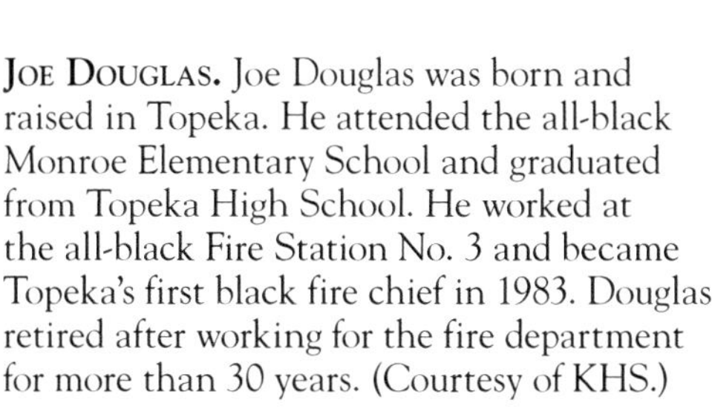

Joe Douglas. Joe Douglas was born and raised in Topeka. He attended the all-black Monroe Elementary School and graduated from Topeka High School. He worked at the all-black Fire Station No. 3 and became Topeka's first black fire chief in 1983. Douglas retired after working for the fire department for more than 30 years. (Courtesy of KHS.)

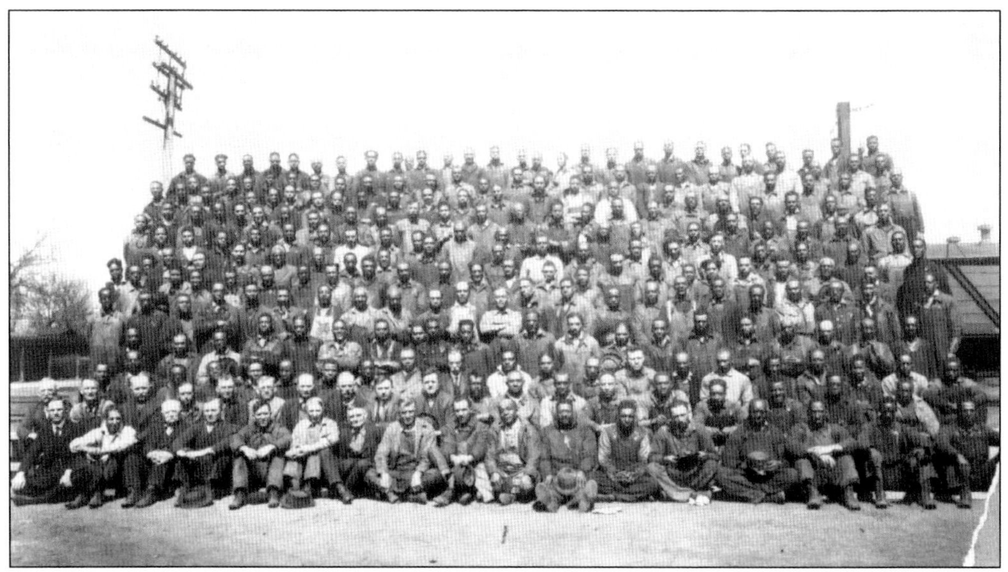

Atchison, Topeka & Santa Fe Employees. The Atchison, Topeka & Santa Fe Railroad Company was the largest employer of black men in Topeka. This photograph shows some of the many African Americans who worked in the shops. More than 75 percent of the employees pictured here are African American. Blacks filled many of the jobs offered by the railroad, working on the assembly line, performing other tasks in the shops, and serving as porters on the trains. (Courtesy of KHS.)

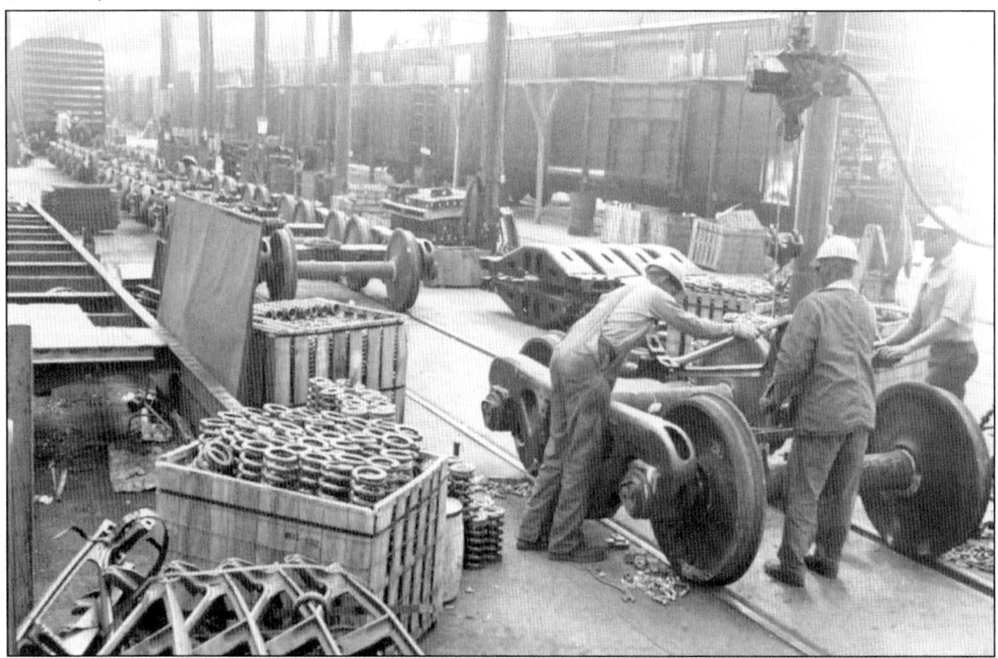

Atchison, Topeka & Santa Fe Shops. The Atchison, Topeka & Santa Fe Railroad began employing African Americans in Topeka as early as the late 1870s. This photograph shows men at the beginning of the assembly line where they built and customized railroad and passenger cars. The Topeka shops, which are now operated by the Burlington Northern Santa Fe Railroad (BNSF), continue to build and repair engines and passenger cars. (Courtesy of KHS.)

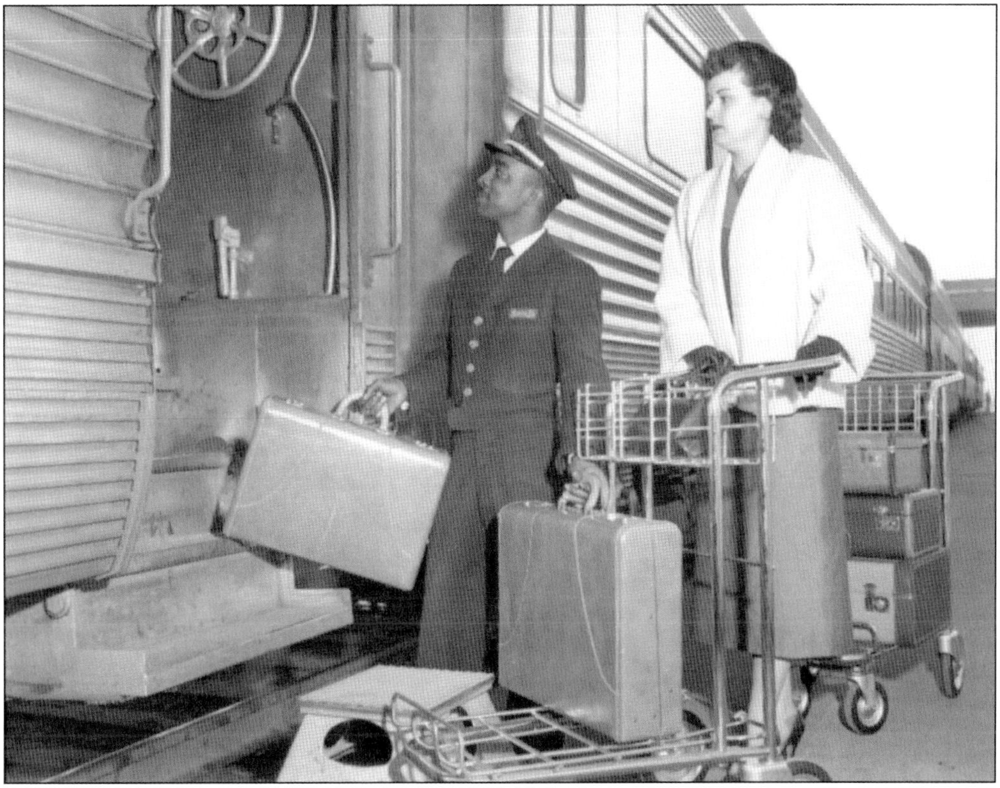

ATCHISON, TOPEKA & SANTA FE PORTER. Some African Americans worked as porters for the railroad. Porters, whose positions were highly respected in the black community, were responsible for taking care of the passengers. They attended to guests in dining cars, sleeper cars, and regular passenger cars. The photograph above shows a porter helping a passenger board the train. (Courtesy of KHS.)

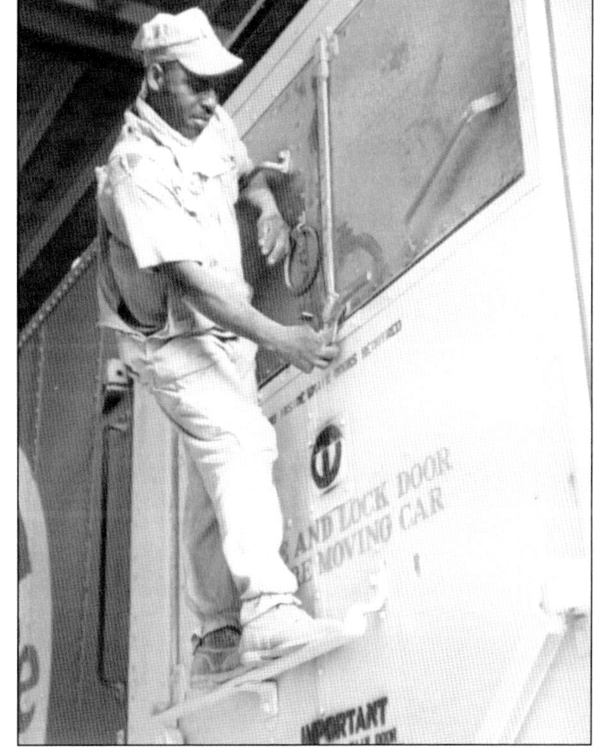

ATCHISON, TOPEKA & SANTA FE WORKMAN. The worker in this photograph was at the end of the assembly line. He is shown inspecting doors, one of the last components installed on the railroad cars. (Courtesy of KHS.)

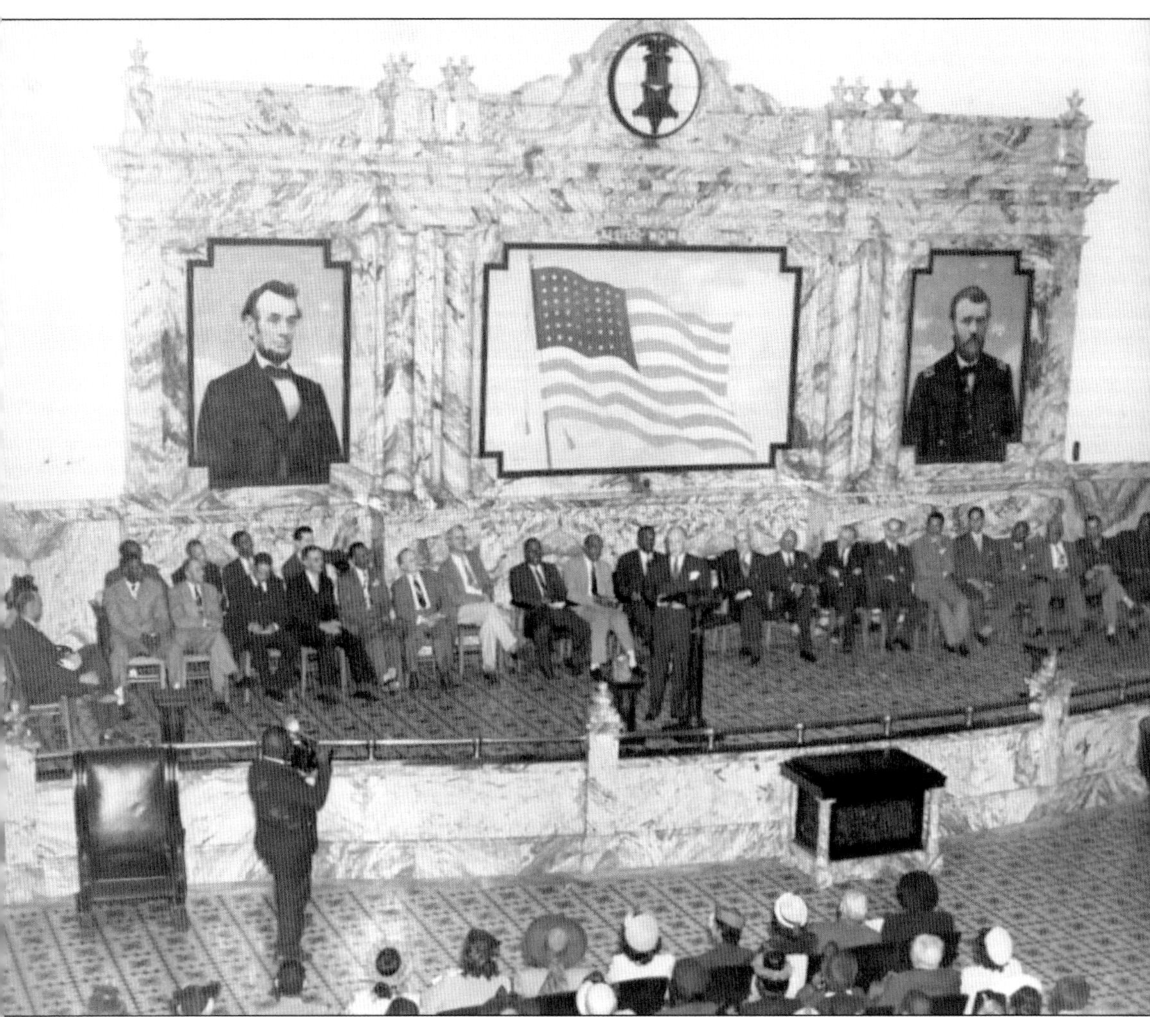

The NAACP. The 1949 meeting of the National Association for the Advancement of Colored People (NAACP) featured the organization's national secretary, Walter White. In this photograph, he is shown giving a speech at a rally in Topeka. This NAACP event was held at the Grand Army of the Republic Memorial Building, which is at Tenth Avenue and Jackson Street, where the Kansas Attorney General's Office is located. He was joined on the stage by former governor Arthur Capper, who was the first president of the Topeka branch of the NAACP and served for more than 30 years on the organization's national board in Washington, DC. Other government and NAACP leaders also attended the event. (Courtesy of KHS.)

McKinley Burnett. As president of the Topeka branch of the NAACP from 1948 to 1963, McKinley Burnett dedicated himself to integrating Topeka's schools and tirelessly petitioned the Topeka Board of Education to end racial segregation. When those efforts did not work, he researched, strategized, and, finally, recruited 13 families to implement a plan that ended in the landmark school desegregation case, *Brown v. Board of Education of Topeka*. The Topeka Public Schools' Burnett Administrative Center, at 624 SW Twenty-fourth Street, was named for him. (Courtesy of Topeka Public Schools.)

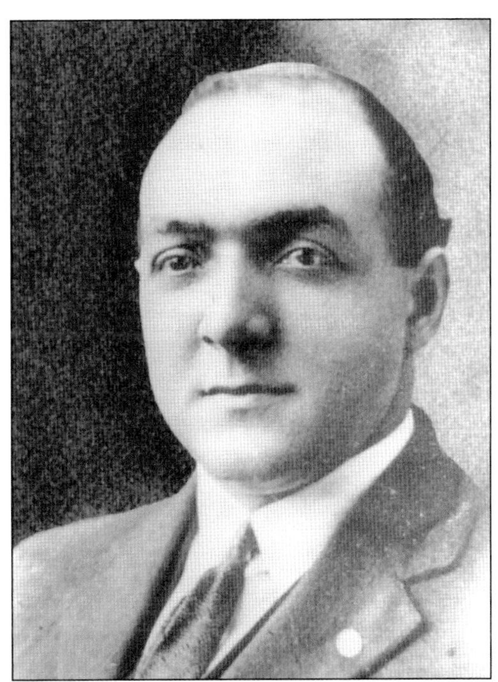

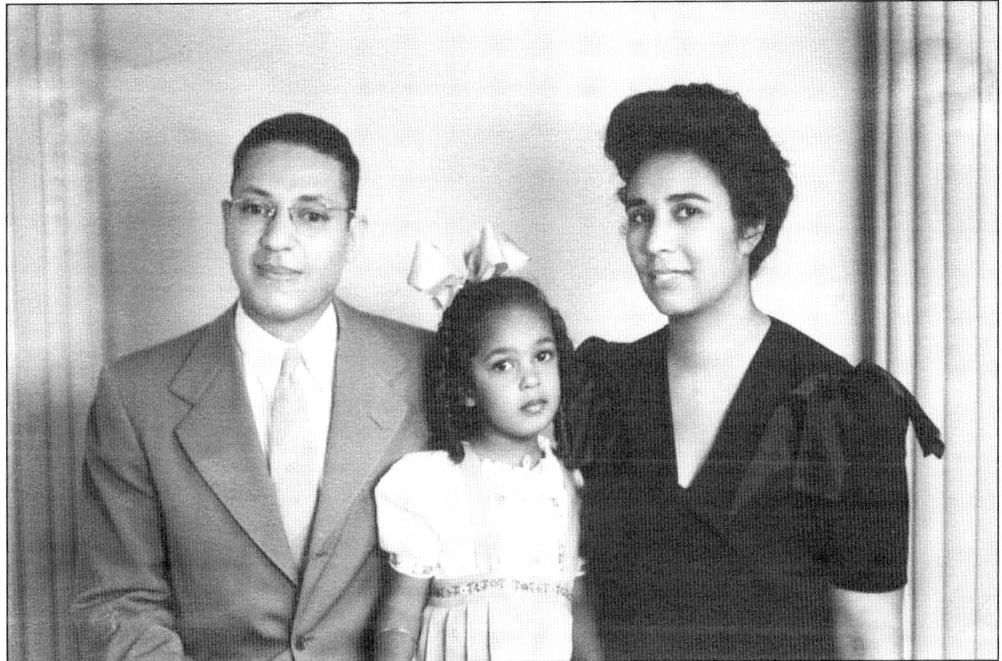

Lucinda Todd and Family. Lucinda Todd was an important part of the *Brown v. Board of Education of Topeka* case. A former schoolteacher, she served as the secretary of the Topeka NAACP. As part of McKinley Burnett's plan, she was one of the 13 volunteers who tried in 1950 to enroll her daughter Nancy in their neighborhood's all-white elementary school. She also petitioned the Topeka School Board to include her daughter in the musical instrument program that had previously only been for white children. Here Lucinda is pictured with her husband, Alvin, and Nancy, their daughter. (Courtesy of KHS.)

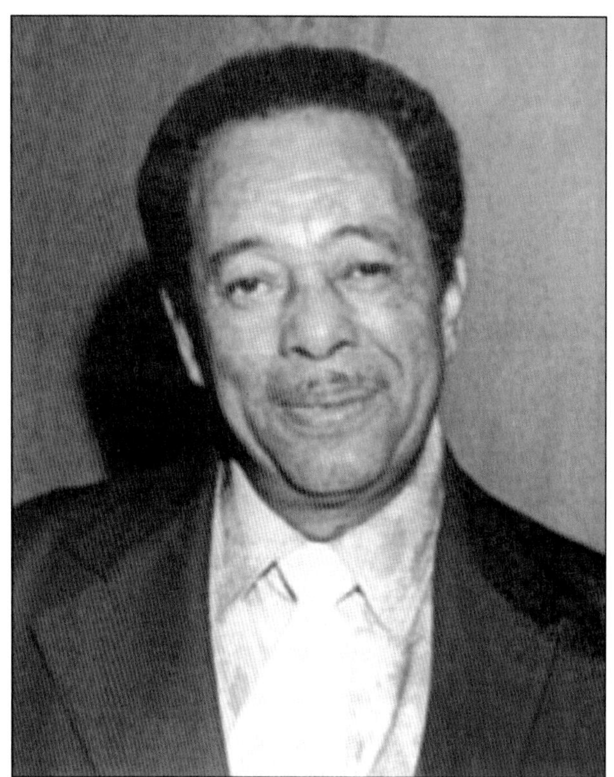

John Scott. John Scott was born in 1919 in Topeka, the son of Elisha and Esther Scott. John attended Topeka Public Schools, graduated from the University of Kansas, and received his law degree from Washburn University School of Law in 1947. He then joined the family law firm and became famous as he and his brother Charles filed the *Brown v. Board of Education of Topeka* lawsuit. John worked for the US Department of Interior for 30 years and retired in 1984. (Courtesy of Topeka Public Schools.)

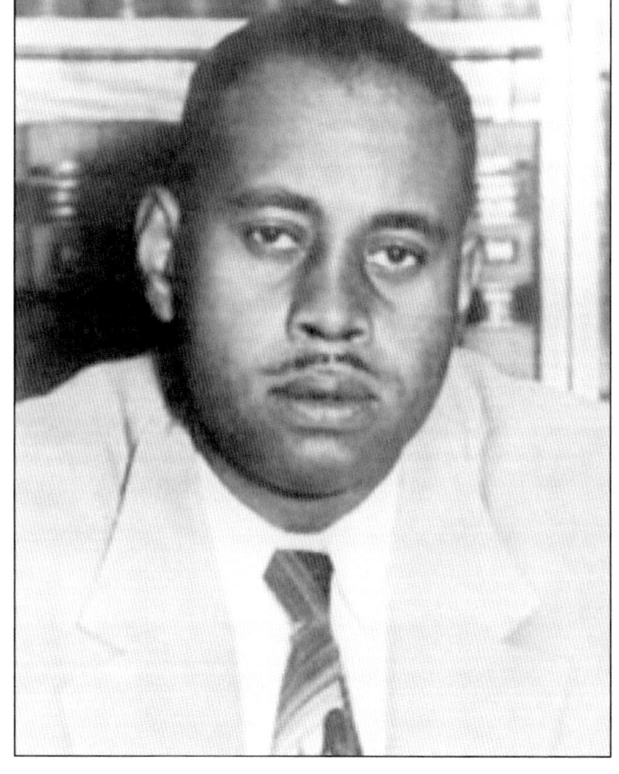

Charles Scott. Born in 1921 and raised in Topeka, Charles Scott, the son of Elisha and Esther Scott, attended Topeka Public Schools. Like his brother John, Charles interrupted his legal education to serve in World War II, then resumed his studies after the war. He graduated from Washburn Law School in 1948 and joined the family law firm, Scott, Scott & Scott. Charles worked on the *Brown v. Board of Education of Topeka* case on the local level before it was appealed to the US Supreme Court. (Courtesy of KSCOLL.)

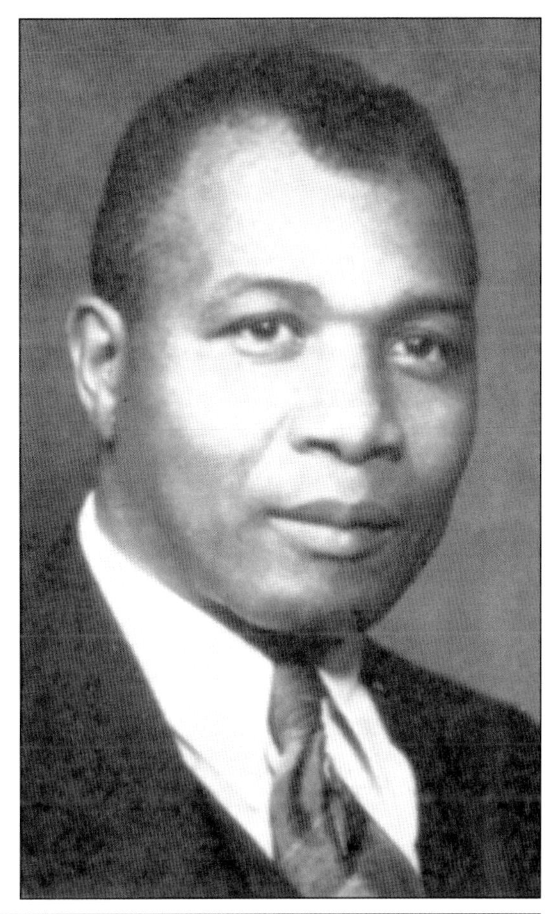

CHARLES BLEDSOE. After attending Washburn between the years of 1931 and 1937, Charles Bledsoe passed the bar exam in 1937 and began practicing law with the Scotts' firm. He served as chairman of the legal committee and as counsel for the plaintiffs of the *Brown v. Board of Education of Topeka* case. Bledsoe is credited with bringing the NAACP attorneys into the case.

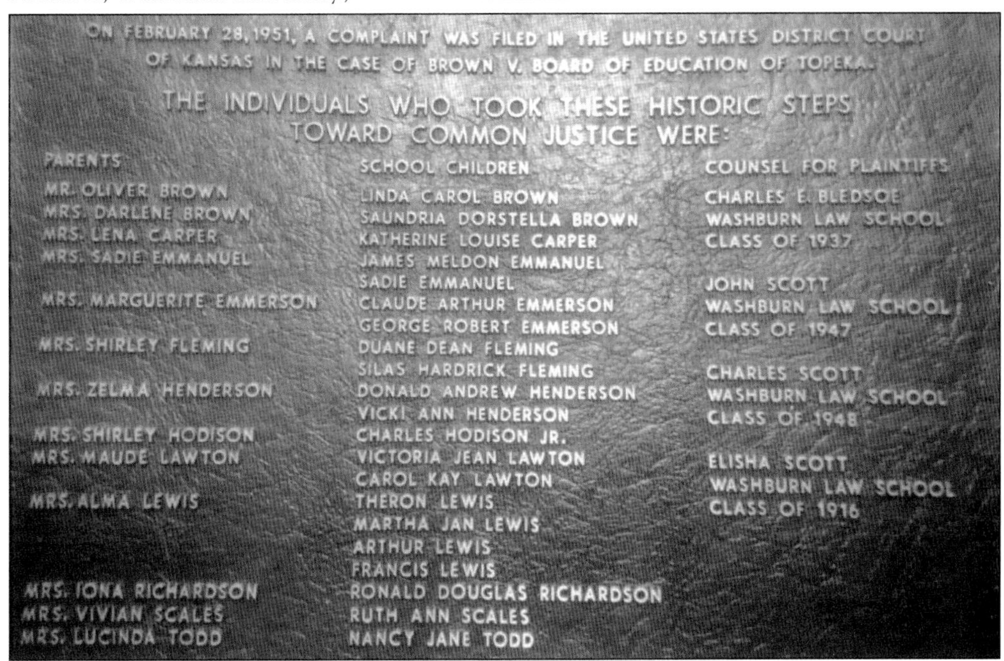

PLAQUE COMMEMORATING *BROWN V. BOARD OF EDUCATION OF TOPEKA*. To commemorate the 30-year anniversary of the *Brown v. Board of Education of Topeka* decision, in 1984 the Washburn University School of Law dedicated a sculpture titled "Common Justice." The accompanying bronze plaque lists the names of the case's plaintiffs and their children, along with the names of the legal counsel who were involved in the case. The plaque, pictured here, and the sculpture are in the main lobby of the law school. (Courtesy of University Archives, Washburn University.)

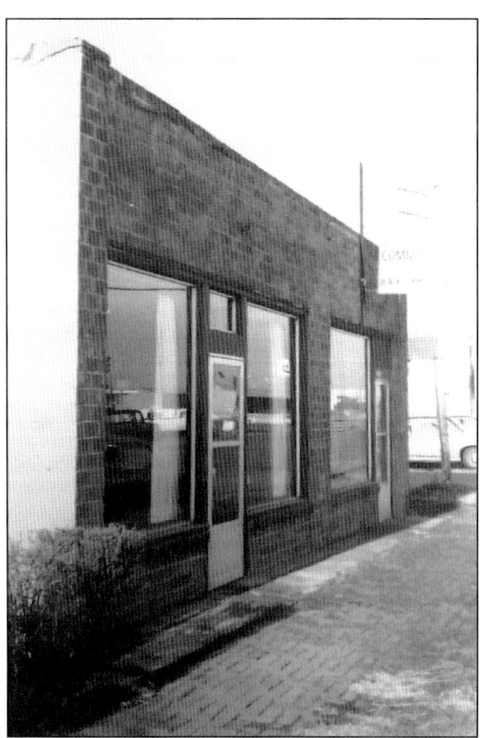

Office of the Coordinating Committee for the Black Community. The Coordinating Committee for the Black Community (CCBC) was founded in 1968 after the death of civil rights leader Dr. Martin Luther King Jr. It was organized by Charles Scott, representatives from Topeka churches, and other members of the black community. The office, which was located at 1009 East Sixth Street and headed by Charles Scott, was the headquarters for civil rights work in Topeka in the 1960s. The CCBC addressed civil rights violations, unfair hiring practices, and other economic issues that required advocacy. (Courtesy of KSCOLL.)

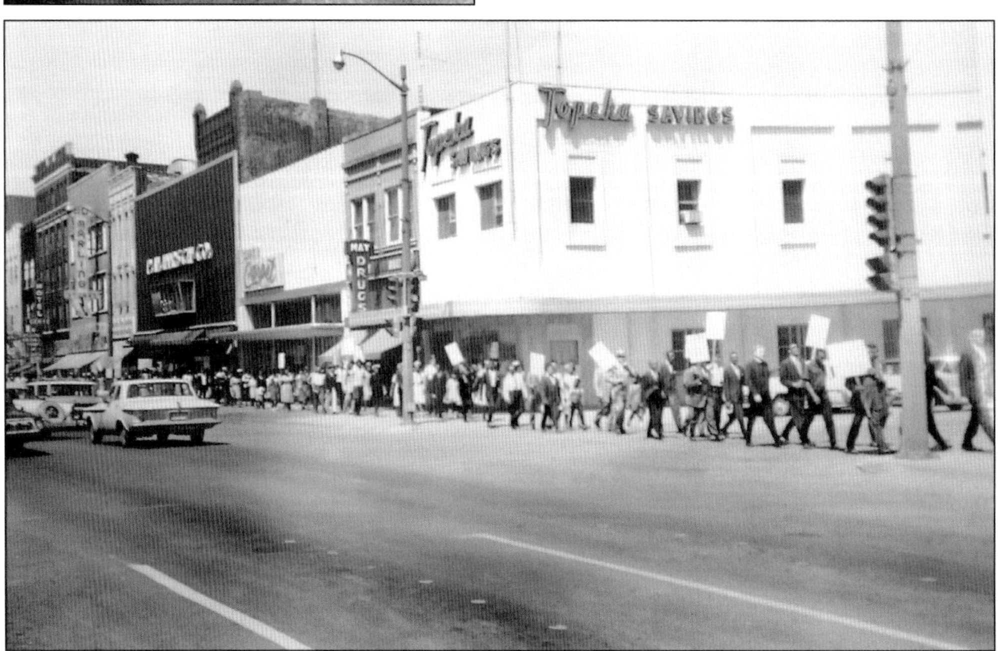

Civil Rights March to the Capitol, 1968. In 1968, Topeka citizens marched south on Kansas Avenue with picket signs to the Kansas State Capitol and stood for a group photograph on the south steps of the building. After the slaying of Dr. Martin Luther King Jr., many members of the community participated in this march against local discriminatory practices. In Topeka, as well as in many communities around the country, King's death was a tragic and sad event. (Courtesy of KSCOLL.)

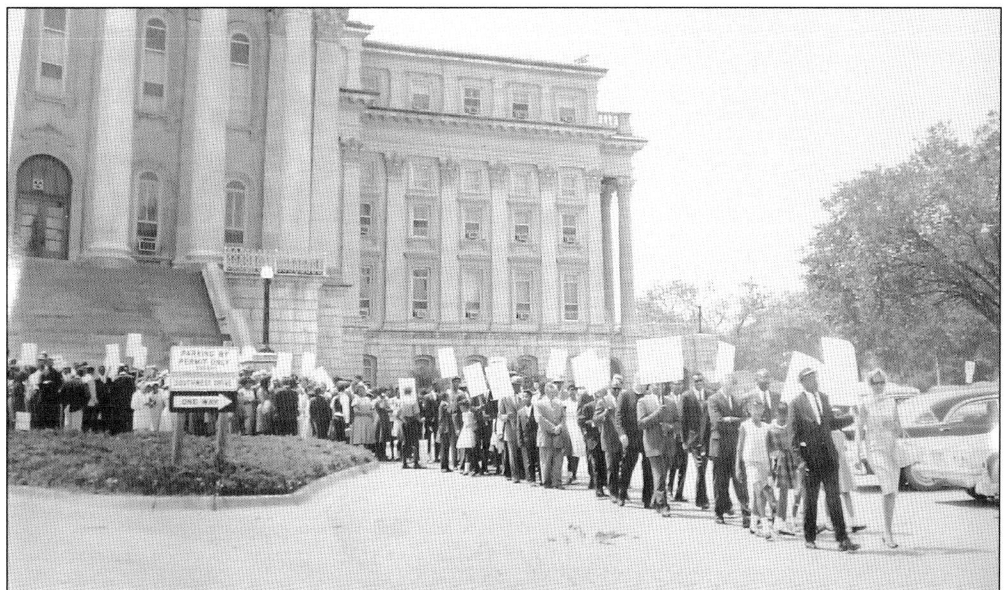

CIVIL RIGHTS MARCH, 1968. The Topeka community, both black and white, marched together to the south side of the statehouse in protest against discrimination in education and employment. The side of the capitol shown in this photograph has been renovated to provide underground parking and no longer looks the same. (Courtesy of KSCOLL.)

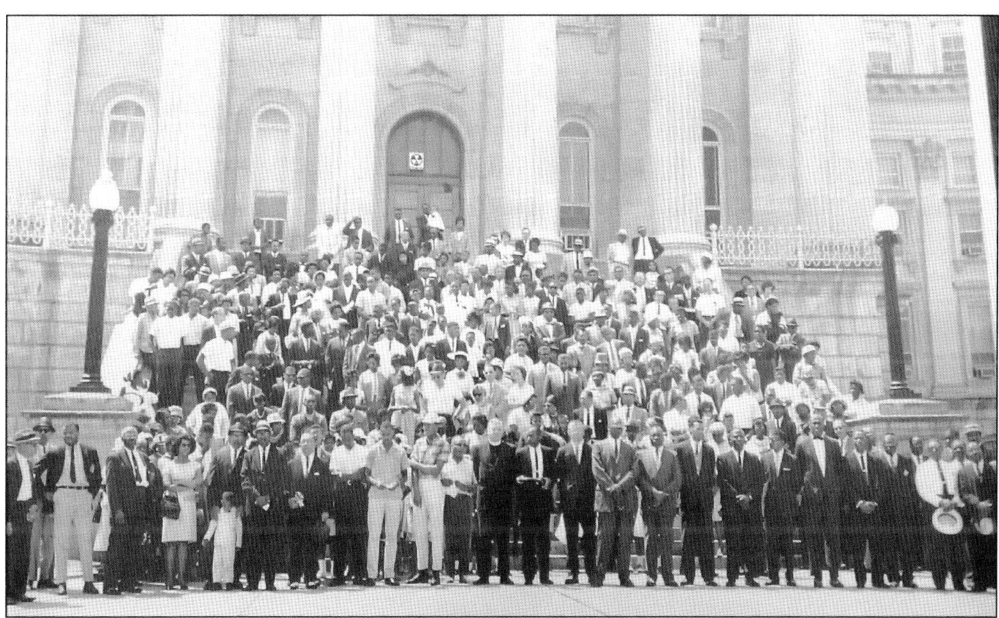

CIVIL RIGHTS MARCH ON THE CAPITOL STEPS, 1968. The marchers stood for a group photograph on the south steps of the Kansas State Capitol. Included in the group were many young men, young women, and children, as well as adults from all walks of life and of all races. They joined together to make a statement against discrimination and senseless violence and for racial tolerance. (Courtesy of KSCOLL.)

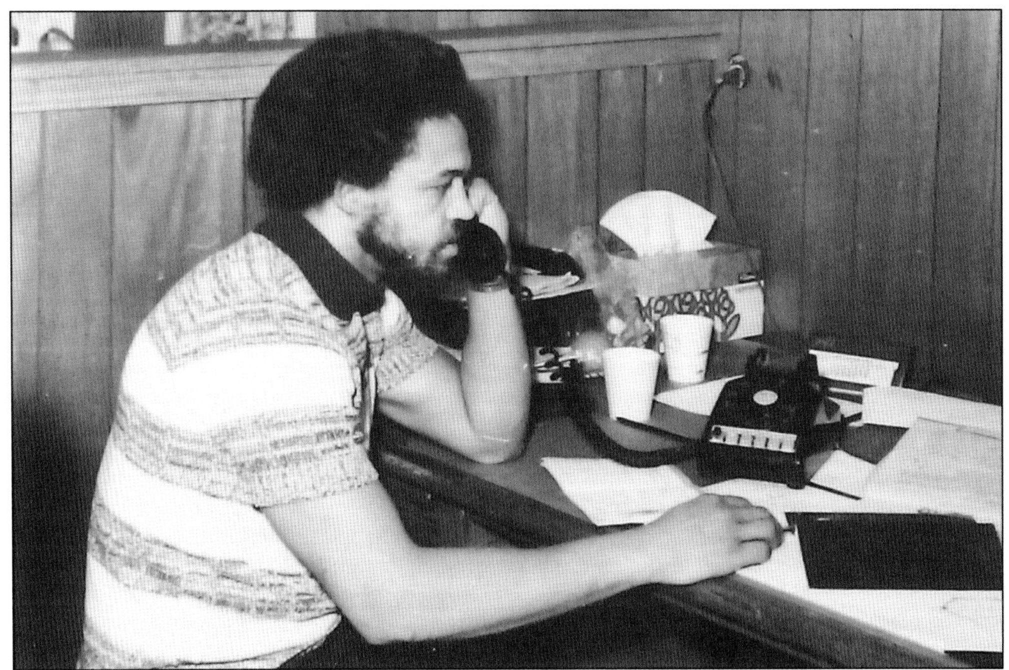

COORDINATING COMMITTEE FOR THE BLACK COMMUNITY. The CCBC conducted community research projects to learn how many blacks were in Topeka. It used such information to determine how many workers were needed to ensure that African Americans in the city received essential services. Pictured above is Arthur Brice, assistant to the CCBC director, Eva Lou Martin. (Courtesy of KSCOLL.)

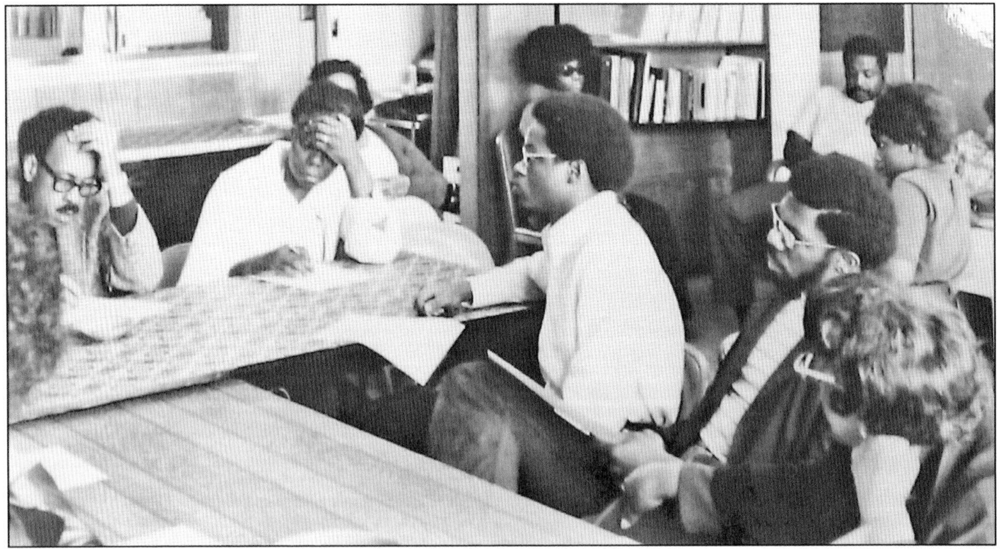

COORDINATING COMMITTEE FOR THE BLACK COMMUNITY STAFF MEETING. The CCBC worked to provide a unified voice through which black people in Topeka could speak out on all issues relating to minorities. Among its many services, it provided information, consultation, and referrals for legal, employment, and discrimination issues. Clockwise from the left are Charles Scott, Ruby Davis, Christine Jackson (behind Ruby), Bernice Steele, Beatrice Jones, Gilbert Parks (in the corner), an unidentified woman, Richard Jones, and unidentified. (Courtesy of KSCOLL.)

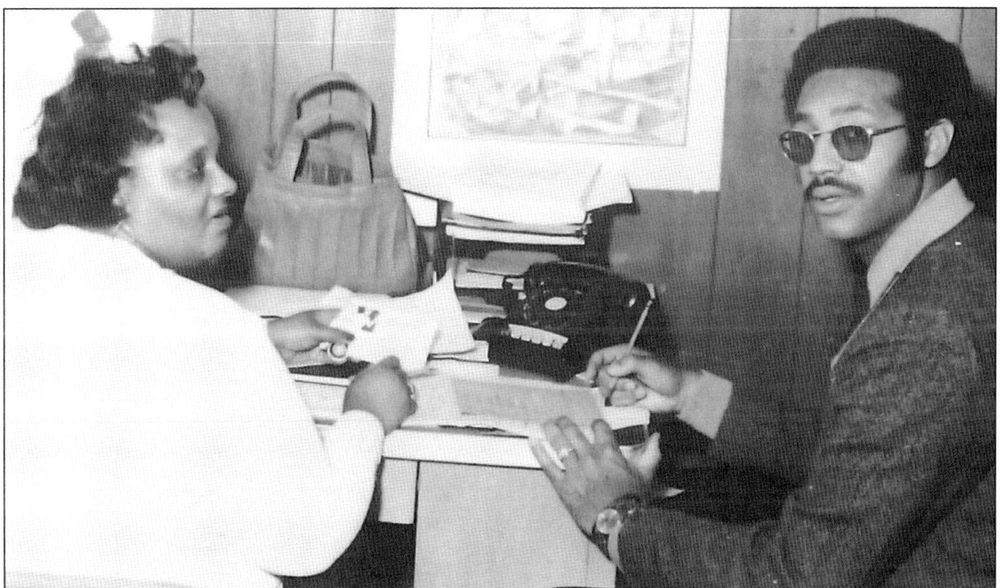

CCBC. Some of the goals of the CCBC were to connect people from East Topeka with programs and services of the public library, support literacy, and work with the chamber of commerce to improve employment for disadvantaged minorities. The CCBC also sought to unify all segments of the black community so that a consensus could be voiced on any issue relating to the general welfare of racial minorities in Topeka. In this photograph, staff members Christine Jackson and Enos Cooper are working on a mailing. (Courtesy of KSCOLL.)

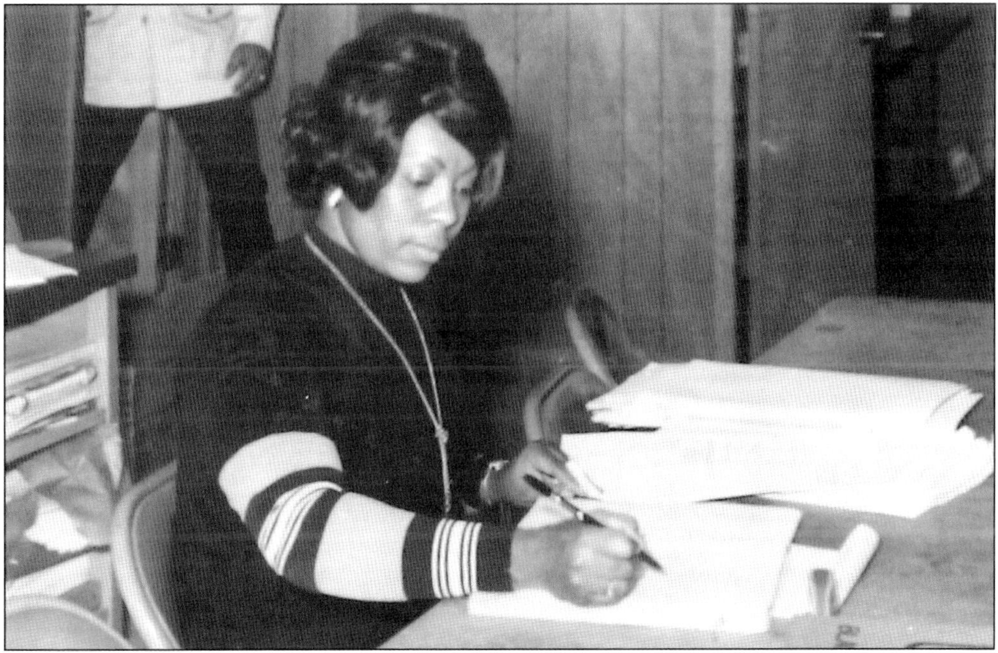

JOANNE MARTIN WITH THE CCBC. The committee wrote grants to cover its expenses and fund the office staff positions, including that of youth coordinator. Its total budget in 1968 was $62,000. JoAnne Martin, pictured here, led the survey committee for CCBC. She was responsible for organizing the efforts to survey the black members of the community. (Courtesy of KSCOLL.)

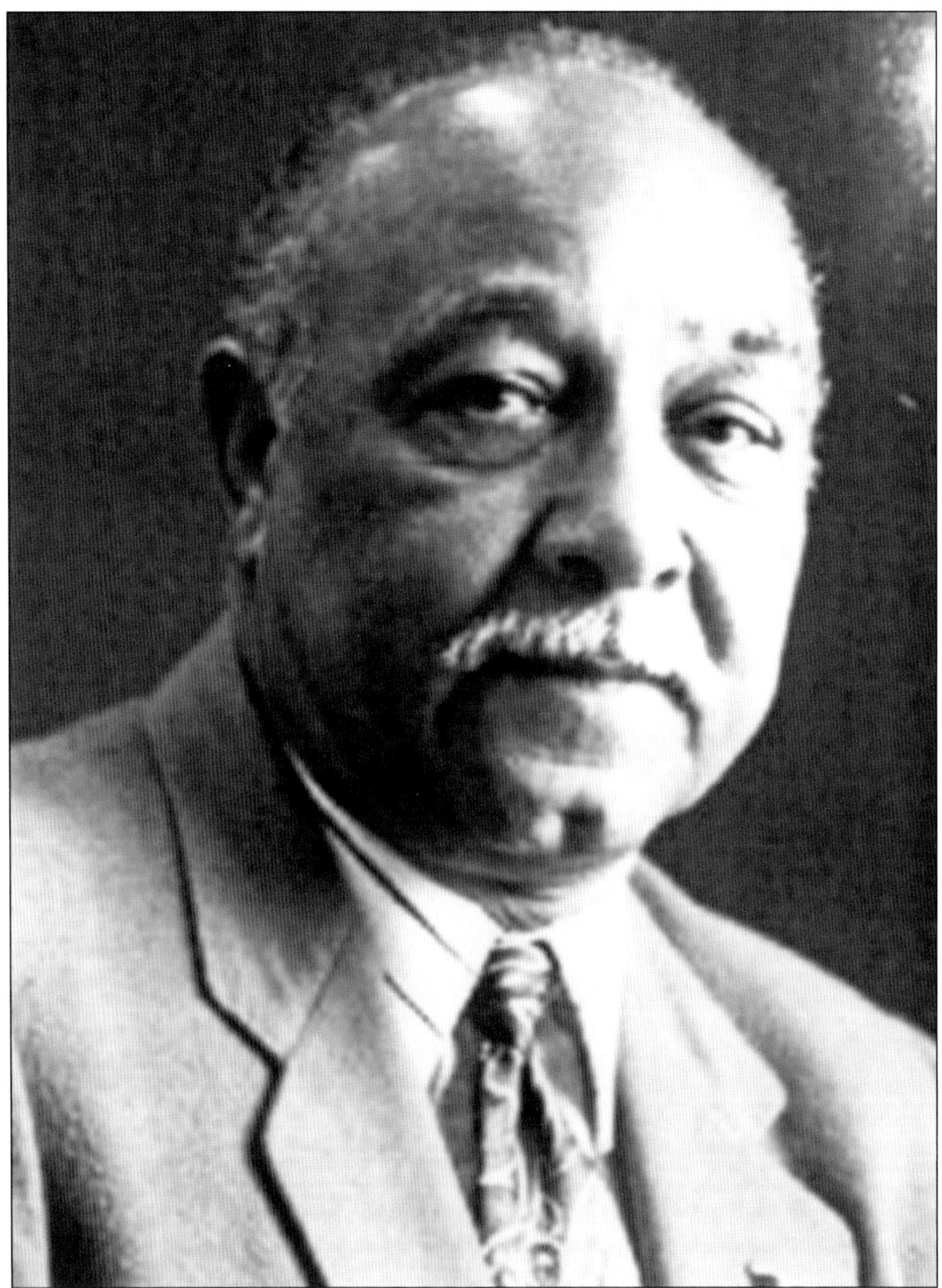

Jack Alexander. Alexander graduated from Topeka High School in 1949 and served as captain of the school's last black basketball team. In 1973, he became the first African American elected to the Topeka City Commission. He was also the first minority appointed to the Kansas Corporation Commission. He later worked as a legislative liaison within the governor's office and served on the Topeka City Council. Alexander also was a leader in several community organizations, including the Topeka NAACP and the United Way of Topeka. (Courtesy of Jack Alexander.)

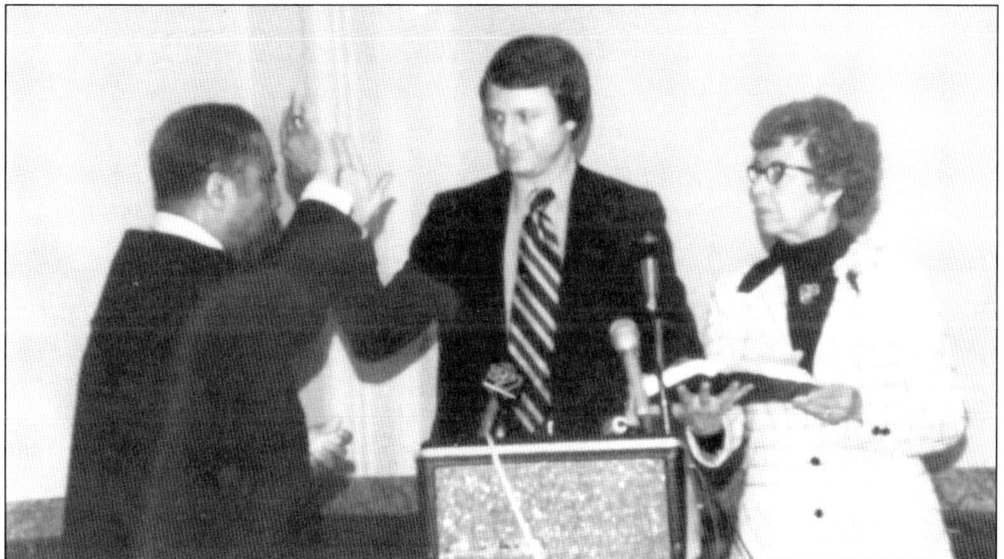

JUSTICE SHERMAN PARKS. Justice Sherman Parks was the first African American to serve on the Kansas Court of Appeals. He was appointed in 1977 and served until his retirement 10 years later. A native Topekan, Parks attended Topeka Public Schools and graduated from Washburn University in 1949. He attended the Washburn School of Law, earned his law degree in 1955, and began his law practice the same year. Parks served as an assistant county attorney for Shawnee County, Kansas assistant attorney general, and in other law-related positions with the state. In this photograph, Parks is being sworn in as a justice on the Kansas Court of Appeals. (Courtesy of KHS.)

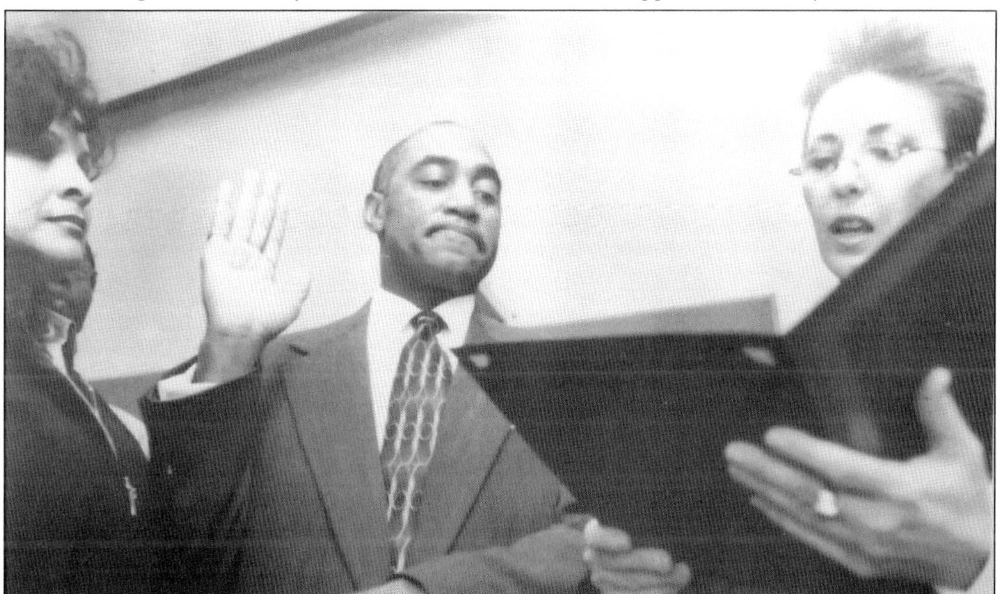

MAYOR JAMES A. MCCLINTON. James A. McClinton served the city of Topeka and state of Kansas for over 20 years in various capacities. His service included positions with the Kansas Department of Corrections, Kansas Neurological Institute, and Kansas Juvenile Justice Authority. He was a member of the Topeka City Council for two terms before becoming mayor. In these capacities, he worked to improve the lives of Topekans. This photograph shows McClinton being sworn in as mayor in 2004 with his wife, Lee, by his side. (Courtesy of KHS.)

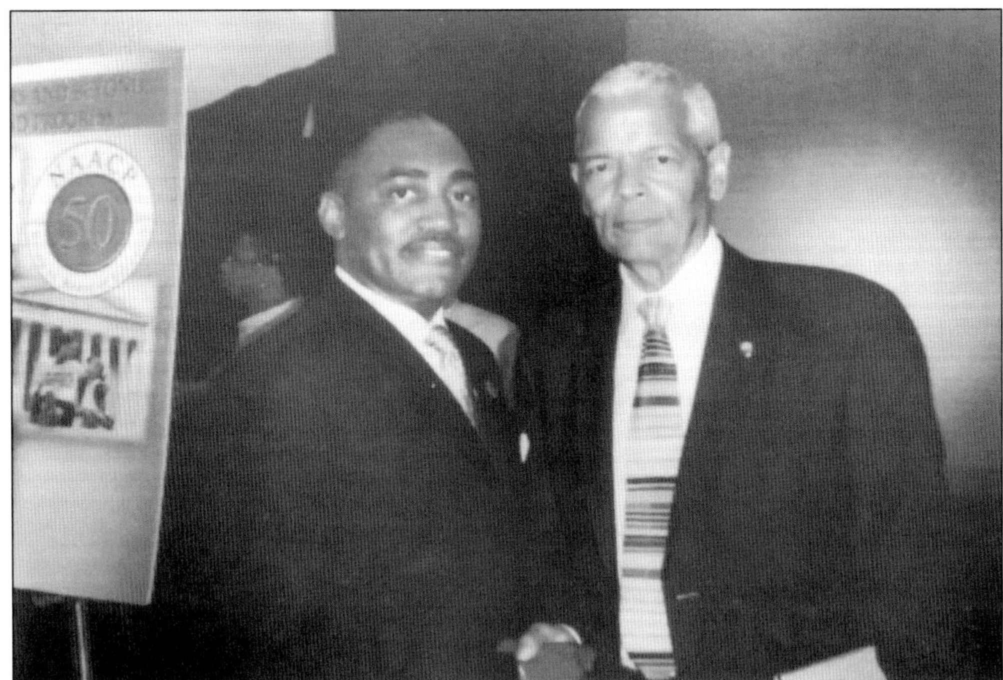

Mayor James A. McClinton and Andrew Young. In 2004, McClinton welcomed the nation to Topeka as he hosted the opening of the *Brown v. Board of Education* National Historic Site. Many people of national prominence were in attendance, including Pres. George W. Bush. In this photograph, McClinton appears with politician, diplomat, activist, and pastor Andrew Young. (Courtesy of KHS.)

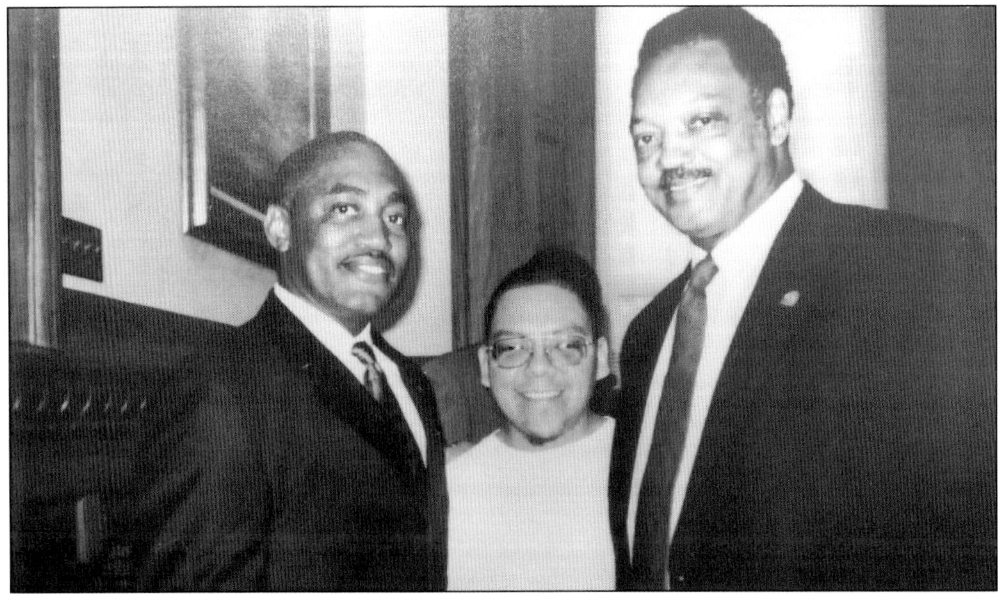

Mayor James A. McClinton and Rev. Jesse Jackson. The 50th anniversary of the *Brown v. Board of Education of Topeka* decision and the formal dedication of the associated historic site attracted many national figures to Topeka in 2004. In this photograph, Mayor James McClinton is seen with political activist Rev. Jesse Jackson. (Courtesy of KHS.)

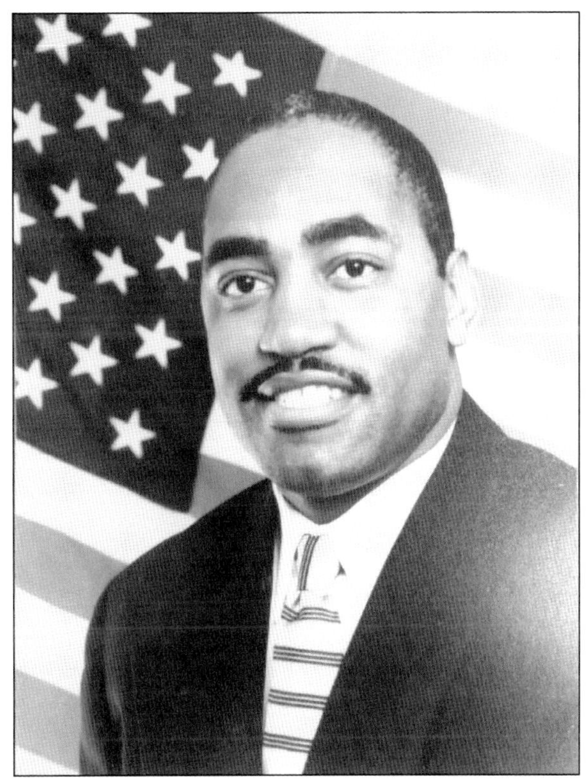

Mayor James A. McClinton. In 2004, McClinton, a man from humble beginnings, became Topeka's 50th mayor and its first black one. He was also the last mayor to serve under Topeka's strong mayor–city council–chief administrative officer form of government. In 2005, the city changed to a city council–city manager form of government that had only a ceremonial mayor. The new mayoral position came with fewer responsibilities and a considerably smaller salary. McClinton declined the ceremonial position and returned to civilian life. This photograph is his official mayoral portrait. McClinton now lives in Dallas, Texas. (Courtesy of KHS.)

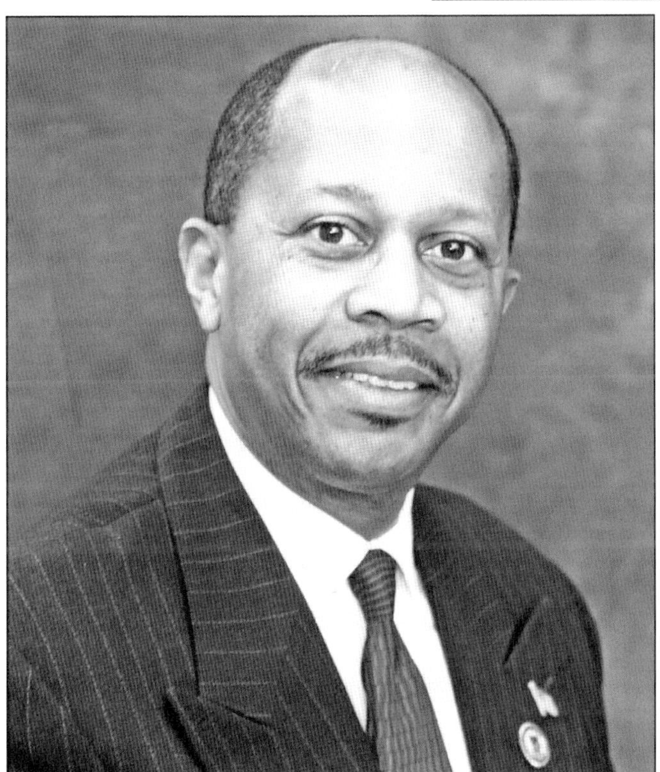

Norton Bonaparte. After Topekans voted in 2004 to change to the city council–city manager form of municipal government, Norton Bonaparte became Topeka's first permanent city manager in 2006. He was appointed by the city council to that position after Topeka's first African American mayor, James McClinton, left office. His previous jobs included city administrator positions in several cities in New Jersey and Maryland. In 2011, he was appointed city manager in Sanford, Florida, where Trayvon Martin was killed in 2012. (Courtesy of City of Topeka.)

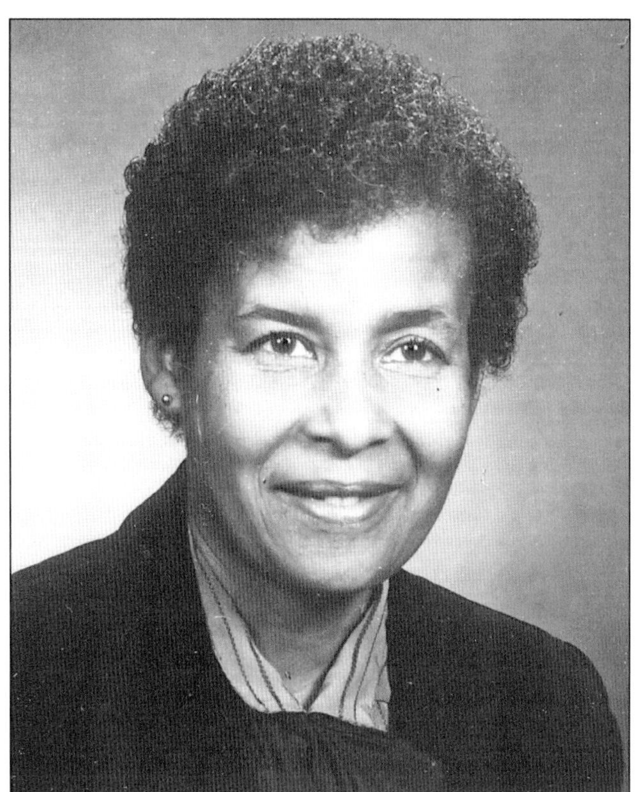

Dr. Kay Meadows. Dr. Kay Meadows was the first African American elected to serve both on the Topeka Board of Education and later as the board's president. She was a strong advocate of educational equity for all children, but especially poor and minority children. A Topeka native, she graduated from Highland Park High School and then from Washburn University. After obtaining her master's and doctorate from Kansas State University, she worked many years in civil rights–related jobs for the State of Kansas. Meadows Elementary School, at 201 SW Clay Street, was named for her. (Courtesy of Topeka Public Schools.)

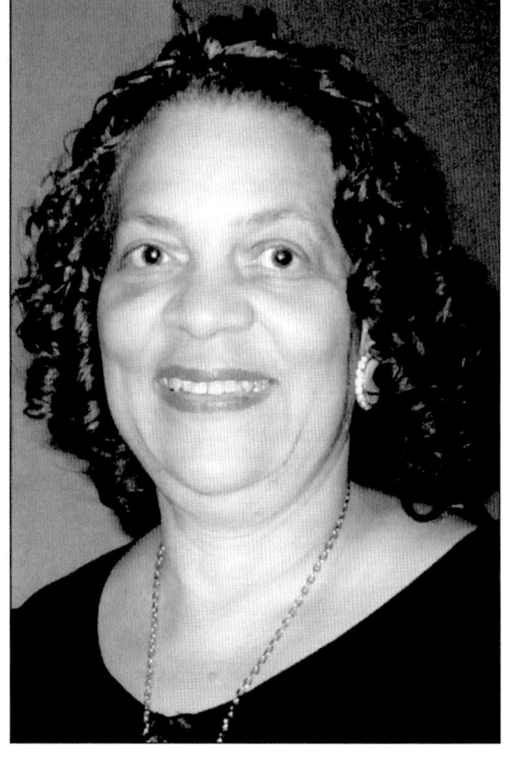

Carolyn Wims-Campbell. The first African American to serve on the Kansas State Board of Education, Carolyn Wims-Campbell was elected to that position in 2008 and reelected in 2012. Previously, she served as president of the Topeka Board of Education and as president of the National Federation of Urban and Suburban School Districts. A recipient of several education and civil rights awards, including the Dr. Martin Luther King Jr. Civil Rights Award presented by the Living the Dream Committee, she has also been actively involved with the YWCA and other community organizations and causes. She is a lifelong member of St. Mark's AME Church. (Courtesy of Kansas State Board of Education.)

Five

Up Until Now
Changing Times

Topeka's black community has changed over the years. Many businesses, job opportunities, neighborhoods, and organizations have changed. Some are still in existence, but others have long since vanished from the Topeka landscape.

For many years, the center of black community activity was the Fourth Street District, on the edge of the Bottoms, where black businesses operated and civic organizations met and were entertained. Once considered the cultural mecca of the black community, the Fourth Street District was demolished as a part of urban renewal.

Over the years, countless people have left Topeka's black community for other areas of the country. However, Topeka continues to have a rich African American heritage that demands attention. Businesses and organizations continue to strive for the viability of the community and the connectivity of its black families. These are the most important values for which previous generations labored and fought.

There are still black neighborhoods in Topeka that have their own character and history. North Topeka, located just across the Topeka bridge, was known as "Sand Town" or "Up in the Sands." It is now known affectionately as "NOTO." Much of East Topeka was called "Mud Town," since there were no paved roads there for many years. Tennessee Town, home to the Exodusters, was once on the western edge of Topeka. It is now part of central Topeka. Each neighborhood has a unique personality and charm. Each strives to enrich the lives of its neighbors with businesses, organizations, and leaders that work together to make Topeka's African American community succeed.

African Americans in the United States have come a long way through much hard work and struggle. Topeka is no exception. Blacks in Topeka have a strong sense of community and family. Many have worked together, prayed together, and developed organizations together to serve each other, teach the youth, and enjoy what life has to offer.

This chapter shows some of the businesses, neighborhoods, leaders, organizations, and events that impacted, changed, and in some cases, enhanced African American life in Topeka in the 20th century.

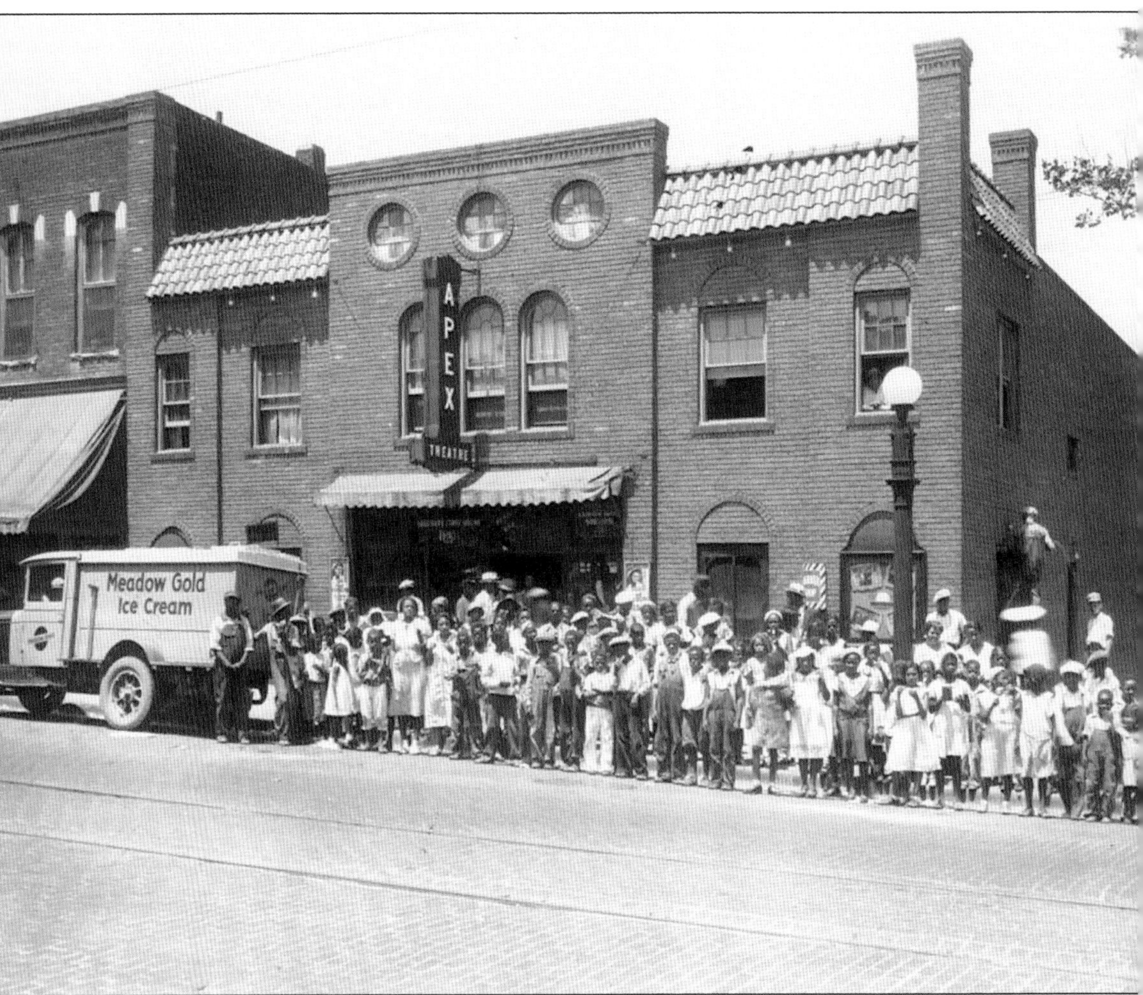

Apex Theater. The Apex was the first Topeka movie theater owned and operated by African Americans. Located at 122 SE Fourth Street, it was the main hangout in Topeka for African Americans, a place for movies as well as for parties to entertain honored guests visiting the city. Harry Abbott was the manager of the Apex Theater in the early 1900s. He also owned a café at 308 Kansas Avenue until he moved to Oklahoma shortly before 1922, when Henry Edward Sheppard bought the Apex. The theater employed the musicians Walter Jones and Julia Stevenson, who played the piano for the silent movies shown in the theater in the early 1900s. W.D. Cooper was the manager, and Emalene Cooper was the assistant manager until Benjamin Payne bought the theater from Sheppard in 1928. (Courtesy of KHS.)

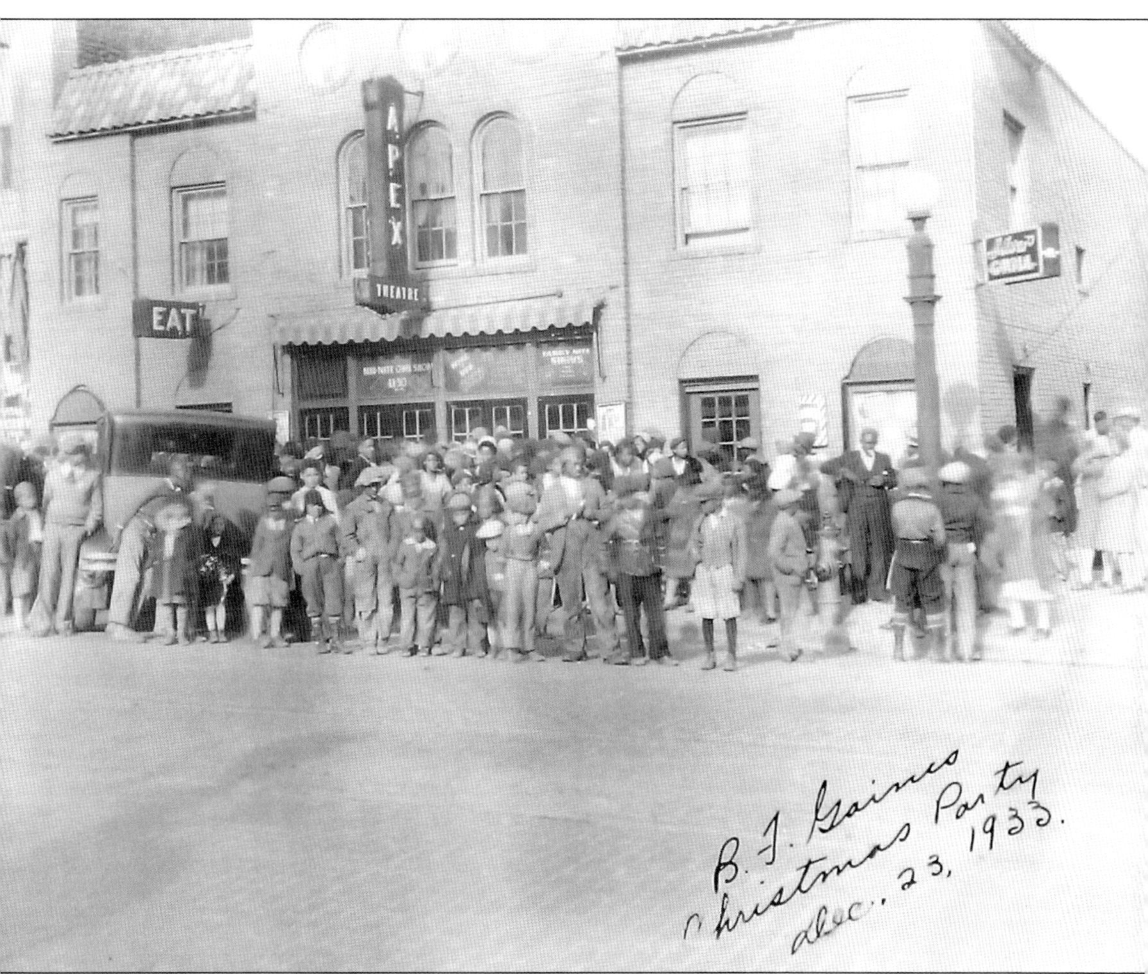

CHRISTMAS PARTY AT APEX THEATER. In 1933, Ben Gaines held a Christmas party for children of Topeka. At the party, children enjoyed ice cream in front of the Apex Theater, as shown in this photograph. One of the popular community activities at the Apex was free movies and ice cream for the children. From the 1940s to the mid-1950s, Dickinson Theatres owned the Apex and renamed it the Ritz. Jessie's Sandwich Shop was located in the same building, just to the west of the theater, under the "eat" sign. (Courtesy of KHS.)

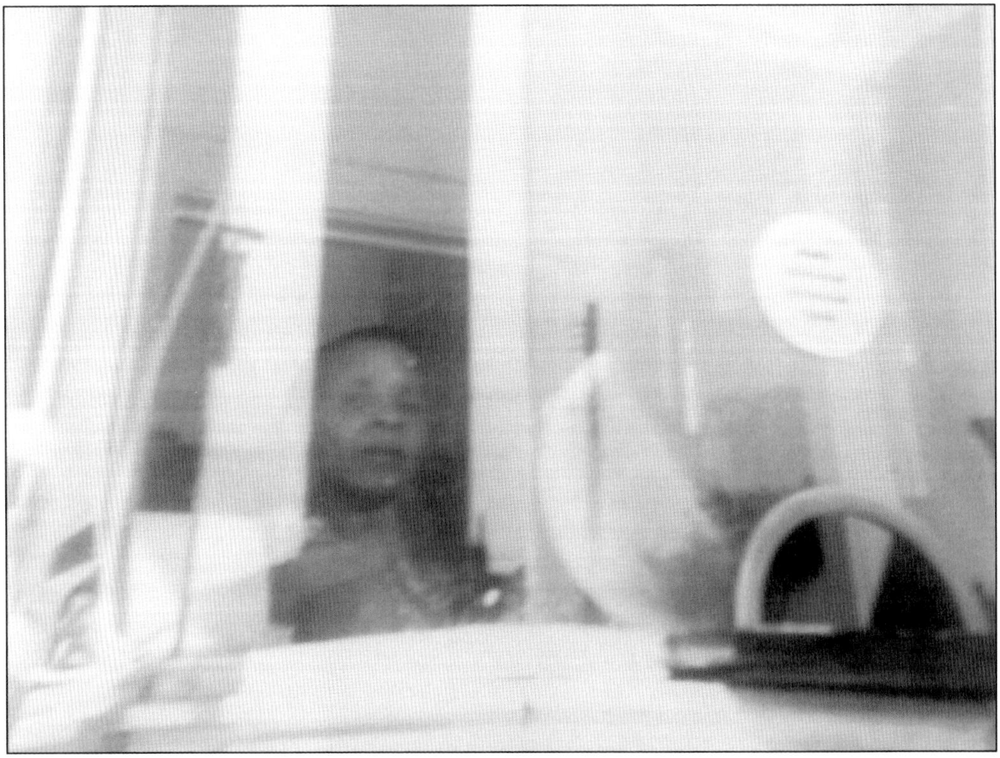

Apex Theater Ticket Window. This photograph is a close-up of the Apex Theater ticket office window that was installed in later years before it was torn down. Mrs. Troupe, seen here, worked in the ticket office for many years. Movies such as *Check and Double Check*, with Amos and Andy and Duke Ellington, played at the Apex in 1932. The theater sponsored activities such as Candy Day, when kids could attend the theater and receive free candy. (Courtesy of Fern Williams.)

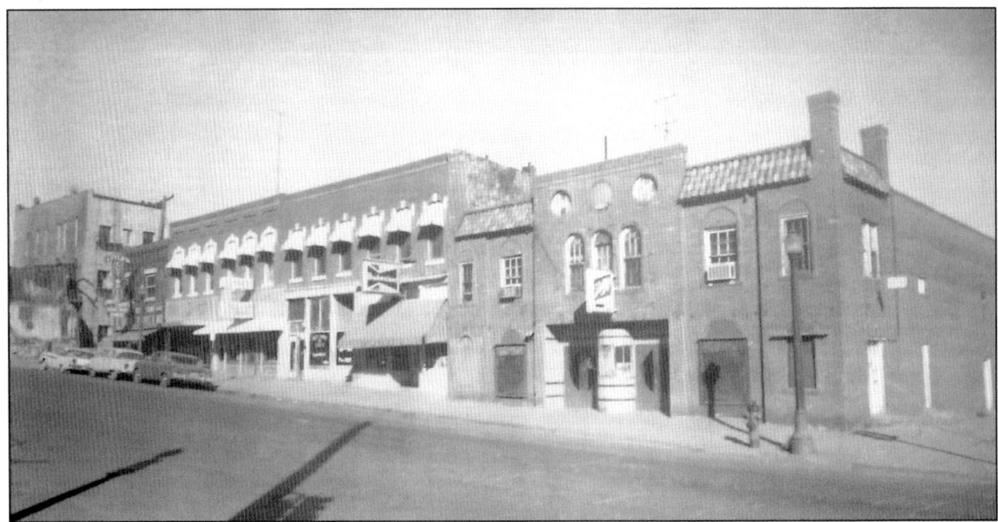

Apex Theater in the 1950s. This photograph of the theater was taken just before urban renewal began in 1958. Businesses were abandoned, and the area no longer enjoyed the appeal that it once had. Lytle's Drug Store is the small building immediately to the left of the row of buildings with awnings. (Courtesy of KHS.)

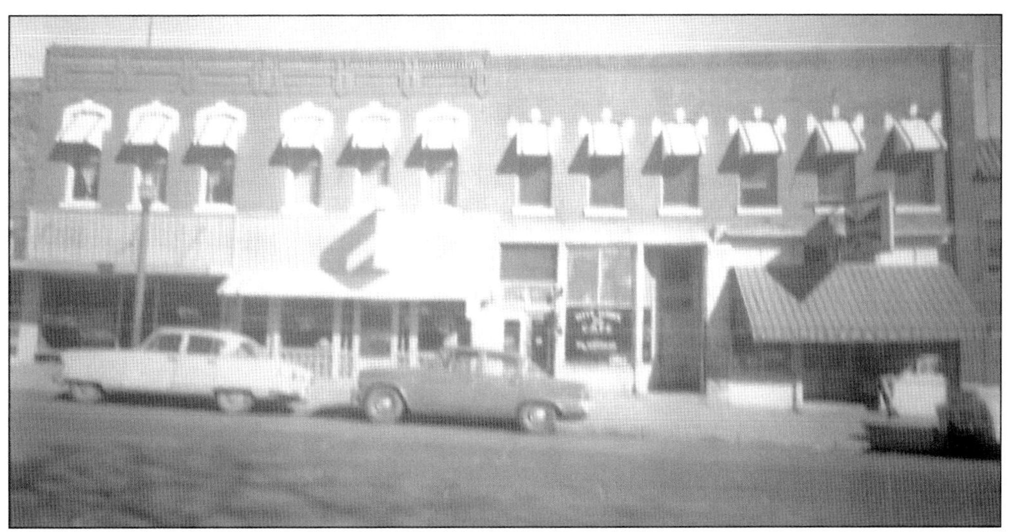

Fourth Street Urban Renewal. The urban renewal program began in 1958 to change the landscape of the main section of town where black businesses were located. The businesses in this once-thriving black hub of the city were encouraged to relocate to other areas of town. This photograph shows what Fourth Street looked like after businesses began moving prior to urban renewal. (Courtesy of KHS.)

113 SE Fourth Street. This building was once part of a flourishing African American business district that had to be abandoned and was then destroyed to make way for an expansion of Topeka's business and industrial area. Hallmark Cards, the Law Enforcement Center, and I-70 are now located in this former African American hub. The area near Fourth and Quincy Streets is now blocked off on the east side of the US Post Office and Federal Courthouse Building. A bank tower, offices, and the Town Site Plaza parking garage were built there. (Courtesy of KHS.)

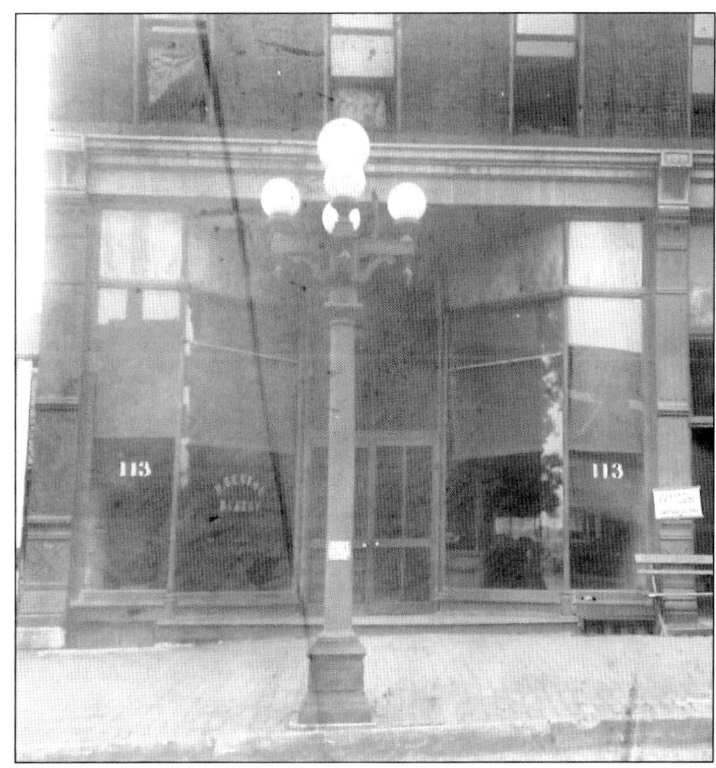

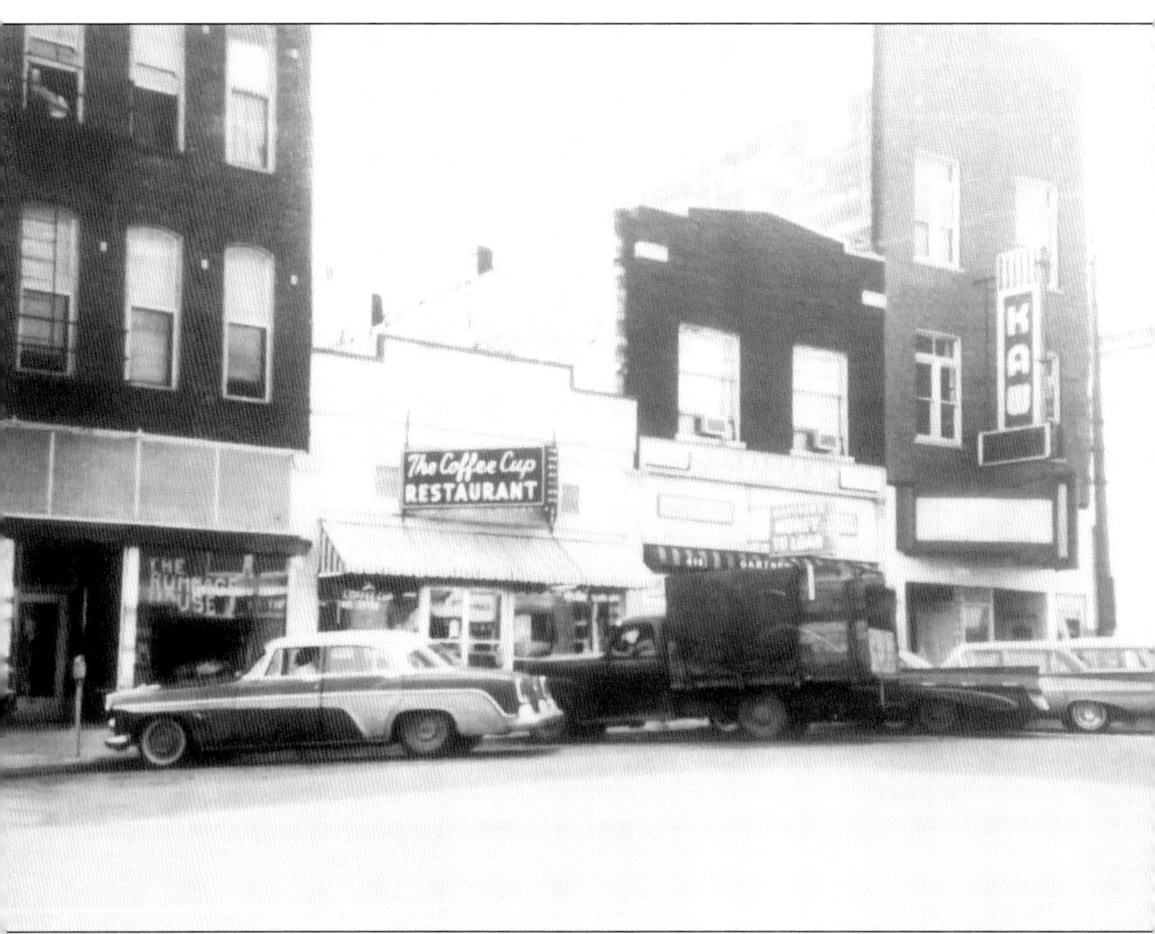

KAW MOVIE THEATER. This side view shows the Kaw Movie Theater. In 1962, this photograph was taken by the city urban renewal program. It was one of the buildings slated to be torn down. In the late 1950s, the Kaw showed movies like *Mark of the Hawk*, which starred Eartha Kitt, Sidney Poitier, and Juano Hernandez. (Courtesy of KHS.)

TENNESSEE TOWN MAP. This map outlines the central part of Topeka, where Tennessee Town was located. Many African Americans lived in this area during the early 20th century. The residents of this historic neighborhood celebrate their history and culture with an annual art festival in the park at Twelfth and Lane Streets, where the Aaron Douglas mural is located. (Courtesy of the author.)

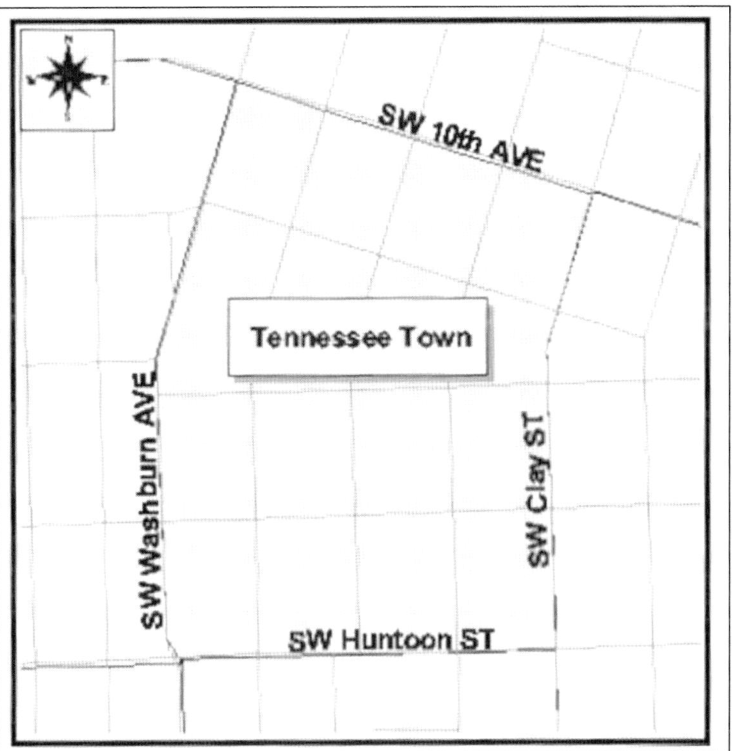

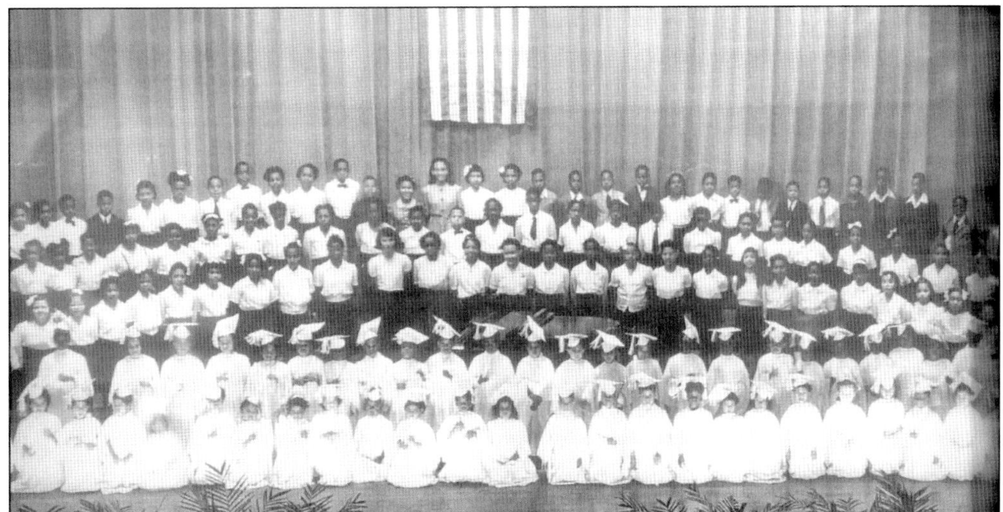

TENNESSEE TOWN CHILDREN. The children in this photograph lived in Tennessee Town and attended the Buchanan Elementary School. They enjoyed happy occasions and school programs that celebrated their community. The building, located at 1195 Buchanan, has been repurposed as a community center and offices for local nonprofits. (Courtesy of Tennessee Town Neighborhood Improvement Association.)

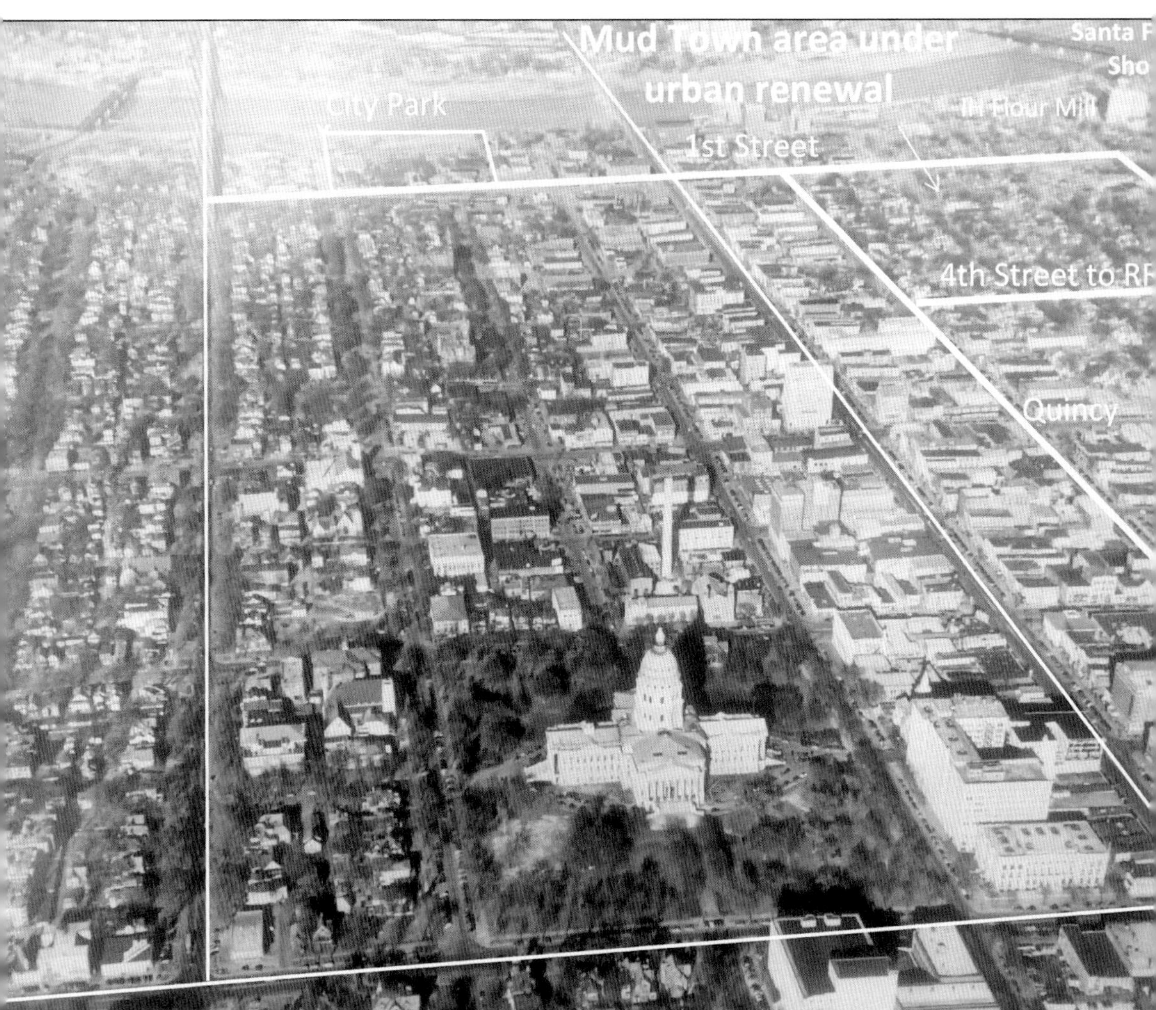

"The Bottoms" Aerial Photo and Map. The area south of the Kansas River and north and east of the capitol was known as "the Bottoms." The Fourth Street District, the black hub of the city, was on the border of the Bottoms. Black businesses operated and organizations met in this area, which was also the entertainment center of the city's African American community. This area was home to many African American and Hispanic families. The City Park is located at the top of this map on First Street. (Courtesy of KHS, boundaries overlaid.)

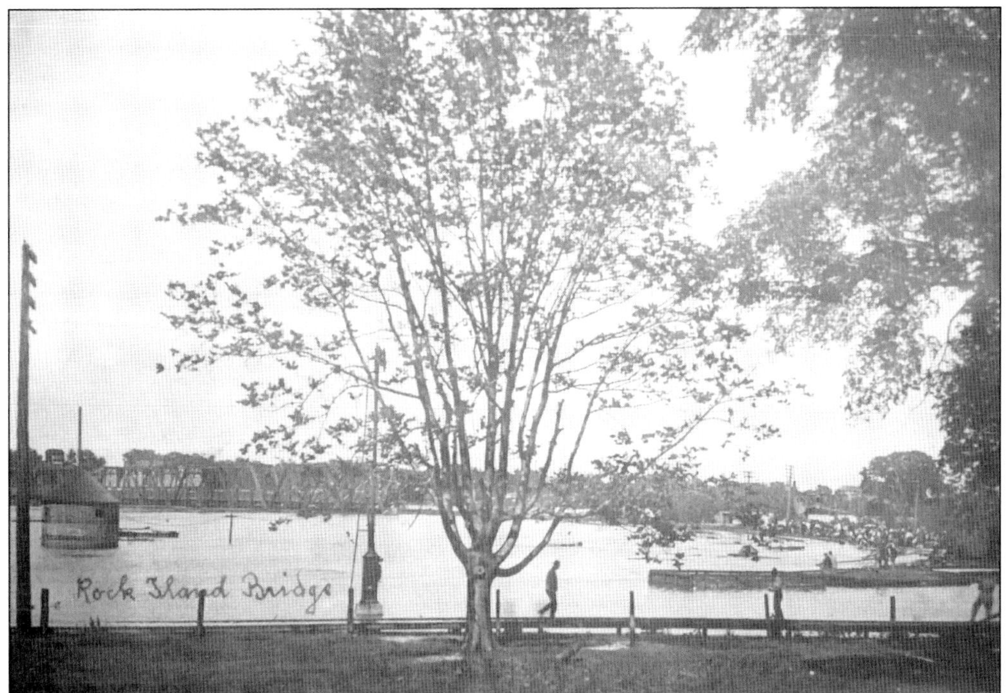

CITY PARK. Located between the Kansas River and First Street, City Park was in the area of Topeka called "the Bottoms." Black churches from all over the city regularly held services, revivals, picnics, and socials there. This photograph is a view from the Rock Island Bridge. (Courtesy of KHS.)

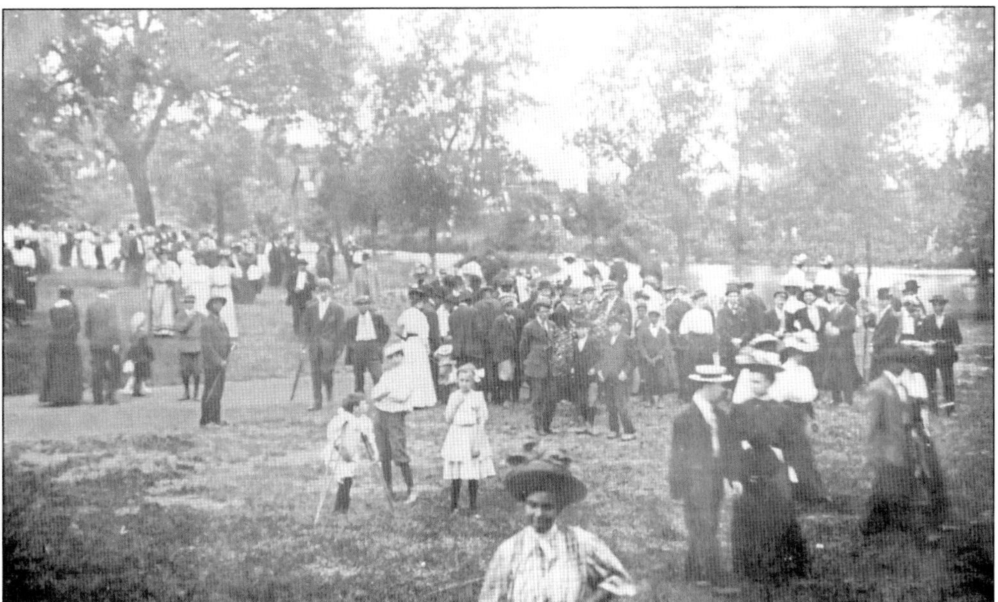

CROWDS AT THE CITY PARK. Churches held many joint events, including concerts and conventions, at City Park. Various other social activities took place in the park, including baseball and, later, swimming. Blacks were only allowed to swim at this location, while whites swam at the Gage Park swimming pool. The City Park was eventually abandoned due to flooding and unhealthy conditions. In this photograph, the community enjoys a Sunday at the park. (Courtesy of KHS.)

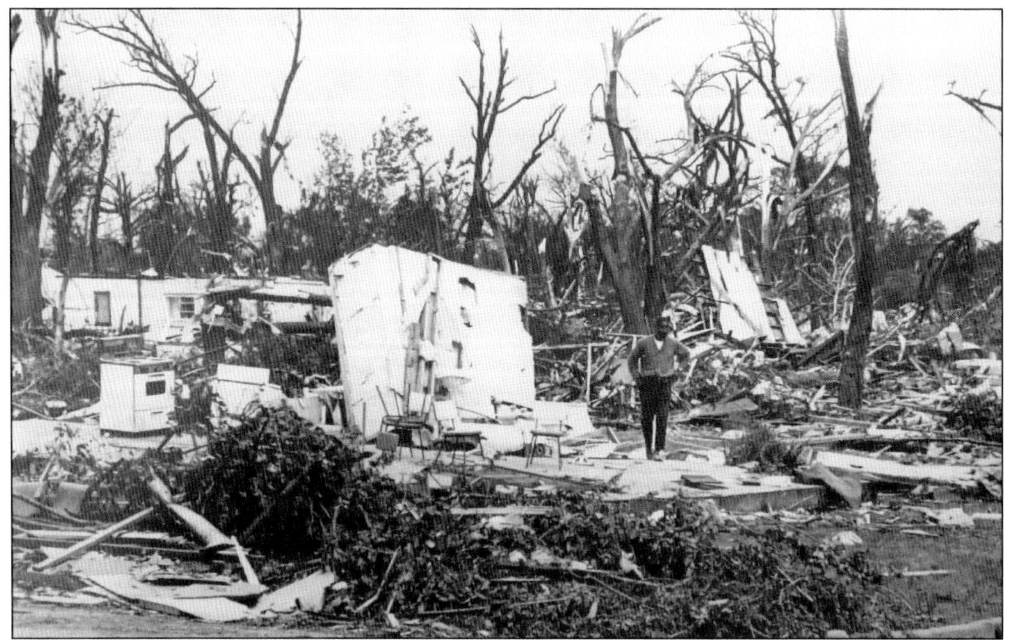

THE 1966 TORNADO IN THE BOTTOMS. The above photograph of a shattered shed in the 400 block of Lake Street in the Bottoms shows the destruction of the 1966 tornado. It went through the south and mid-section of Topeka before tearing through the northeast section of town. The photograph below shows what was left of Tom Coleman's house at 232 Lime Street. He stands in his yard with devastation all around him. (Both photographs courtesy of KHS.)

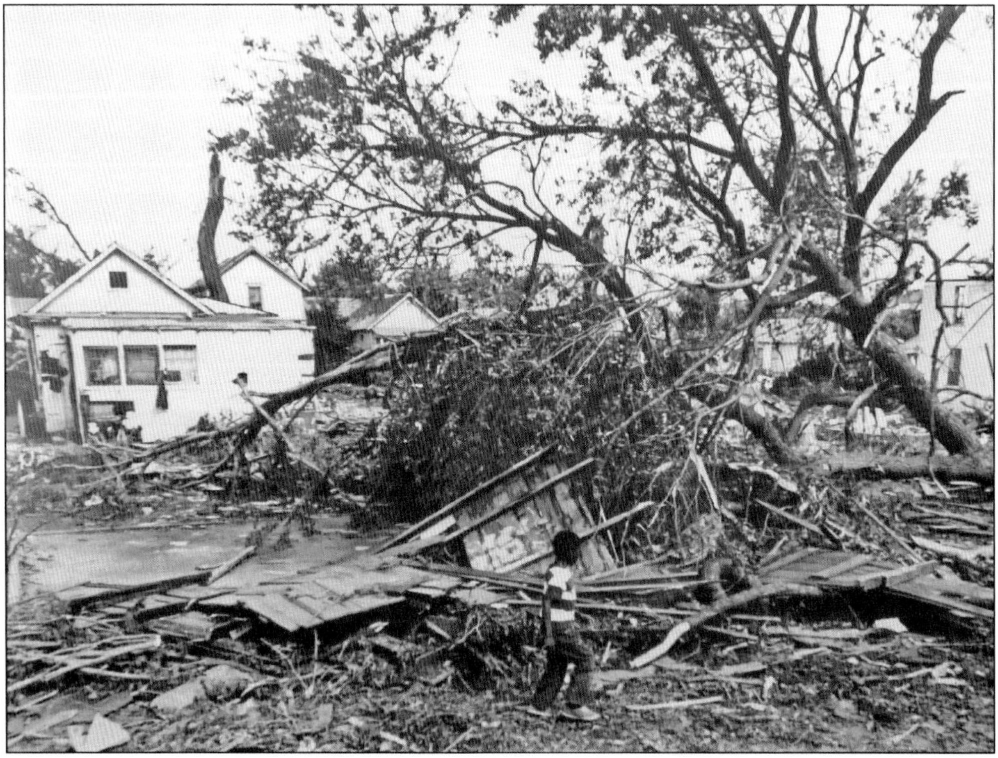

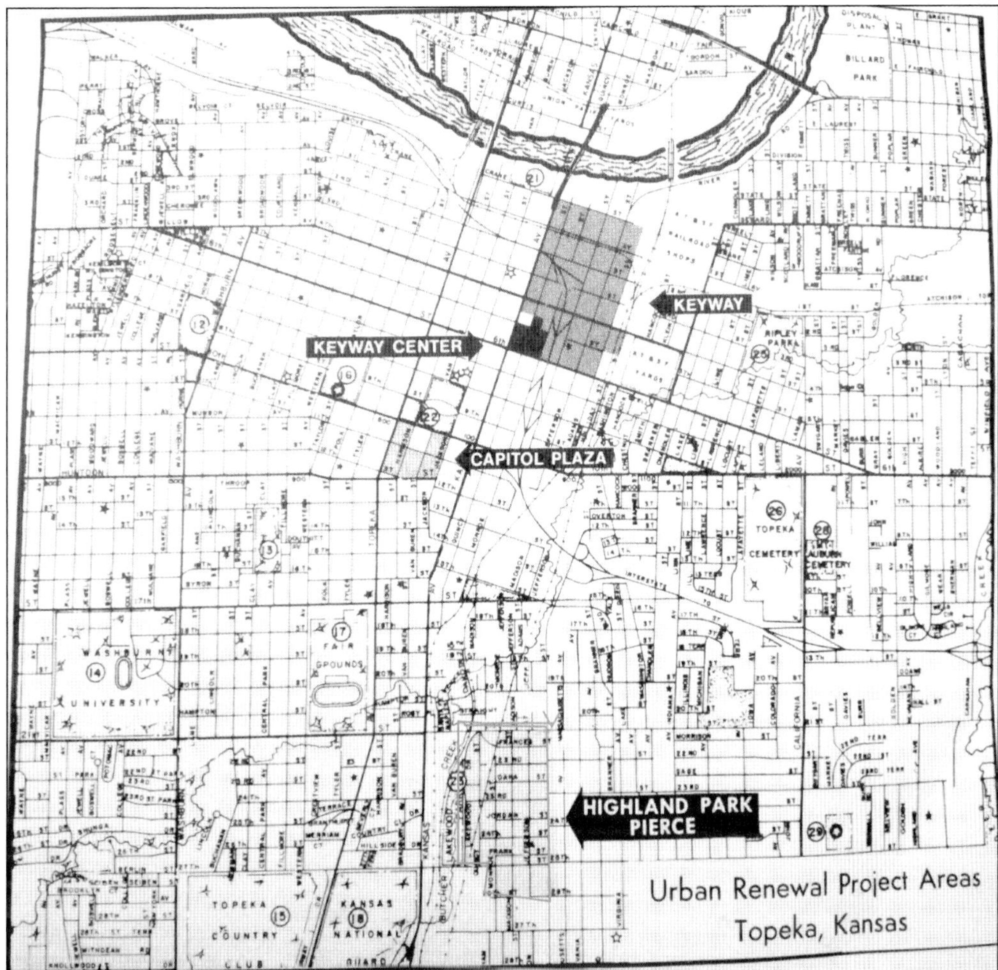

Pierce's Addition and Urban Renewal Map. The East Topeka area from Lakewood to Massachusetts Streets and between Twenty-first and Twenty-sixth Streets is known as Pierce's Addition. In the early 1970s, the US Department of Housing and Urban Development began urban renewal projects in this area and other parts of Topeka to rehabilitate old homes, build new properties, and relocate residents. This map shows the various projects throughout the city, including the Fourth Street District, labeled here as the new Keyway area, and the Capital Plaza area on the fairgrounds. (Courtesy of Tishara Hale.)

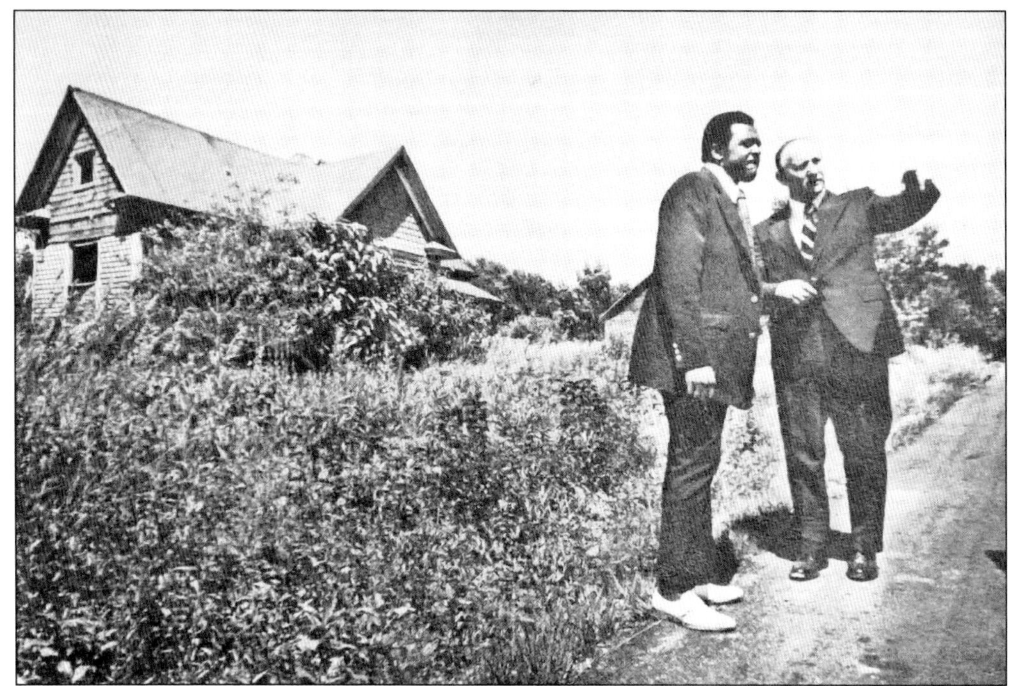

Pierce's Addition Urban Renewal. Representatives elected by the residents of the area gave input to HUD about its various projects. Urban renewal changed the landscape of the black community in East Topeka. Not everyone thought that it was good for African Americans; some felt that the process broke up the black community and dislocated families. In the photograph above, Sen. James Pearson (right) discusses the problems with project director Earl Jackson at Twenty-fifth and Adams Streets. Below, the Project Area Committee reviews HUD proposals. (Both photographs courtesy of Tishara Hale.)

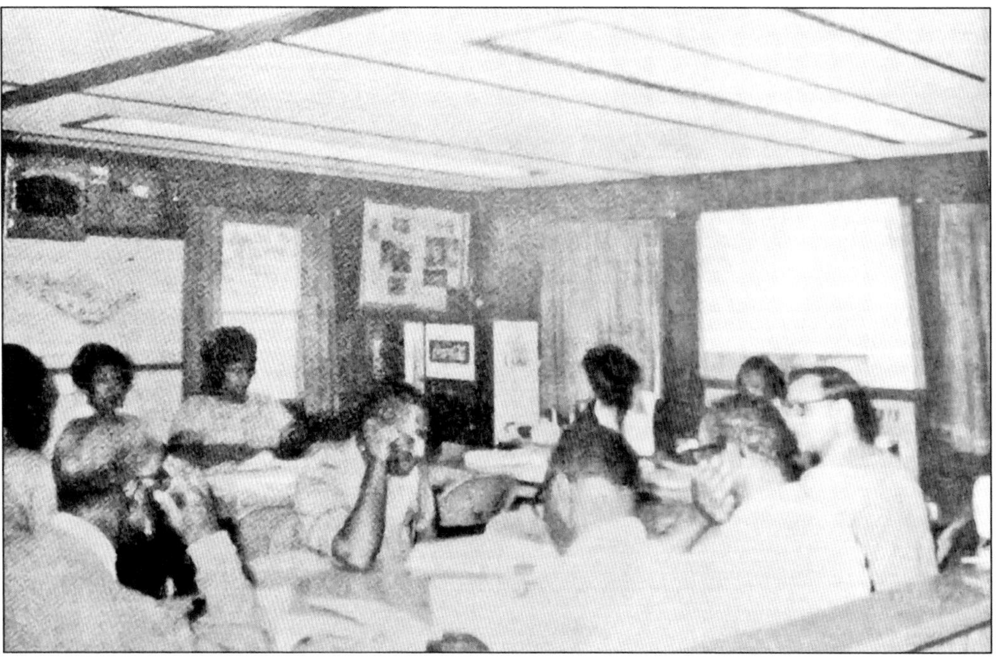

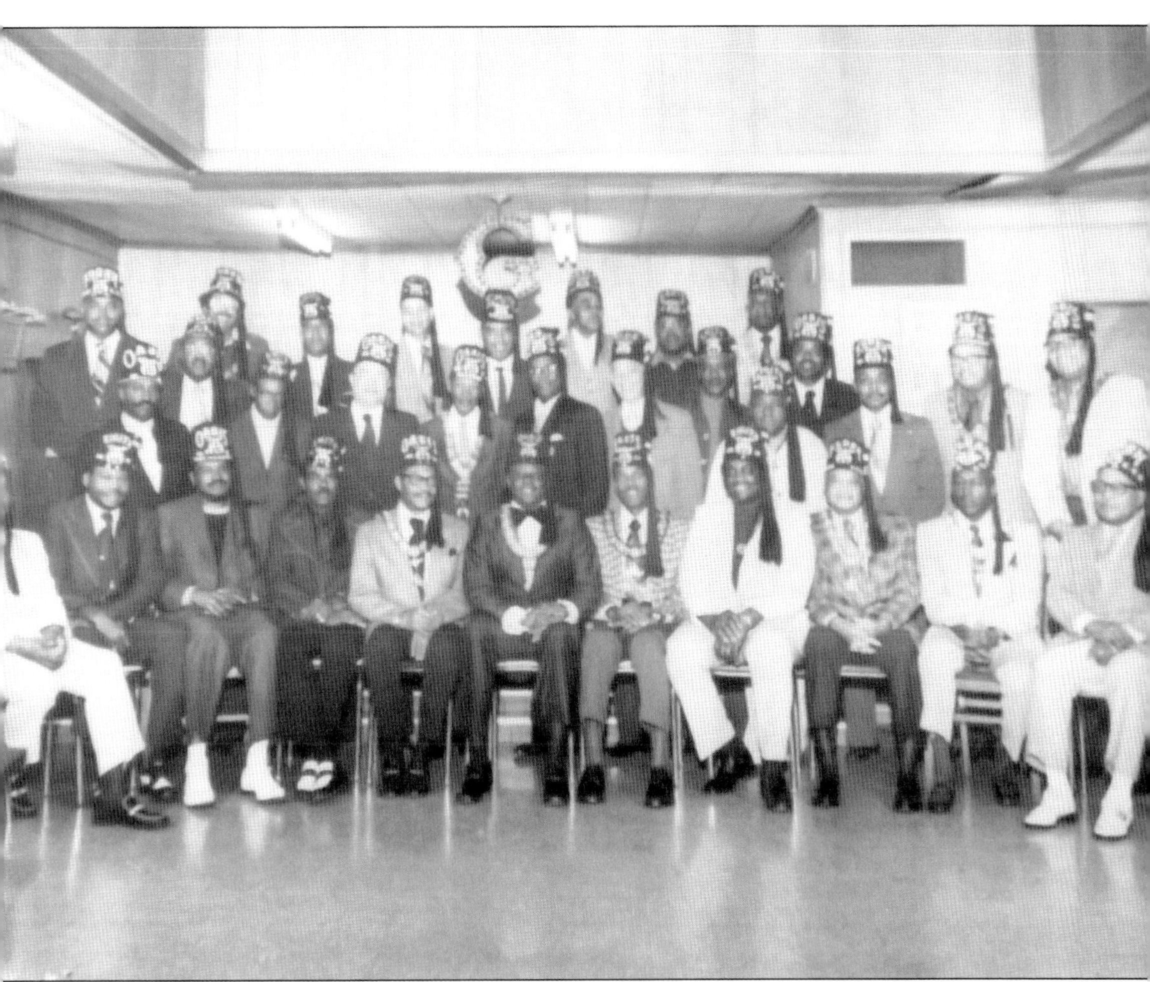

Oasis Temple No. 29. The Shriners from the Ancient Egyptian Arabic Order of Nobles of the Mystic Shrine are pictured here in the Metropolitan Hall at 404 Kansas Avenue, where they regularly met (in the Fourth Street District). The organization was established before 1928 as a benevolent organization of men who wanted to help their community. Attorney Charles Scott was one of Topeka's prominent African American men who were very active in the Shriners' lodge. (Courtesy of KSCOLL.)

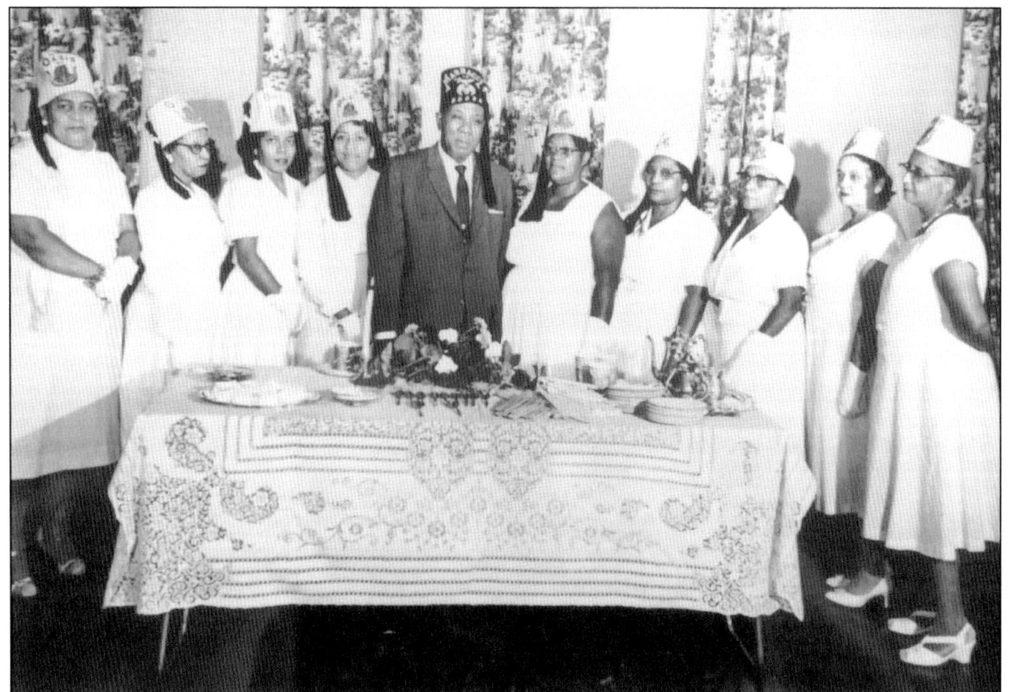

Lady Shriners. Many of the Lady Shriners were the wives of the members of the Oasis Lodge No. 29 Shriners. Like those men, the women also worked to help their community and raise money for the various activities that they sponsored. Here, the ladies are pictured with the potentate before serving a meal during one of their meetings in the 1950s. (Courtesy of KSCOLL.)

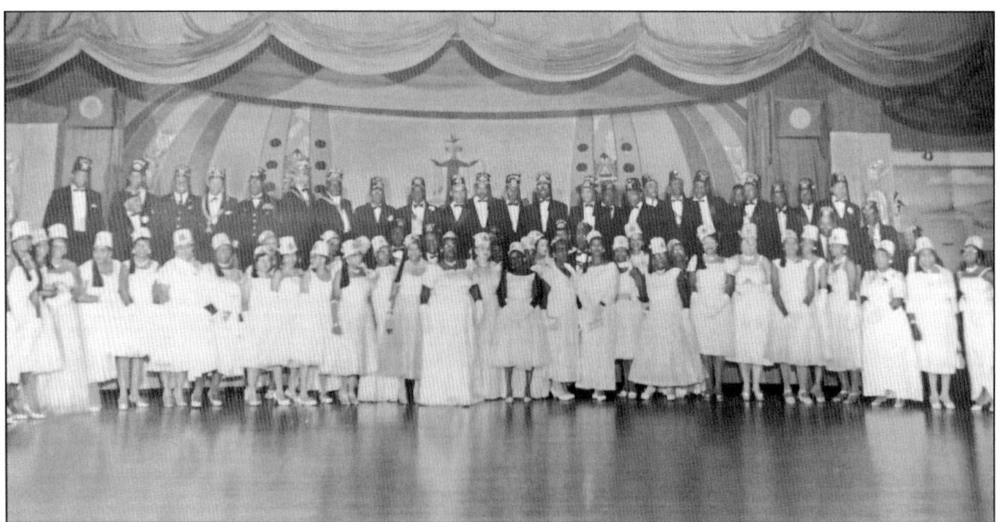

Shriners Potentate's Ball. Meadow Acres was a dance hall located on South Topeka Boulevard, just south of Twenty-ninth Street. In the 1950s, this area was considered to be outside the Topeka city limits. Many special occasions took place there, including this Oasis Lodge No. 29 Shriners Potentate's Ball. The ballroom featured elaborate decorations and a large dance floor. Meadow Acres was also the venue for big bands and concerts by acts such as Ike and Tina Turner and Ray Charles. (Courtesy of KSCOLL.)

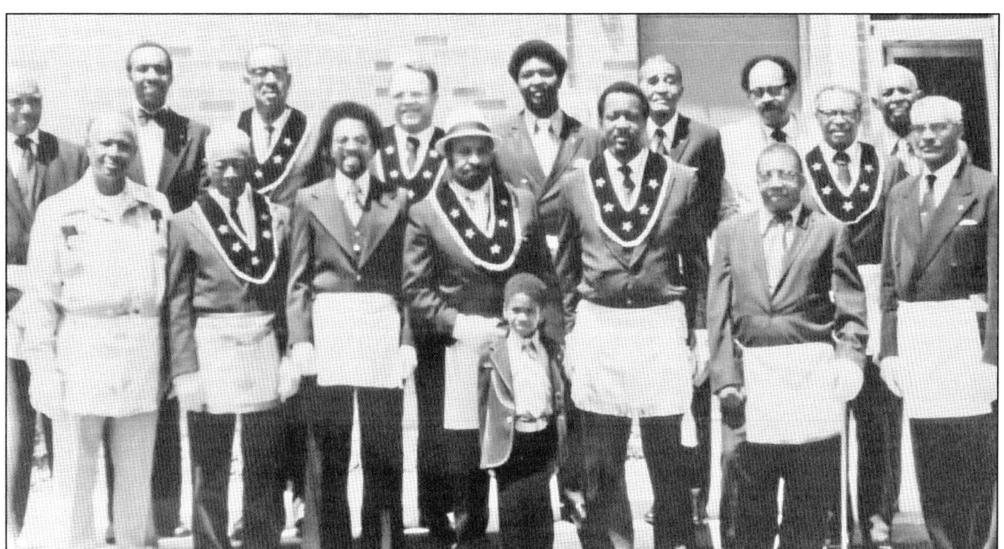

Prince Hall F&AM Lodge. The Prince Hall Free and Accepted Mason Lodge was established in Topeka before 1928, according to the city's 1928 *Colored City Directory*. Through the years, the Masons have had a strong presence in the black community. Many African American leaders belonged to the Freemasons and participated in the burial rites for its members. Members supported the community by helping those who were less fortunate. Some of the men who belonged to the Masons also belonged to other lodges. (Courtesy of KSCOLL.)

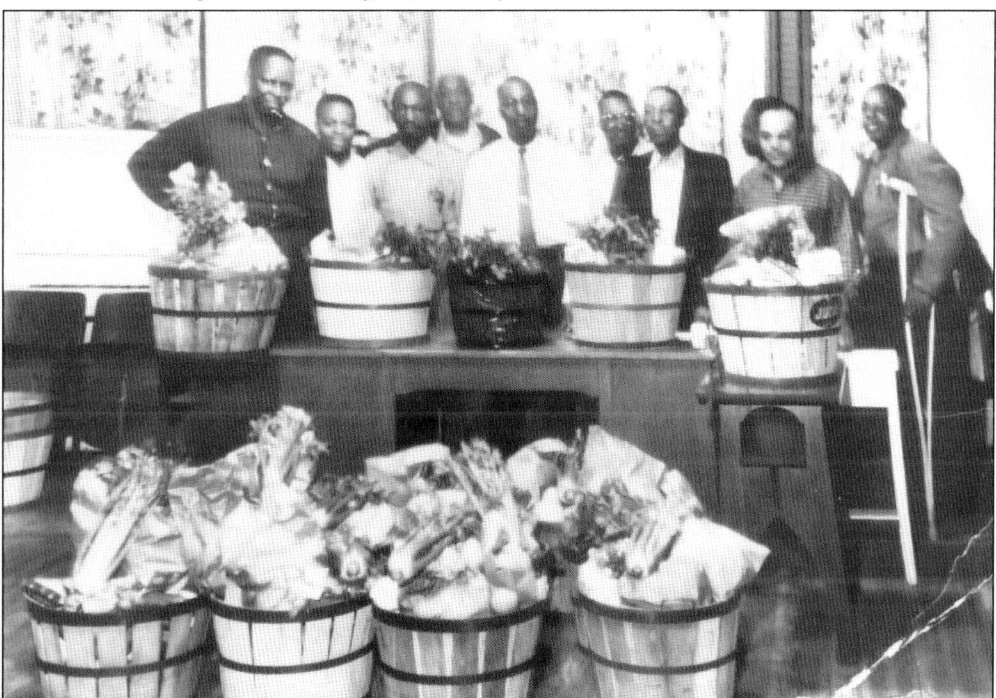

Elks Club. The Elks Club has been one of Topeka's African American men's groups since 1965. Dedicated to the welfare of their members and the needy, the Elks have worked to help the community in various ways. In this photograph, they are shown collecting food in their building at Third and Jackson Streets to give to local people in need. (Courtesy of KSCOLL.)

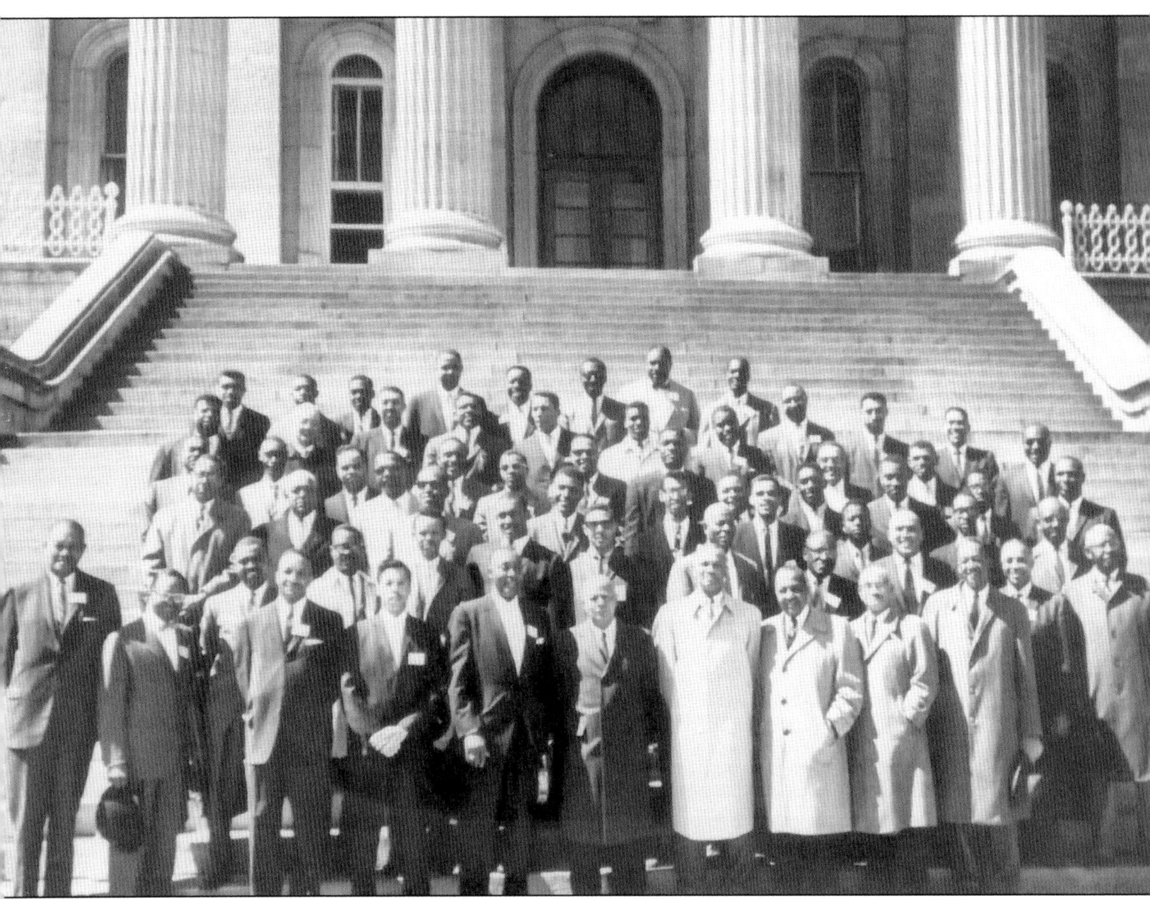

Kappa Alpha Psi Officials. The Kappa Alpha Psi fraternity officials convened in Topeka in the late 1950s. Many of these men were part of the Topeka chapter of the fraternity. This photograph was taken on the south steps of the Kansas State Capitol during one of their conferences. (Courtesy of KSCOLL.)

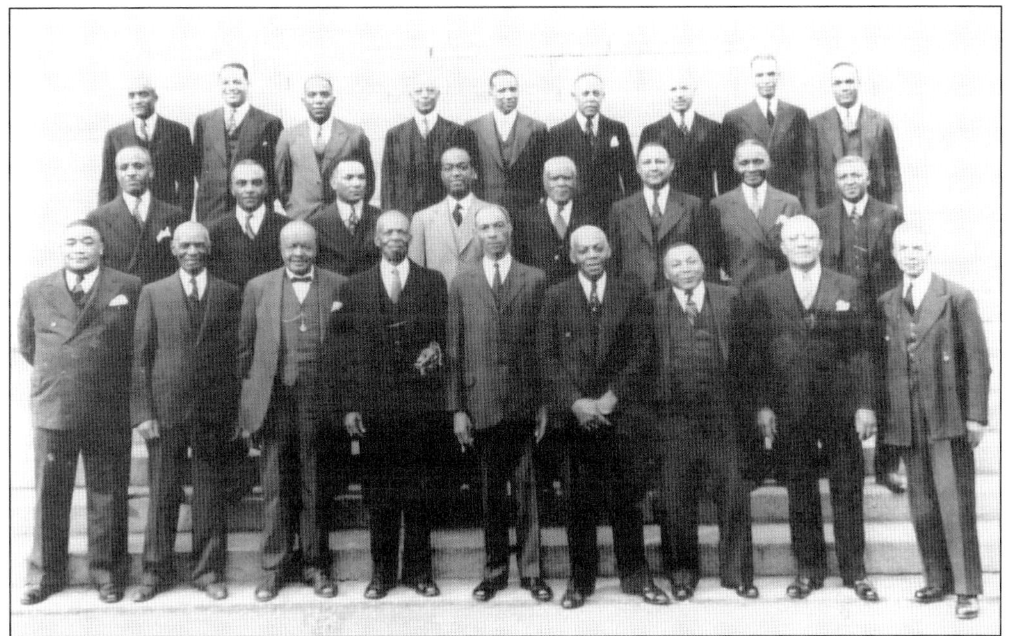

Kappa Alpha Psi Members. The members of the Topeka chapter of the "Kappas," as they were nicknamed, stood for a photograph in the 1950s. (Courtesy of KSCOLL.)

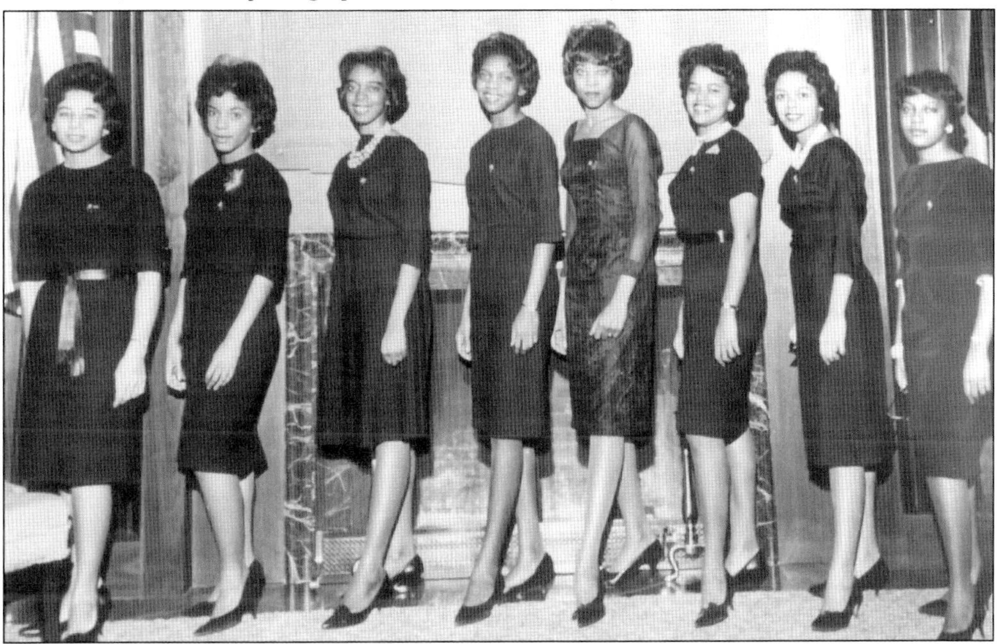

Alpha Kappa Alpha Sorority, Upsilon Chapter. The Alpha Kappa Alpha sorority was founded in 1908 in Washington, DC, at Howard University. The Topeka Upsilon chapter was formed on the Washburn campus and was dedicated to "global leadership through timeless service." In this photograph, which was taken in the 1960s, the ladies make a striking pose. Today, the "Alphas" continue the traditions of their early sorority sisters. From left to right are Joyece Holland, Marybelle Sayer, Larna Hayes-Arrington, two unidentified women, Kathy Hayes, and two unidentified women. (Courtesy of KSCOLL.)

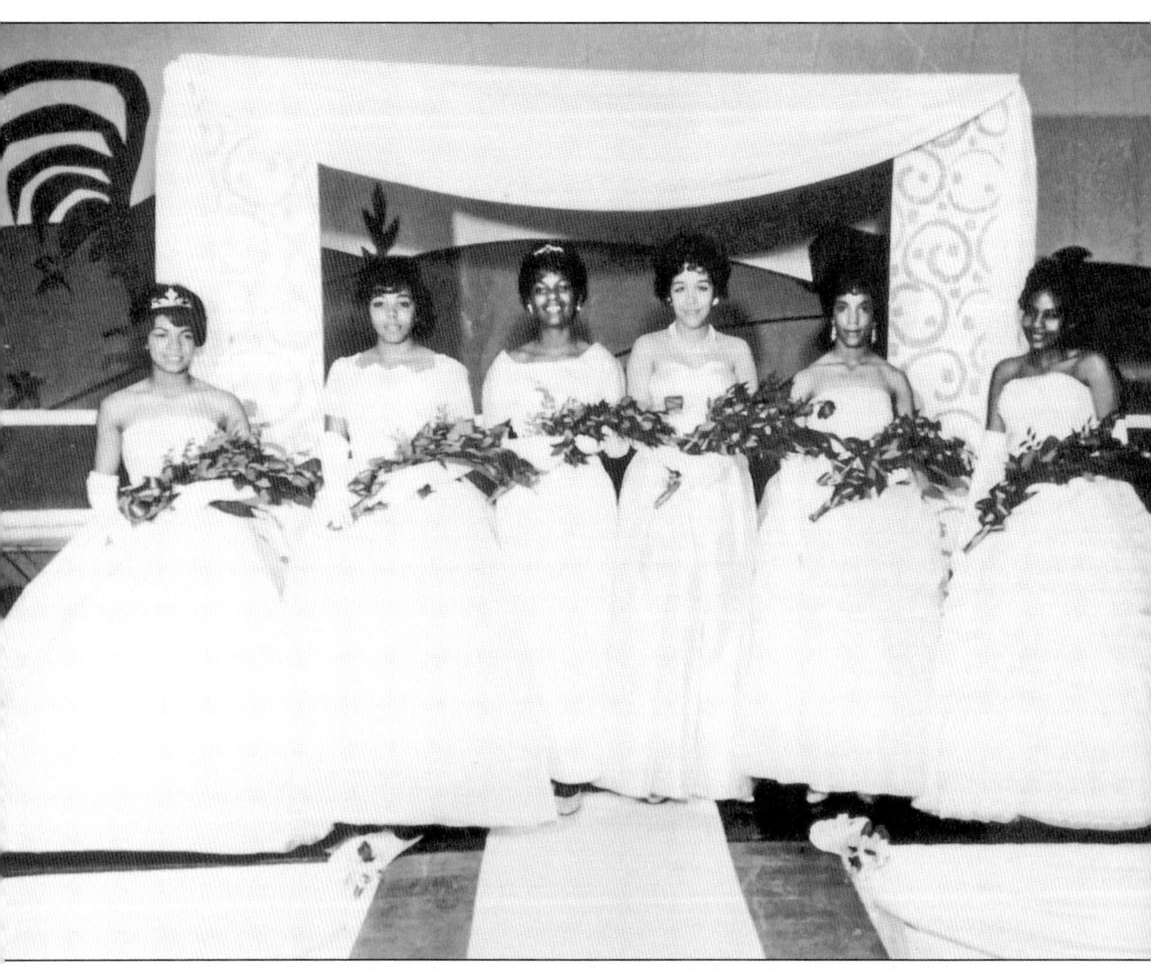

LINKS DEBUTANTE BALL. The Links organization has been dedicated to the youth of the community. The debutante ball was both a major annual event in the black community and an important event in a young woman's life. (Courtesy of KSCOLL.)

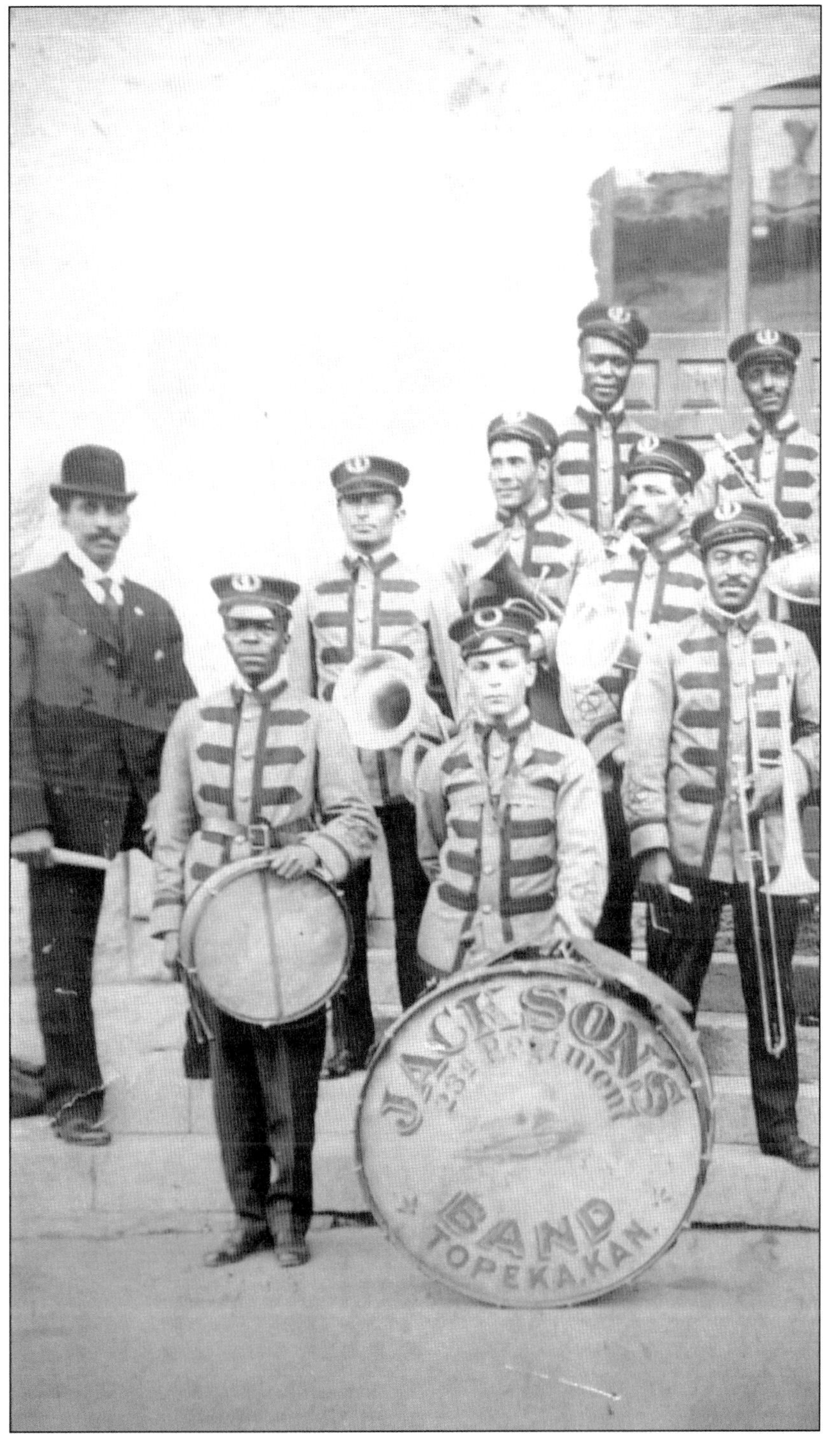

JACKSON'S 23RD REGIMENT BAND. This band, which was under the direction of Prof. E.W. Jackson, was the regimental band for the all-black 23rd Kansas Volunteers during the Spanish-American War. After the war, it became known as Jackson's Band and played in many venues in Topeka and in the black community. (Courtesy of Linda Brown Thompson.)

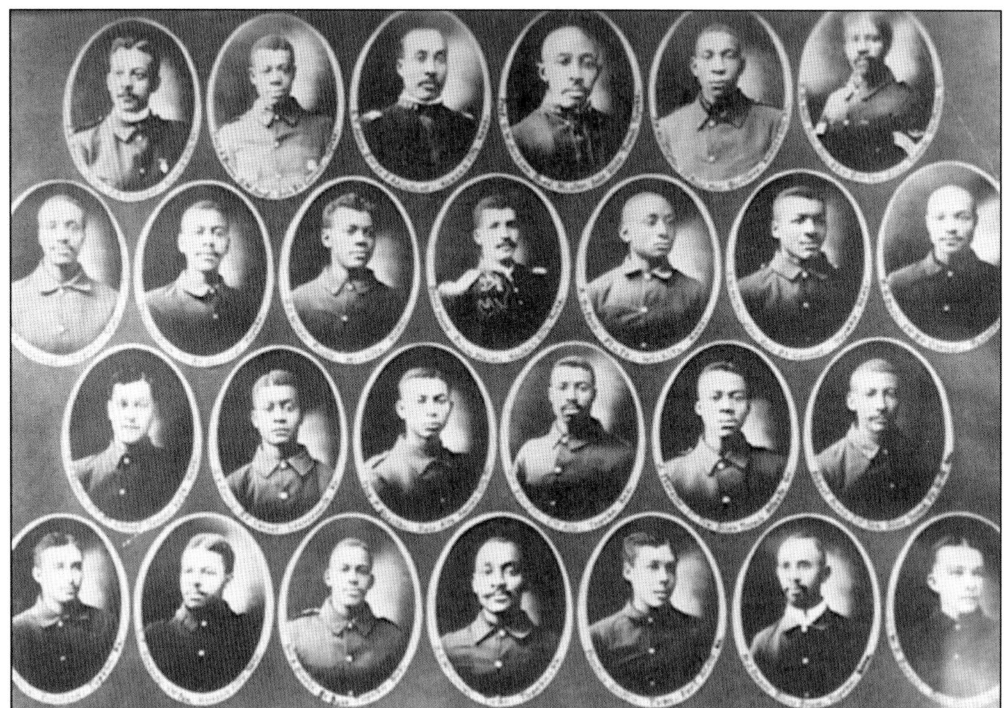

JACKSON'S 23RD REGIMENTAL BAND. In these formal photographs of the members of the 23rd Regimental Band, each member's portrait is annotated with his name, instrument, and hometown. Begun in 1890 in Topeka as Jackson's Dispatch Band, this group enlisted in the military during the Spanish-American War as the regimental band for the all-black 23rd Kansas Volunteers. The band was commanded by Lt. Adj. S.T. Jones and was directed by Prof. E.W. Jackson. Lt. Col. James Beck was the regimental commander. (Courtesy of KHS.)

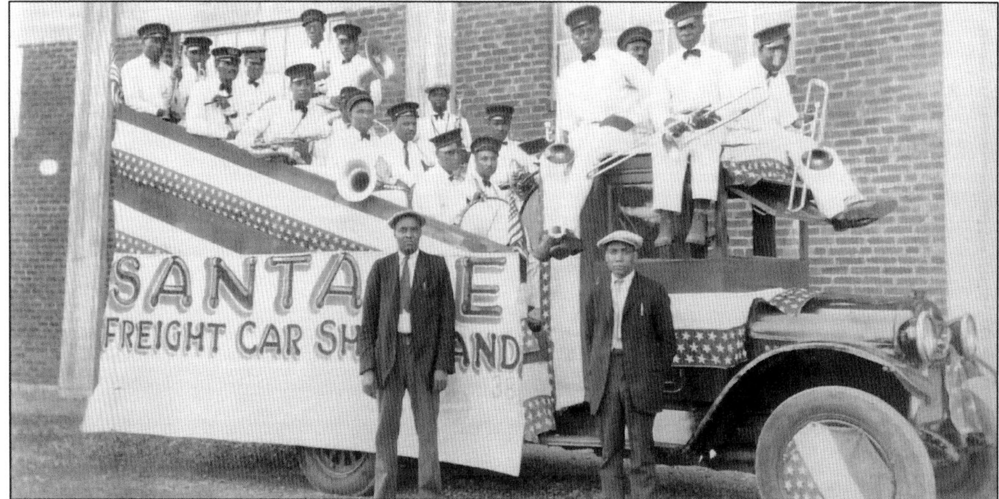

SANTA FE FREIGHT CAR SHOP BAND. The Atchison, Topeka & Santa Fe band was started in 1911, when the Santa Fe shops opened. Over the years, the band has changed its name from Santa Fe Freight Car Shop Band to Topeka Shop Band to Topeka Santa Fe Band, its current name. The band continues to perform and played 15 venues in the 2013 season. This 1928 photograph shows some of the band members in a local parade. (Courtesy of KHS.)

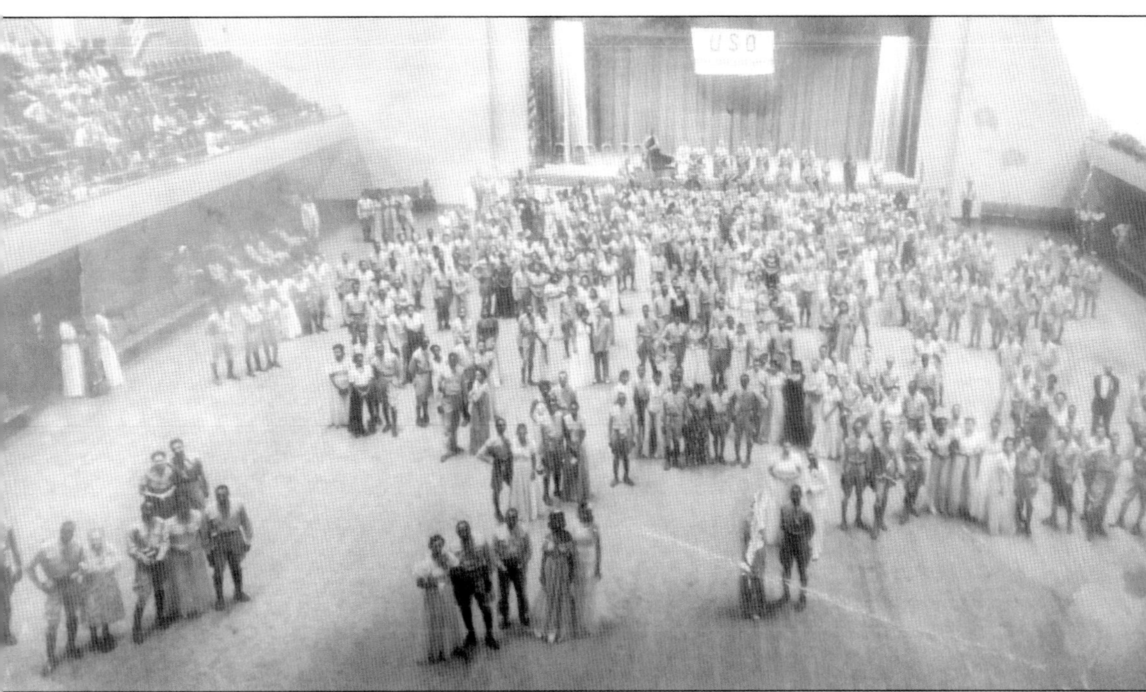

USO Dance at Meadow Acres. Scenes like the one in this 1940s photograph of the Meadow Acres Ballroom in South Topeka were common during World War II. Soldiers spent their leave and "rest and relaxation" time at social gatherings such as this. This image shows most of the soldiers in their uniforms and many young women with whom the servicemen could dance and socialize. (Courtesy of Judy Billings.)

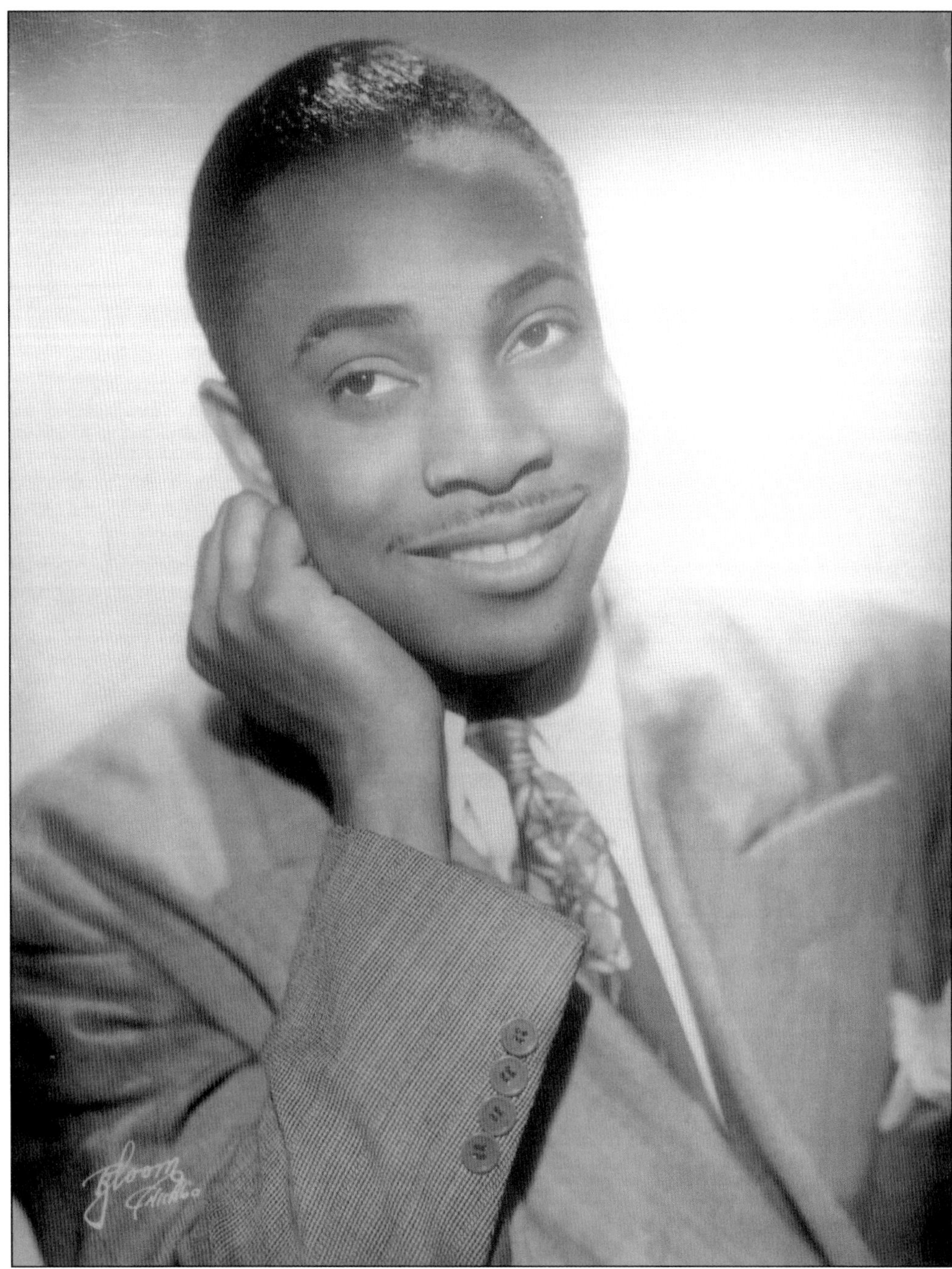

YOUNG ARNOLD DWIGHT "GATEMOUTH" MOORE. Born in 1913 in Topeka to Robert and Georgia Moore, Arnold Dwight Moore attended Topeka Public Schools. As a youth, he earned a reputation as a child singer and entered and won many amateur contests. When he was teenager, he went to Kansas City and sang in the famous Eighteenth and Vine District. When he had the chance to sing for a traveling carnival, his life changed forever. Nicknamed "Gatemouth," he became a popular blues singer. (Courtesy of Rosalind Moore Wynne.)

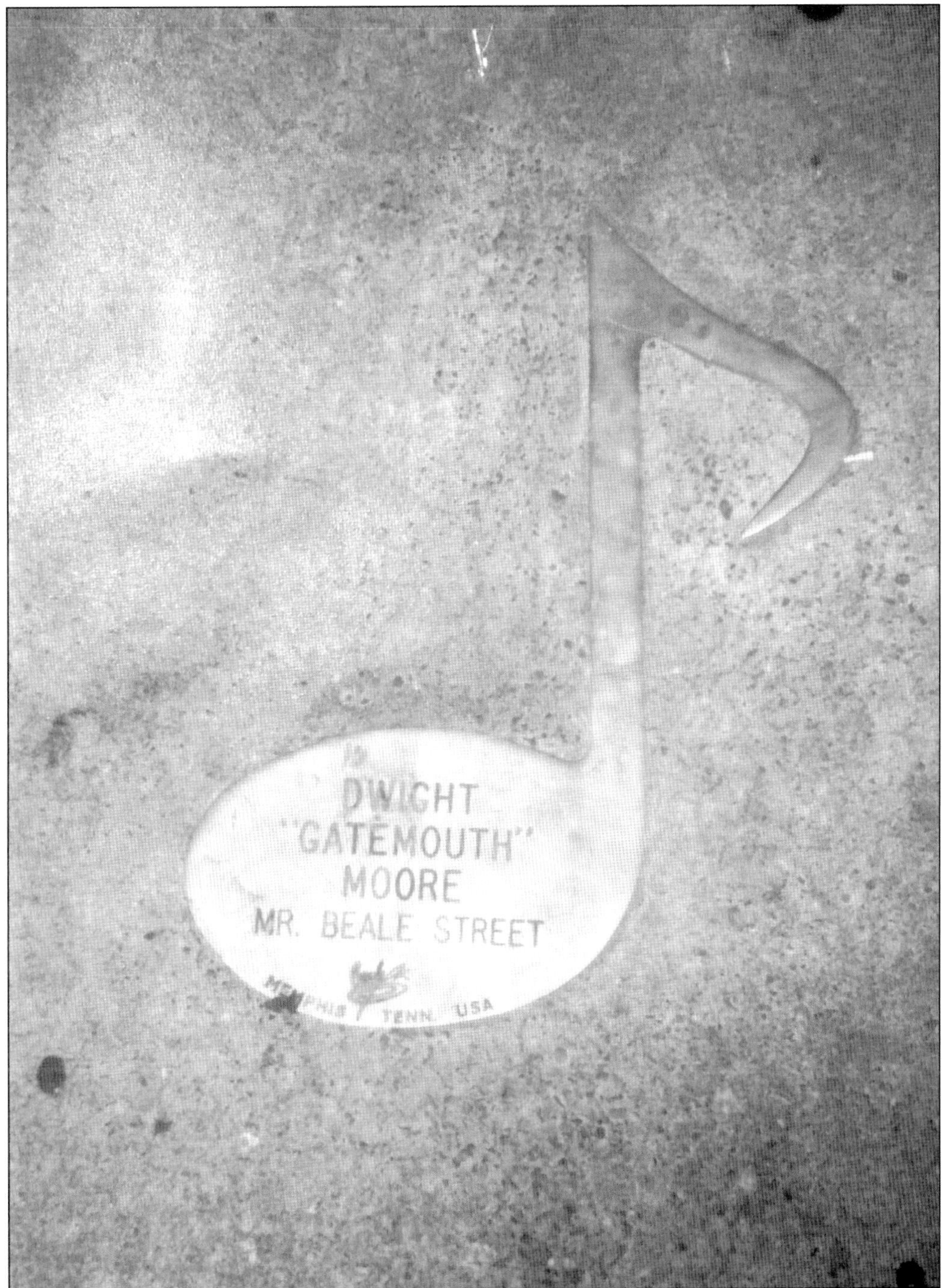

Gatemouth Moore on Beale Street. Gatemouth Moore was a Topeka-born blues singer who played many venues around the country, including Kansas City and Chicago. The first blues singer to perform at Carnegie Hall, he was considered the best blues singer by Count Basie. Popular during the 1940s, Moore recorded on the Black Swan Records label and had a long singing career. In 1996, a brass note dedicated to Moore, pictured here, was placed on the Beale Street Walk of Fame in Memphis, Tennessee. (Courtesy of Rosalind Moore Wynne.)

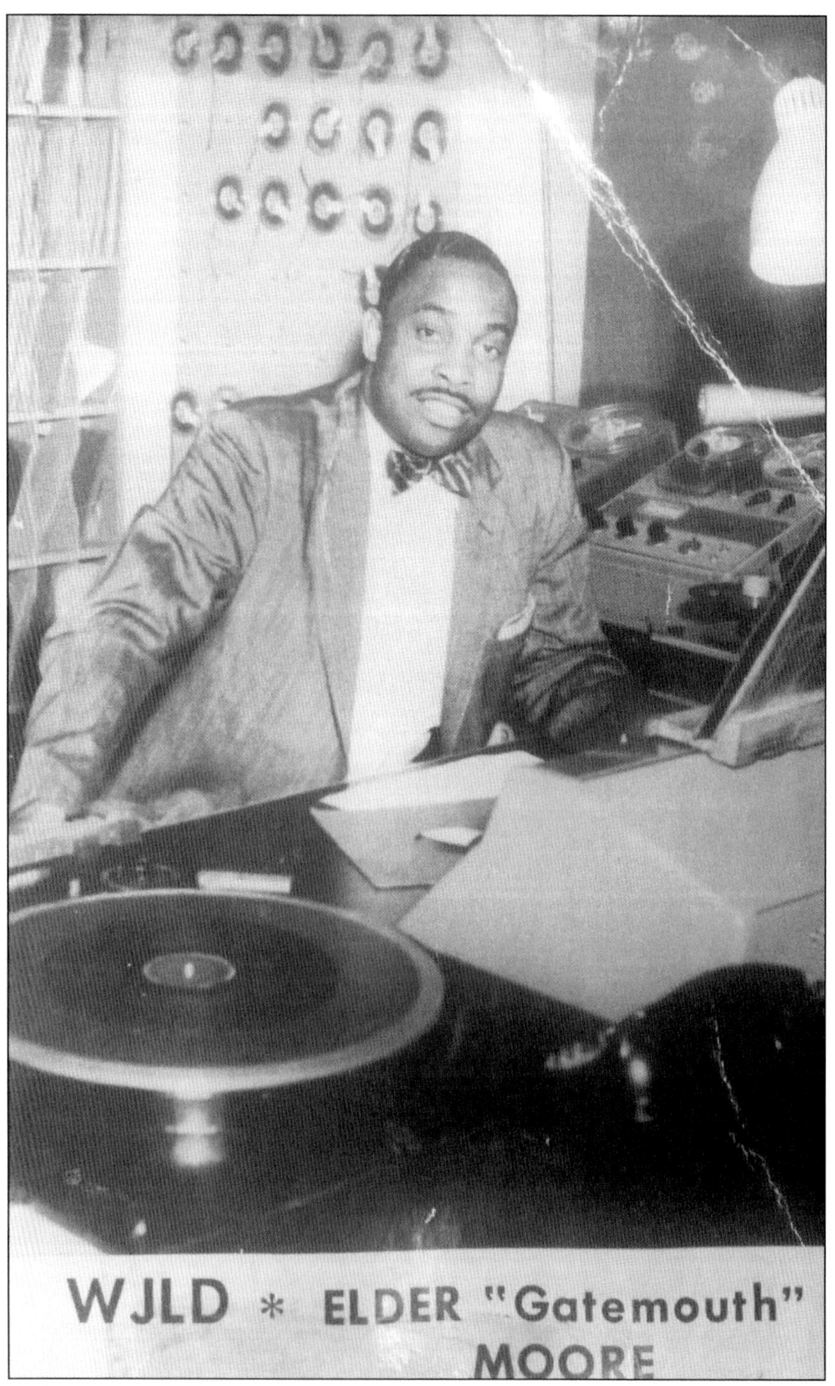

Preacher Gatemouth Moore. In 1949, Gatemouth Moore felt called to preach, and he spent the rest of his life promoting the gospel and singing gospel music. His gospel music and preaching were carried on many radio stations. Here, he is pictured on a 1956 promotional postcard for gospel station WJLD in Birmingham, Alabama. He was known for his lively sermons and once staged his own funeral, which included his spectacular entrance out of a coffin. (Courtesy of Rosalind Moore Wynne.)

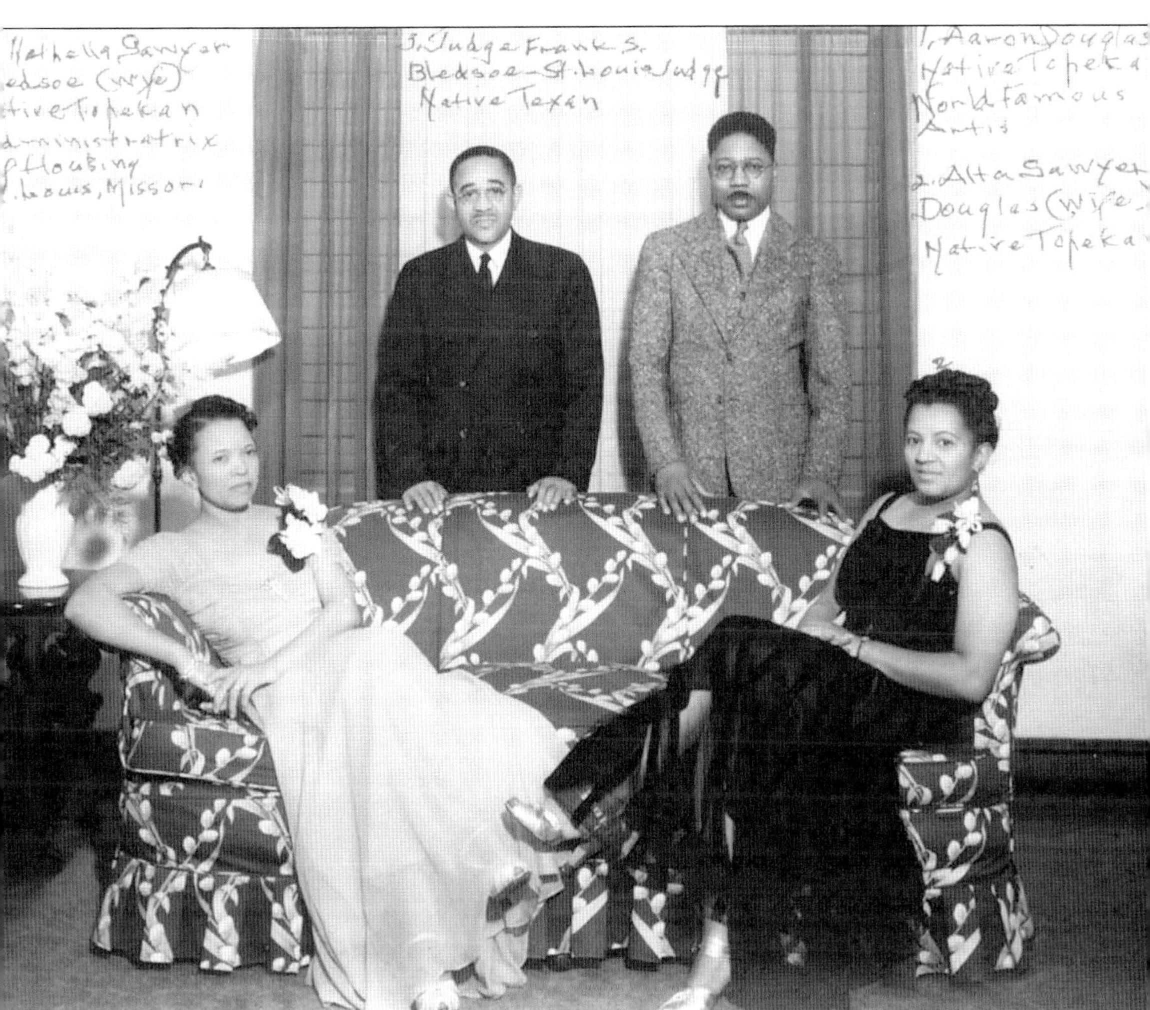

AARON DOUGLAS. Native Topekan Aaron Douglas became known as the "Father of African Art." He moved to Harlem, where he became the first president of the Harlem Artists Guild. He taught in the art department of Fisk University for 29 years. A copy of his work is in the Aaron Douglas Art Park on Twelfth Street between Washburn Avenue and Lane Street in Topeka, the site of the annual Aaron Douglas Art Fair. Pictured here are, from left to right, Nathella Sawyer-Bledsoe; Frank S. Bledsoe; Aaron Douglas; and Alta Sawyer-Douglas, his wife. (Courtesy of TSCPL.)

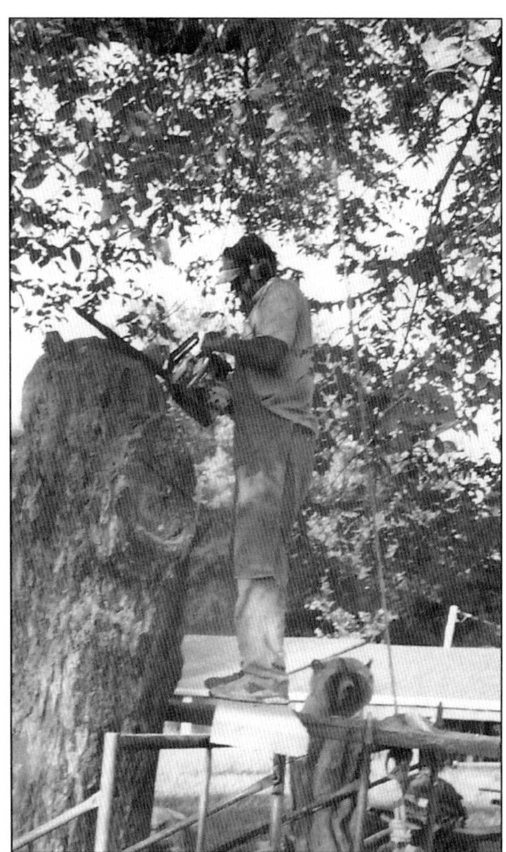

James Hale. Following his tour of duty in Korea in 1961, James Hale completed his Air Force service at Topeka's Forbes Field. While in Topeka, he studied welding at a local technical school and sculpting at Washburn University. He began creating many lifelike metal wildlife sculptures, some of which are on display at the Wildlife & Parks Office in Pratt, Kansas, and the Milford State Fish and Game Information Center. Hale switched from metal to wood because he could complete the sculptures 10 times faster. Shown here is an 18-foot-tall wood sculpture that Hale made from an elm stump and completed for Topeka's Ward-Meade Park in 1997. (Courtesy of the Hale children.)

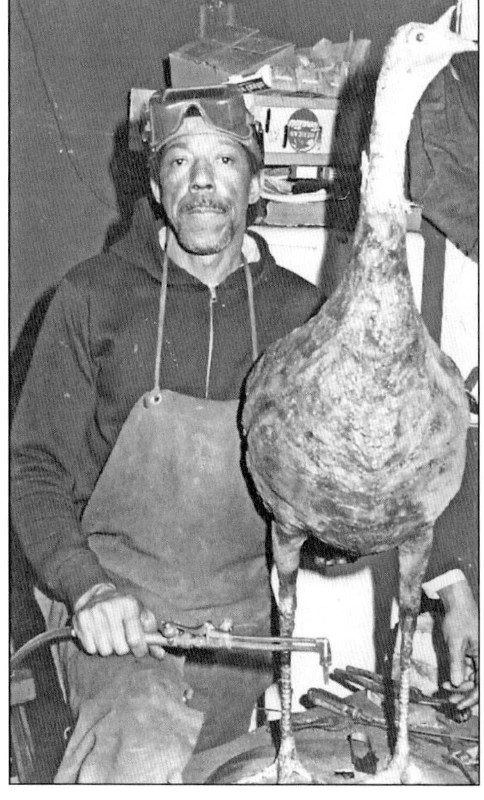

James Hale Art. Welding sculpture was the first art Hale created. It took weeks—sometimes months—to complete. In this photograph, Hale stands with one of his works, a lifelike replica of a wild turkey. Hale has produced hundreds of pieces of art and sold them across the country. Some of his artwork can be found in Topeka at the homes of his children. (Courtesy of the Hale children.)

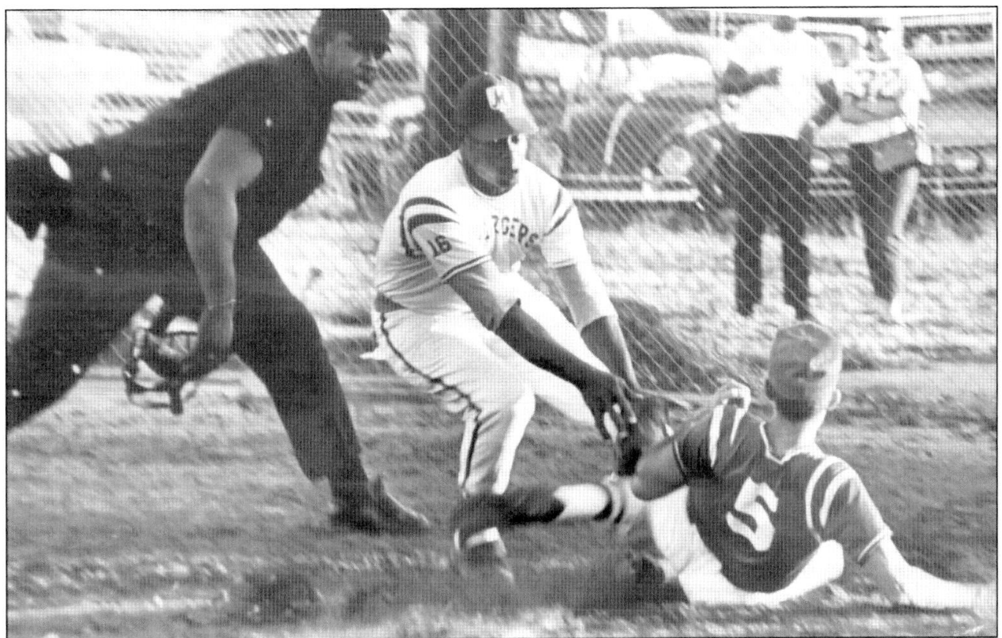

JOE DOUGLAS. Joe Douglas was called the "Babe Ruth of Topeka baseball." In this 1968 action photograph, Douglas, who is playing for the Metzger team, is tagging a player out. The umpire is Harold Adams. (Courtesy of the *Topeka Capital-Journal.*)

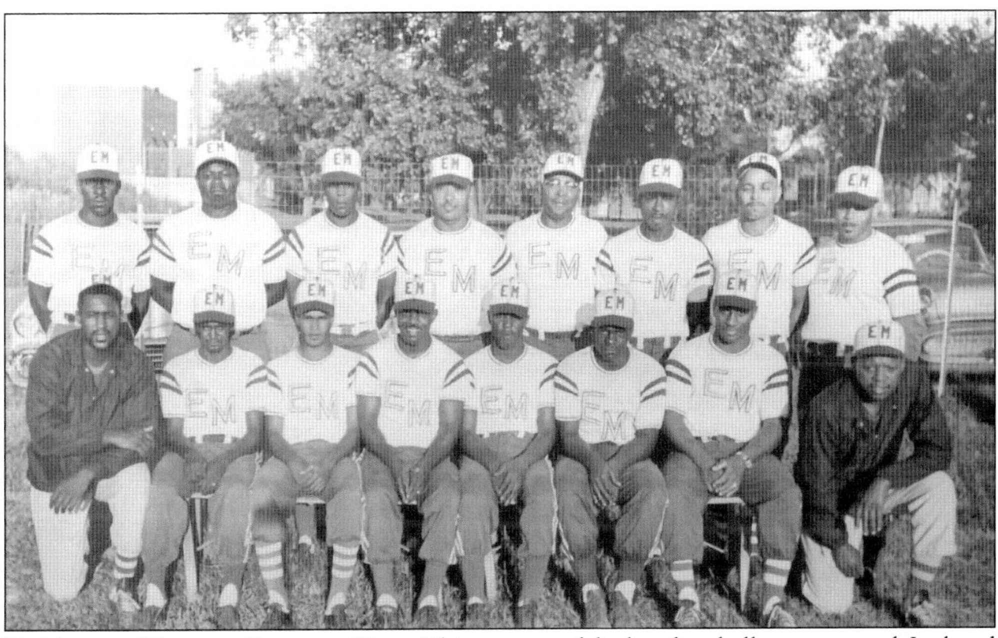

ED MARLING HORNETS BASEBALL TEAM. This was one of the best baseball teams around. It played both white and black teams locally and regionally. The players are, from left to right, (first row) Bob Bradford, Keith Miller, Roy Miller, Jackie Wright, Larry Wooldridge, and Jake Mitchell; (second row) David Perkins, Milo Mitchell, Gene Brooks, Tom Hardy, Oliver Brown Jr., Earnest Moore, Jack Alexander, and Wilbur Douglas. The coaches are unidentified. (Courtesy of KHS.)

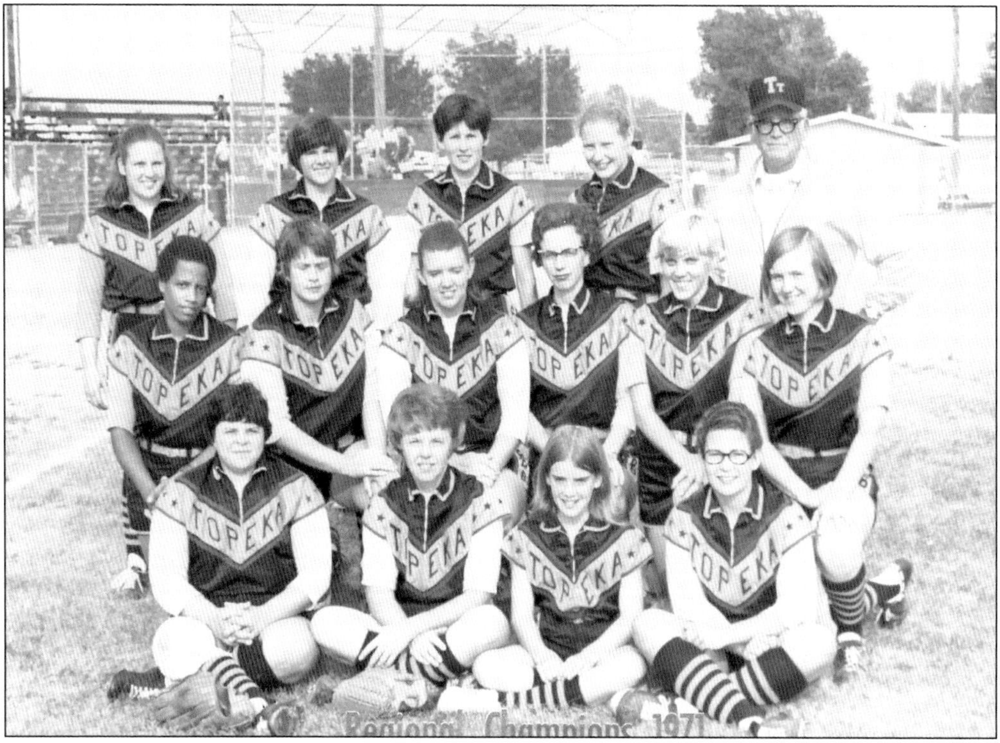

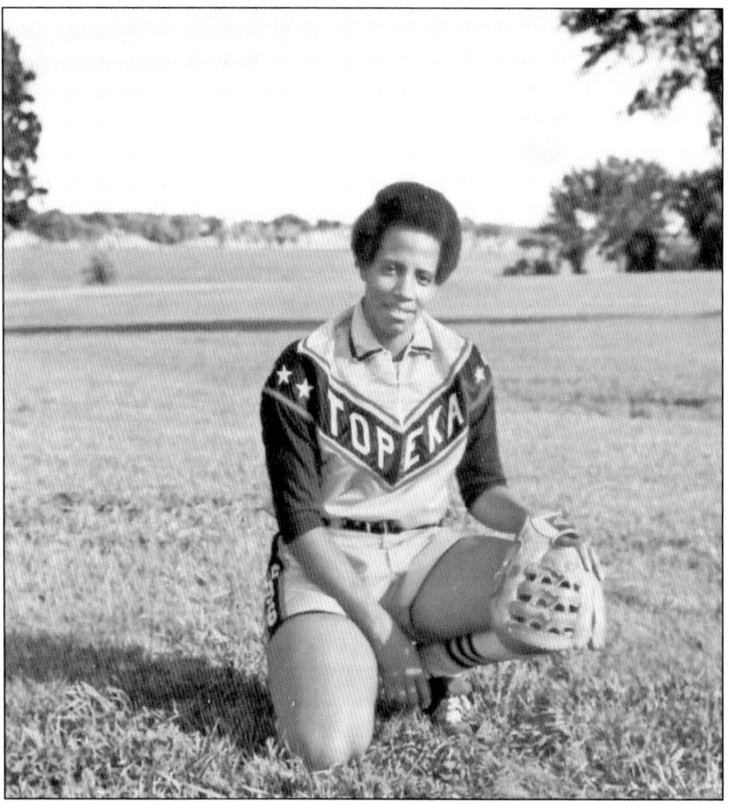

GLORIA GRAVES AND THE TEAMSTERETTES. The only African American to play for both the Topeka Teamsterettes and the WIBW-TV women's softball teams, pitcher Gloria Graves led the Teamsterettes to the regional and national championships in 1970. Although there were few African Americans who played women's softball at the time, Graves said she didn't experience any problems from other players. She did say, though, that she occasionally heard negative comments from the stands. (Both photographs courtesy of Phyllis Fast.)

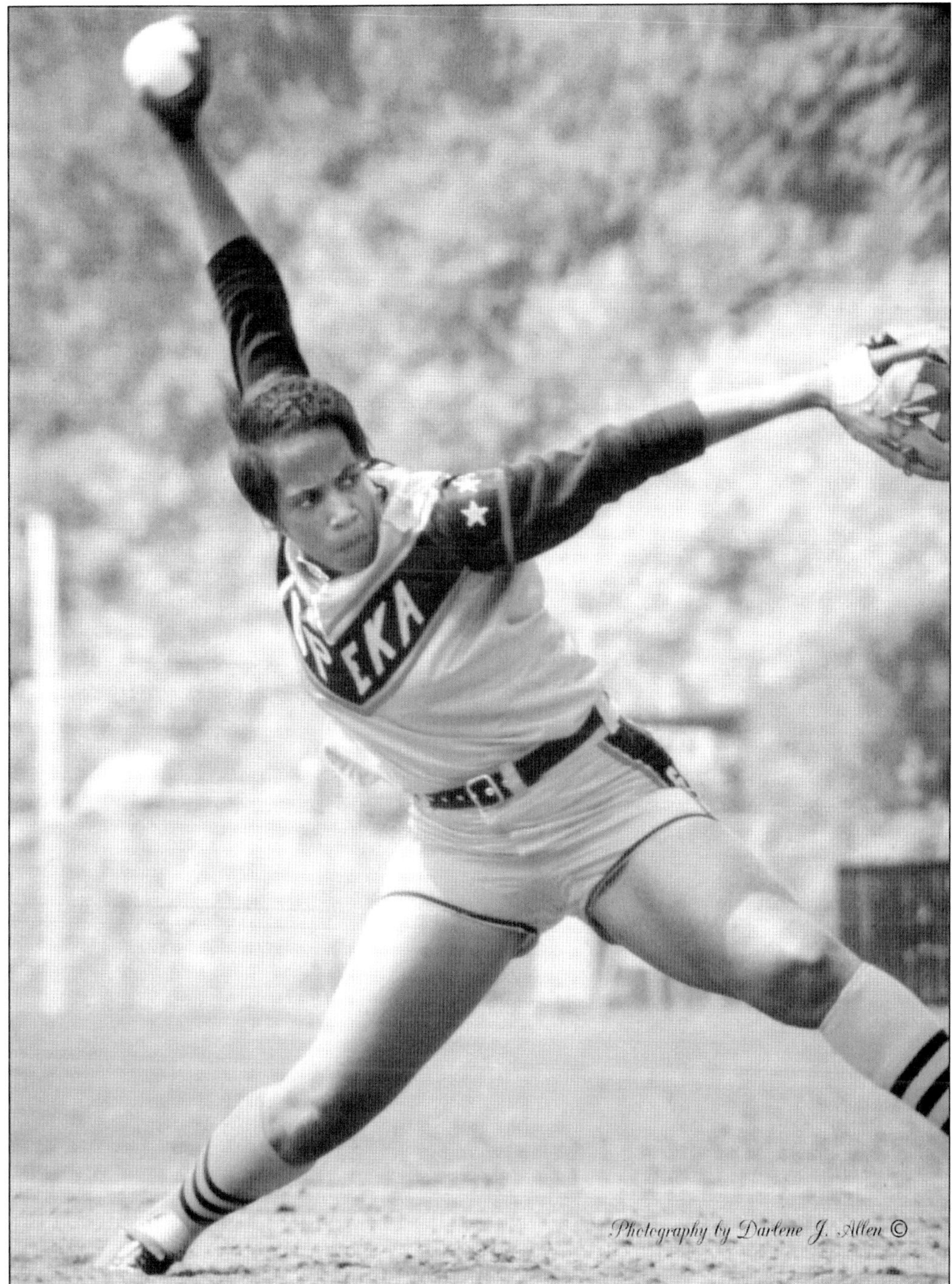

Gloria Graves. A 1970 graduate of Topeka High School, Gloria Graves later was a pitcher for the University of Kansas women's softball team and was selected to the 1977 collegiate Big Eight Championship All-Tournament Team. She was known, feared, and sometimes considered controversial because of her sidearmed pitching. (Courtesy of Phyllis Fast.)

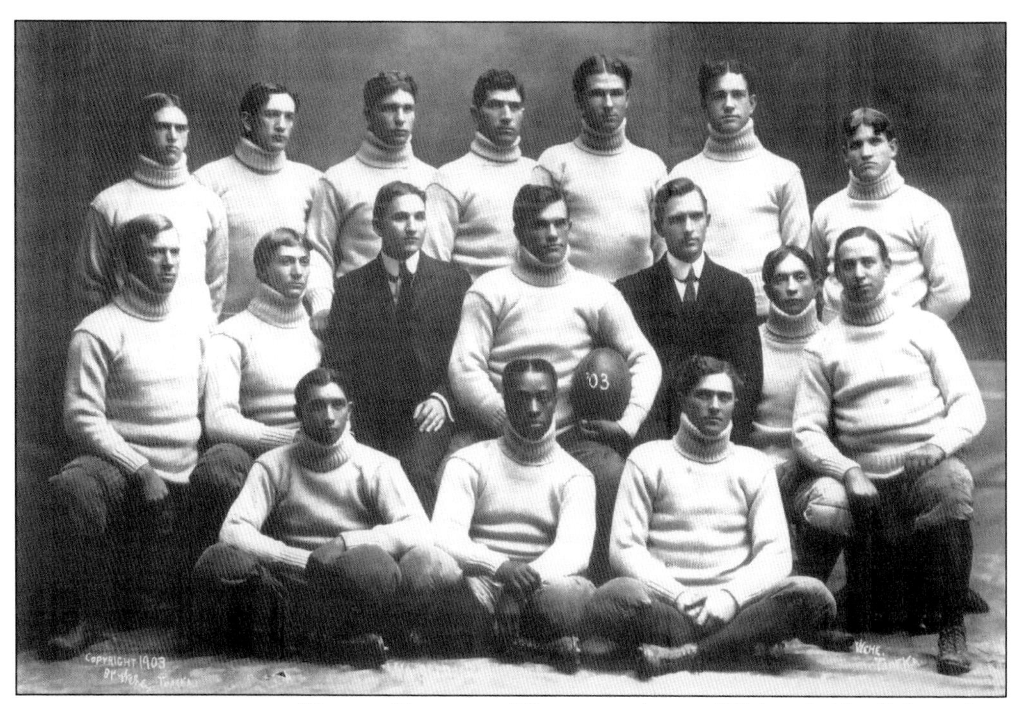

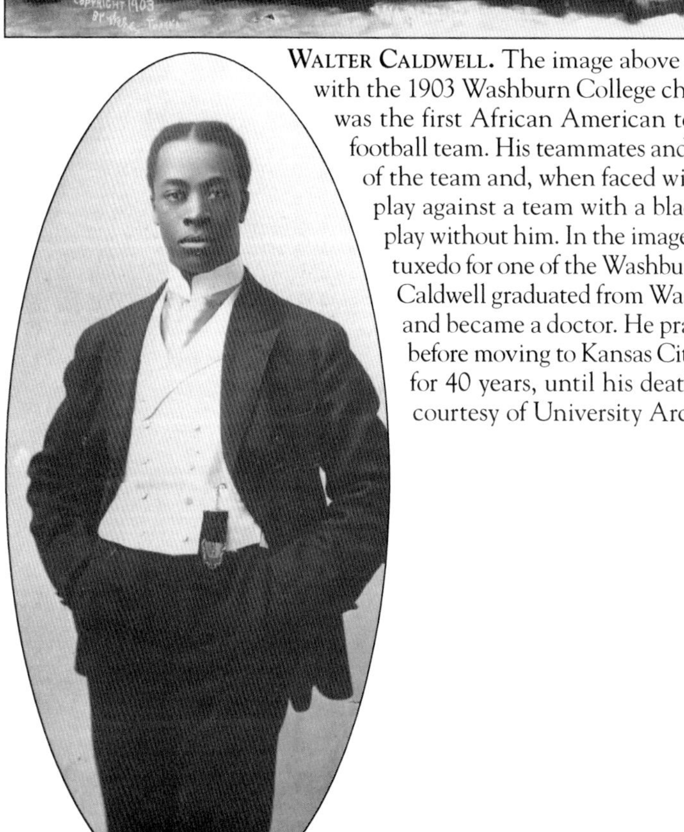

WALTER CALDWELL. The image above of Walter Caldwell shows him with the 1903 Washburn College championship football team. He was the first African American to play on Washburn College's football team. His teammates and coach considered him the star of the team and, when faced with other teams who refused to play against a team with a black player, his coach refused to play without him. In the image on the left, Caldwell donned a tuxedo for one of the Washburn football team's formal affairs. Caldwell graduated from Washburn Medical School in 1913 and became a doctor. He practiced in Topeka for two years before moving to Kansas City, where he practiced medicine for 40 years, until his death in 1959. (Both photographs courtesy of University Archives, Washburn University.)

ARTHUR FLETCHER. A Washburn University athlete and graduate, Arthur Fletcher played professional football for the Los Angeles Rams and was the first African American to play for the Baltimore Colts. He later went on to serve four US presidents and was involved in politics for many years. His positions included assistant secretary of wage and labor standards in the Department of Labor, deputy presidential advisor for Urban Affairs, and chairman of the US Civil Rights Commission. He served as a delegate to the UN and became the executive director of the United Negro College Fund in 1972, helping coin its slogan: "A mind is a terrible thing to waste." He is considered the "father of affirmative action." The 1950 photograph at right shows him in his Washburn football uniform. He is pictured below in 1970. (Both photographs courtesy of University Archives, Washburn University.)

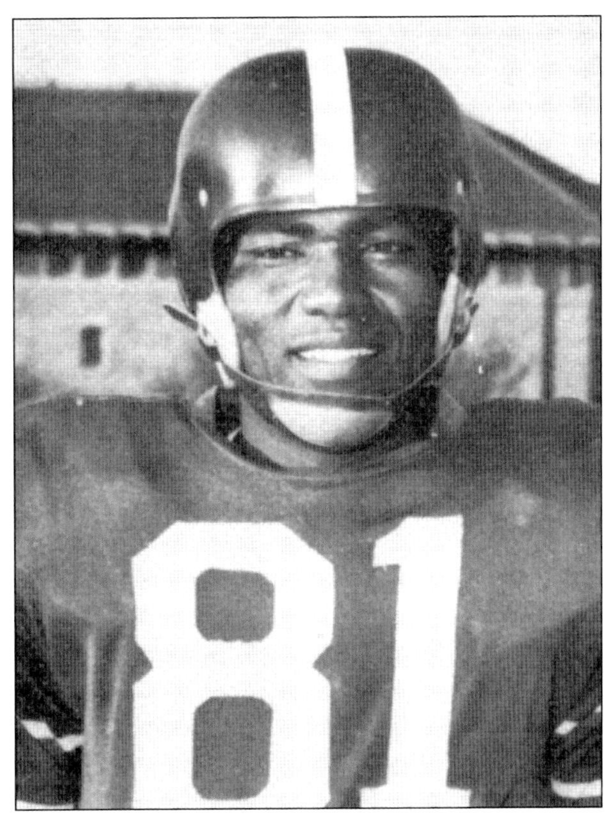

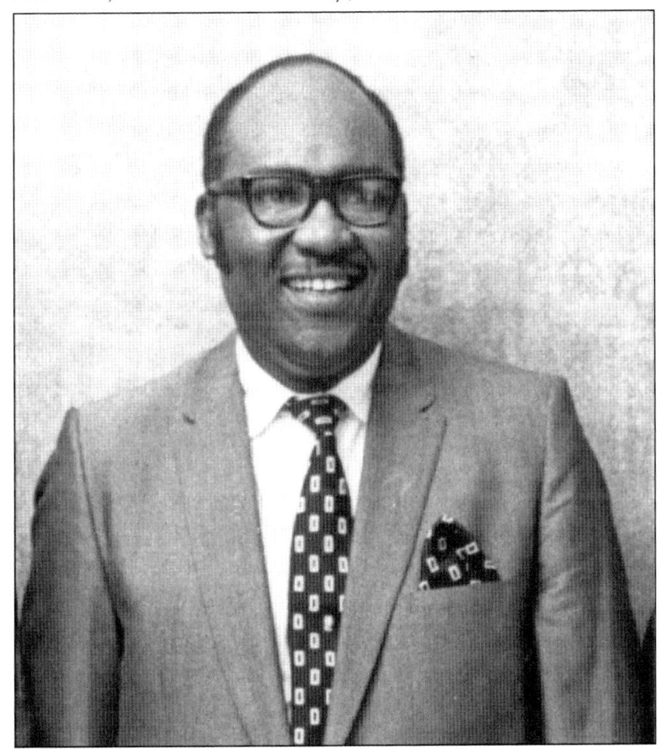

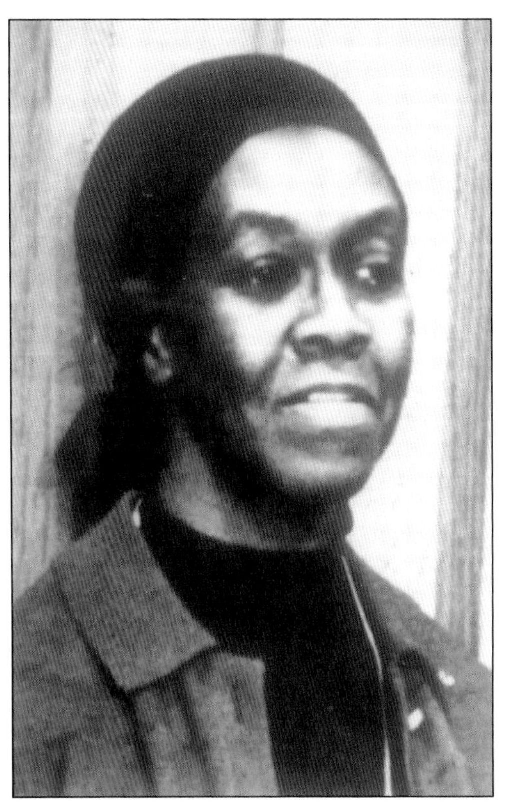

Gwendolyn Brooks and Langston Hughes. Though she spent only a few years of her life in Topeka, Gwendolyn Brooks (left) was born there in 1917 and claimed Topeka as her home. She and fellow poet Langston Hughes (below) were important black writers who contributed much to the genre of poetry. They both spent their early years in Topeka, where their families also resided. In 1983, Brooks, who had previously received the Pulitzer Prize for Poetry, was invited to Washburn University to receive an honorary degree. Langston Hughes was a leader of the Harlem Renaissance, a social activist, novelist, playwright, and columnist—in addition to being a poet. (Brooks photograph courtesy of University Archives, Washburn University; Hughes photograph courtesy of KHS.)

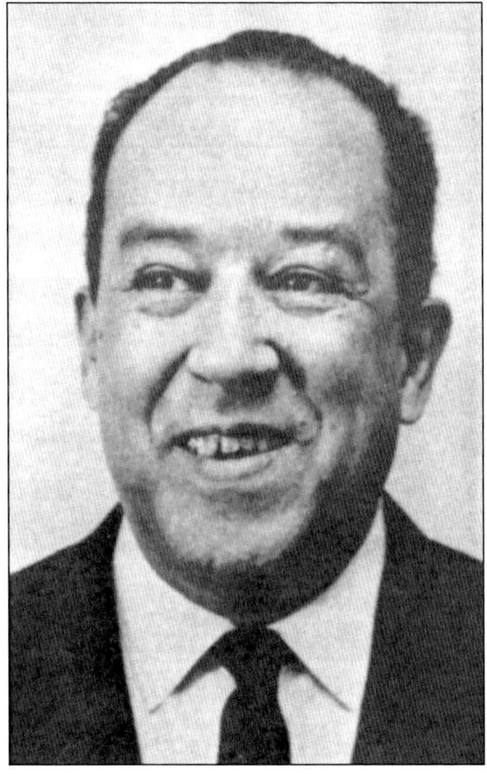

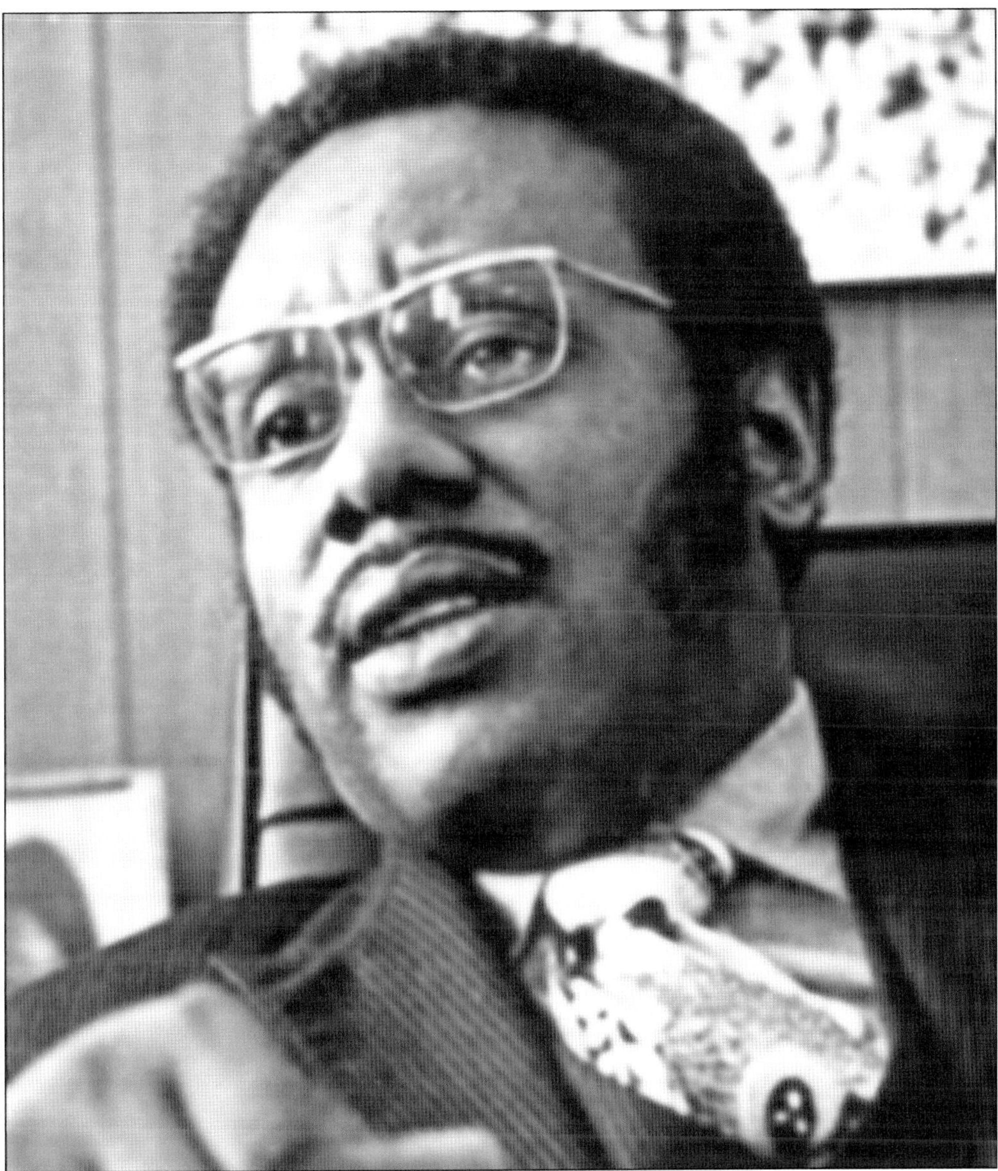

Samuel C. Jackson. Samuel C. Jackson was a prominent attorney and civil rights leader. He graduated from Topeka High School in 1947 and earned his undergraduate degree from Washburn University in 1951 and his law degree from the Washburn School of Law in 1954. He worked in the Topeka law firm of Scott, Scott & Scott and was an attorney for the Kansas State Welfare Department. After serving as the president of the Topeka branch of the NAACP in the 1960s, he later served on the national level for the NAACP. He was appointed by Pres. Lyndon Johnson as one of the original members of the Equal Employment Opportunity Commission in 1965 and was named by Pres. Richard Nixon as the assistant secretary of the US Department of Housing and Urban Development in 1969. Topeka's Samuel C. Jackson Park, at 1220 SE Tenth Avenue, was named for him. (Courtesy of the Washburn University School of Law.)

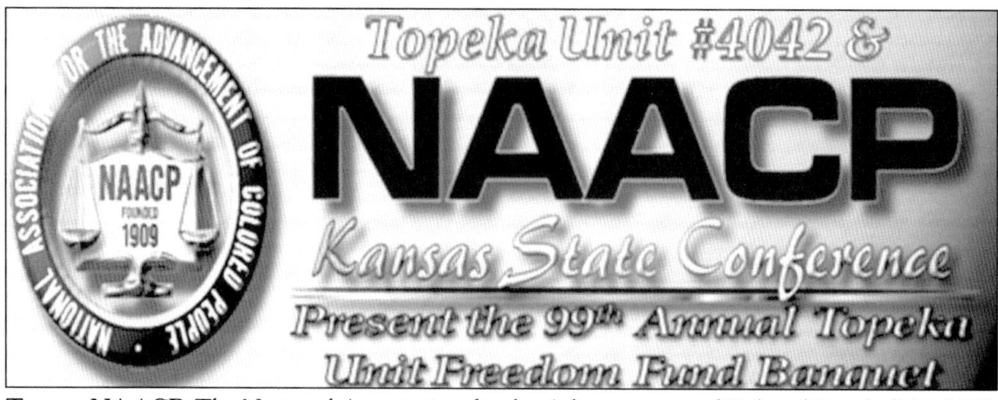

TOPEKA NAACP. The National Association for the Advancement of Colored People (NAACP) was founded in 1909. Its mission is to ensure the political, educational, and socio-economic equality for all persons and to eliminate racial hatred and racial discrimination. The Topeka branch, No. 4042, was the first branch organized in Kansas and was granted its charter in 1913. The first officers of Topeka Unit No. 4042 were Arthur Capper, chapter president (who was also governor of Kansas and US senator); Nathaniel Sawyer, chairman of the executive committee; Rev. George G. Walker, treasurer; and Julia B. Roundtree, secretary. (Courtesy of Topeka NAACP.)

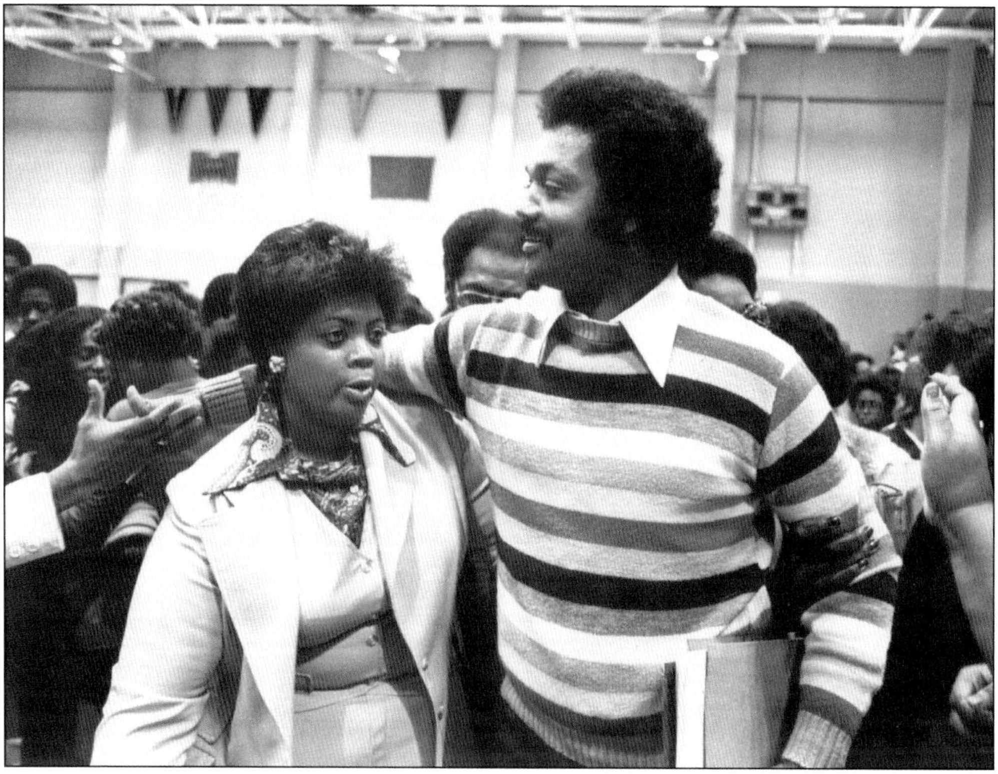

LINDA BROWN AND JESSE JACKSON. Following the famous *Brown v. Board of Education of Topeka* case, in which her father was the lead plaintiff, Linda Brown has traveled the country speaking about the case and about her experiences. This photograph of Brown and Rev. Jesse Jackson, which was taken in the auditorium of Highland Park High School after Reverend Jackson spoke there, shows Brown greeting Jackson as he made his way through the crowd. (Courtesy of Linda Brown-Thompson.)

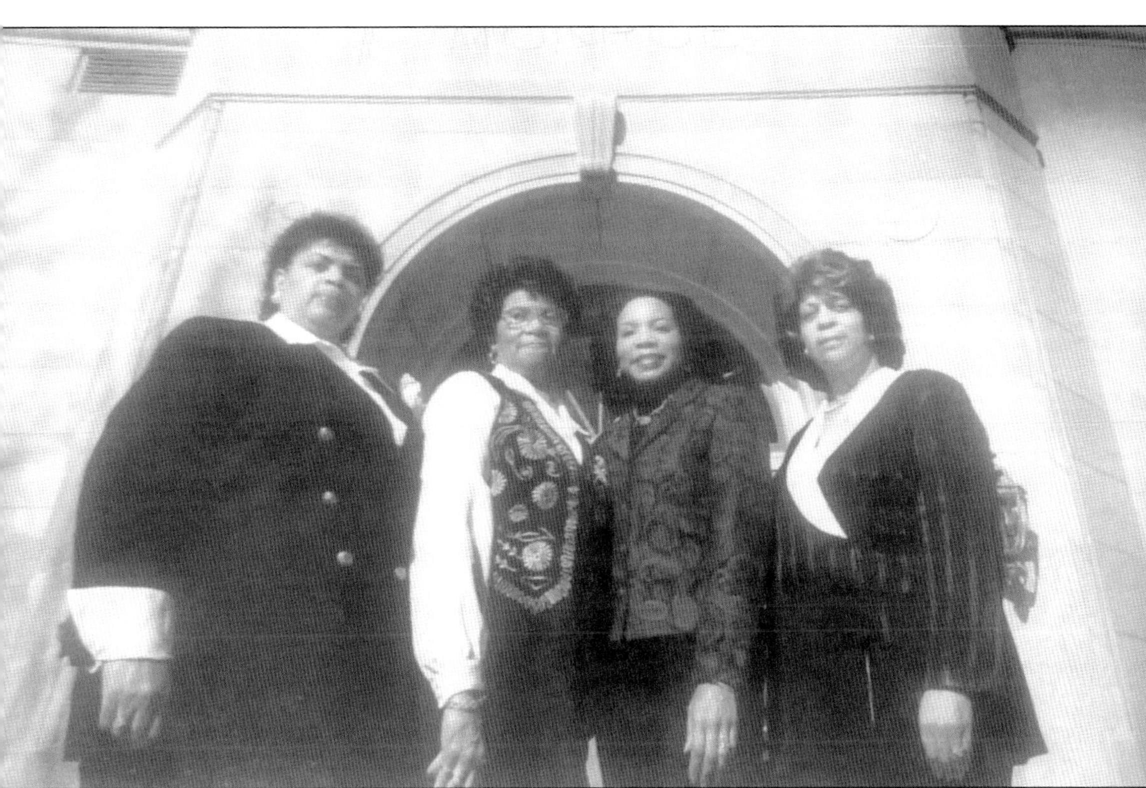

Brown Foundation. The Brown Foundation was established in 1988 by the Oliver Brown family to commemorate the 1954 *Brown v. Board of Education of Topeka* case and US Supreme Court decision. The foundation has annually sponsored a forum of speakers, entertainment, and educational programming in conjunction with Washburn University. In 2004, fifty years after the *Brown v. Board* decision, the organization was successful in getting a National Historic Site designation for the Monroe School building. The site is now operated by the National Park Service. Pictured here are the founding members of the Brown Foundation. Leola Montgomery, second from left, was the wife of Oliver Brown. Their daughters, from left to right, are Linda Brown-Thompson, Cheryl Brown-Henderson, and Teri Brown-Tyler. (Courtesy of the *Topeka Capital-Journal.*)

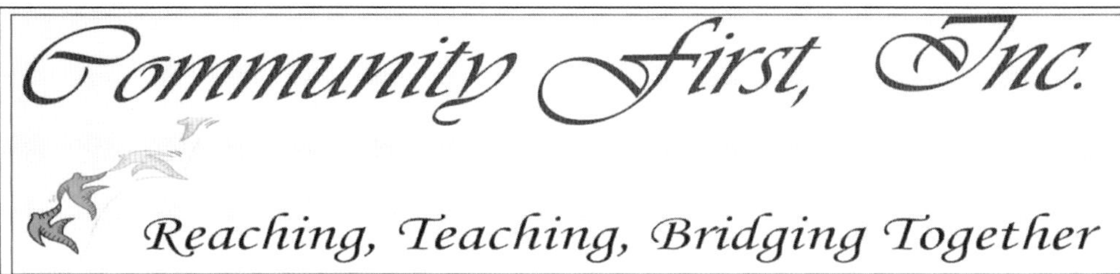

COMMUNITY FIRST, INC. In 1999, Faith Temple Church of God in Christ founded Community First to meet the needs of children, promote ongoing community development, enhance community-planning processes, and promote opportunities for Topeka citizens. The organization works to develop healthy families, promote positive adolescent growth, and enhance intergenerational relationships. Community First operates the Abbott Community Center, located at 1112 SE Tenth Street, which offers year-round programs for youth. (Courtesy of Community First, Inc.)

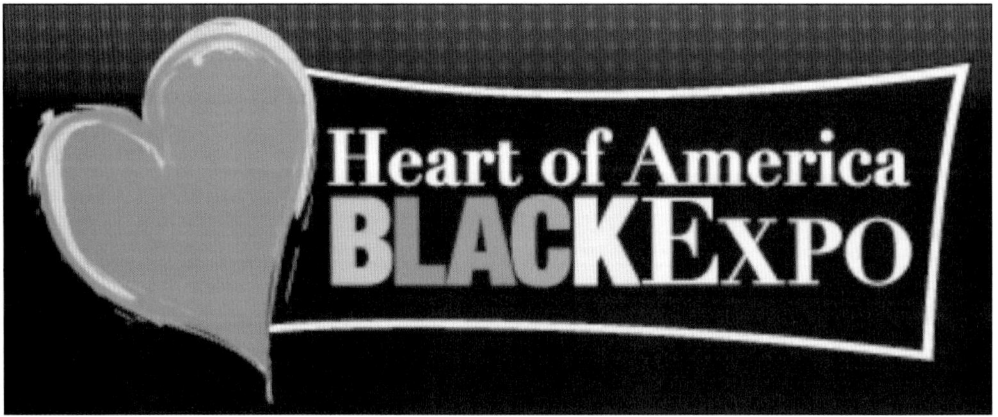

BLACK EXPO. Originally organized in 2004 by Curtis Pitts, the Heart of America Black Expo is a cultural event designed to create positive race relations throughout the Topeka area and the Midwest. The Heart of America Black Expo hosts annual conferences on leadership, fatherhood, parenting, and economic development. In 2011, the Heart of America Black Expo celebrated the *Brown v. Board of Education of Topeka* decision, local community leaders, and improvements in race relationships. The event, called Grantfest (named after the local philanthropist Grant Cushinberry), brought the community together in celebration of the achievements of Topeka's African Americans. (Courtesy of Curtis Pitts.)

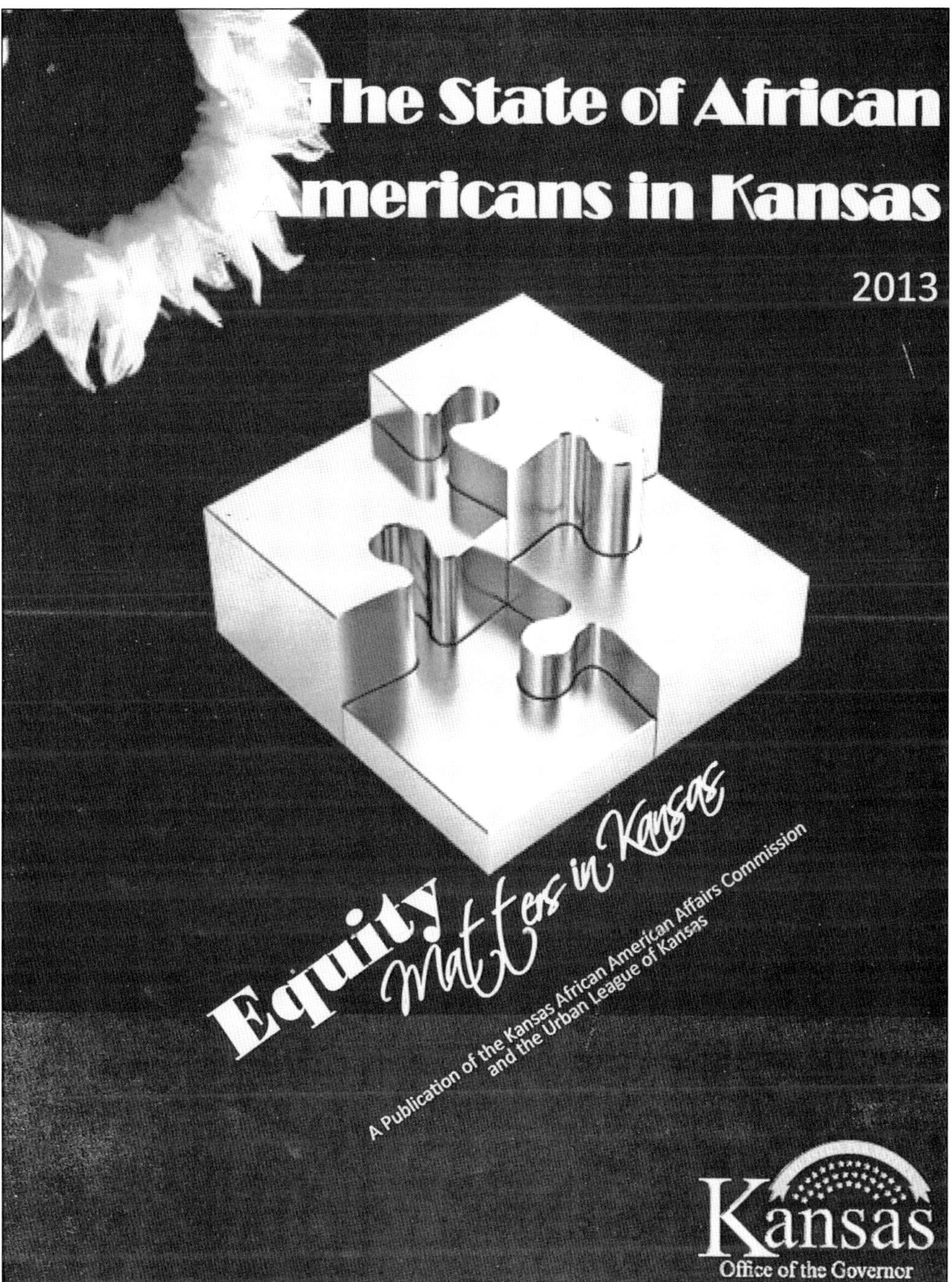

Kansas African American Affairs Commission. The Kansas African American Affairs Commission (KAAAC) was created in 1997, when Gov. Bill Graves signed a bill authorizing it into law. In 2004, Gov. Kathleen Sebelius signed into law a bill allowing the commission to serve officially as the governor's liaison to the African American communities throughout the state. The commission, whose members are appointed by the governor, works in conjunction with other state and local entities to provide equity to the black community. (Courtesy of Kansas African American Affairs Commission.)

Discover Thousands of Local History Books Featuring Millions of Vintage Images

Arcadia Publishing, the leading local history publisher in the United States, is committed to making history accessible and meaningful through publishing books that celebrate and preserve the heritage of America's people and places.

Find more books like this at
www.arcadiapublishing.com

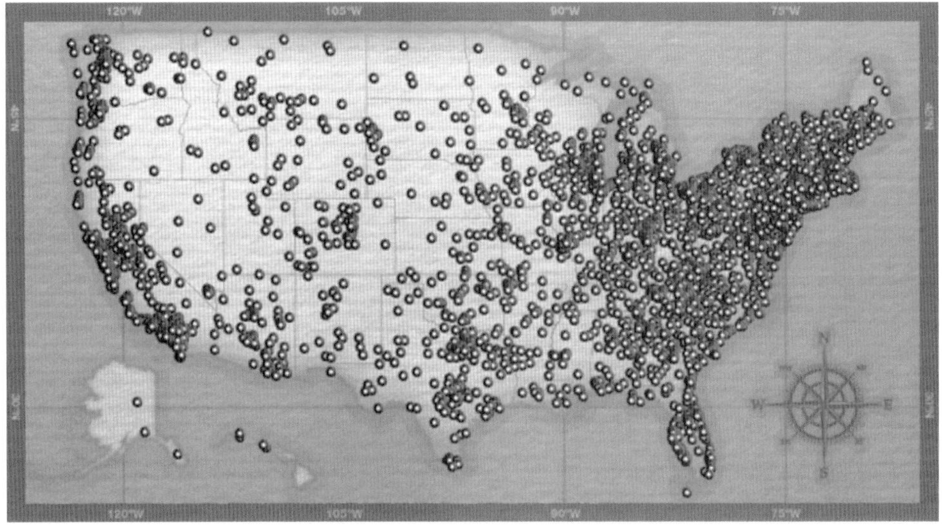

Search for your hometown history, your old stomping grounds, and even your favorite sports team.

Consistent with our mission to preserve history on a local level, this book was printed in South Carolina on American-made paper and manufactured entirely in the United States. Products carrying the accredited Forest Stewardship Council (FSC) label are printed on 100 percent FSC-certified paper.

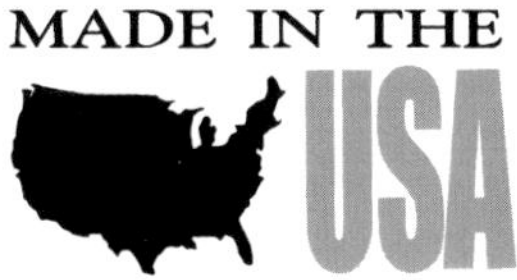